Parallel Port Complete

Programming, Interfacing, & Using the PC's Parallel Printer Port

Jan Axelson

Lakeview Research
Madison, WI 53704

Lakeview Research
5310 Chinook Ln.
Madison, WI 53704
USA
Phone: 608-241-5824
Fax: 608-241-5848
Email: info@lvr.com
WWW: http://www.lvr.com

14 13 12 11 10 9 8 7 6

Products and services named in this book are trademarks or registered trademarks of their respective companies. The author uses these names in editorial fashion only and for the benefit of the trademark owners. No such use, or the use of any trade name, is intended to convey endorsement or other affiliation with the book.

ISBN 0-9650819-1-5

Manufactured in the United States of America

Table of Contents

Introduction

From its origin as a simple printer interface, the personal computer's parallel port has evolved into a place to plug in just about anything you might want to hook to a computer. The parallel port is popular because it's versatile—you can use it for output, input, or bidirectional links—and because it's available—every PC has one.

Printers are still the most common devices connected to the port, but other popular options include external tape and disk drives and scanners. Laptop computers may use a parallel-port-based network interface or joystick. For special applications, there are dozens of parallel-port devices for use in data collection, testing, and control systems. And the parallel port is the interface of choice for many one-of-a-kind and small-scale projects that require communications between a computer and an external device.

In spite of its popularity, the parallel port has always been a bit of a challenge to work with. Over the years, several variations on the original port's design have emerged, yet there has been no single source of documentation that describes the port in its many variations.

I wrote this book to serve as a practical, hands-on guide to all aspects of the parallel port. It covers both hardware and software, including how to design external circuits that connect to the port, as well as how to write programs to control and monitor the port, including both the original and improved port designs.

Who should read this book?

The book is designed to serve readers with a variety of backgrounds and interests:

Programmers will find code examples that show how to use the port in all of its modes. If you program in Visual Basic, you can use the routines directly in your programs.

For **hardware designers,** there are details about the port circuits and how to interface them to the world outside the PC. I cover the port's original design and the many variations and improvements that have evolved. Examples show how to design circuits for reliable data transfers.

System **troubleshooters** can use the programming techniques and examples for finding and testing ports on a system.

Experimenters will find dozens of circuit and code examples, along with explanations and tips for modifying the examples for a particular application.

Teachers and students have found the parallel port to be a handy tool for experiments with electronics and computer control. Many of the examples in this book are suitable as school projects.

And last but not least, **users**, or anyone who uses a computer with printers or other devices that connect to the parallel port, will find useful information, including advice on configuring ports, how to add a port, and information on cables, port extenders, and switch boxes.

What's Inside

This book focuses on several areas related to the parallel port:

Using the New Modes

Some of the most frequently asked parallel-port questions relate to using, programming, and interfacing the port in the new, advanced modes, including the enhanced parallel port (EPP), the extended capabilities port (ECP), and the PS/2-type, or simple bidirectional, port. This book covers each of these. Examples show how to enable a mode, how to use the mode to transfer data, and how to use software negotiation to enable a PC and peripheral to select the best mode available.

Visual Basic Tools

Microsoft's Visual Basic is one of the most popular programming languages for PCs, and this book includes programming tools to help in writing Visual-Basic programs that access the parallel port. One tool is a Visual-Basic form that enables users to find, select, and test the parallel ports on a system. You can use the form as a template, or beginning form, for applications you write. Also included is a set of routines that simplify reading and writing to the parallel port's registers and reading and changing individual bits in a byte.

Because Visual Basic doesn't include functions for performing simple reads and writes to a port, the companion disk included with this book includes DLLs that add these abilities to Visual Basic. Versions are included for use with both 16-bit and 32-bit programs.

Applications

Besides the general-purpose programming tools, I've included a variety of example circuits with Visual-Basic code for controlling and monitoring external circuits. The examples include popular applications such as switching power to a load, reading analog signals, expanding the number of inputs and outputs that the port can access, and interfacing to a microcontroller circuit. One example shows how to use the parallel port to communicate with chips that use a synchronous serial interface. A chapter on real-time control shows how to write programs that trigger on external events, such as a signal transition at the parallel port or time or calendar information. There's a discussion and examples of using the parallel port as the power source for low-power external circuits.

Cables and Interfacing

The proper cable can mean the difference between a link that works reliably and one that doesn't. This book shows how to choose an appropriate parallel-port cable, and how to design the circuits that interface to the cable.

PC-to-PC Communications

Although the parallel port was originally intended as an interface between a PC and a printer or other peripheral, it's also become a popular interface for transferring information between two PCs. This book shows how to set up a PC-to-PC link using the parallel ports and either the operating system's built-in tools or your own programs.

About the Program Code

Every programmer has a favorite language. The choices include various implementations of Basic, C/C++, and Pascal/Delphi, and assembly language.

For the program examples in this book, I wanted to use a popular language so as many readers as possible could use the examples directly, and this prompted my decision to use Microsoft's Visual Basic for Windows. A big reason for Visual Basic's popularity is that the programming environment makes it extremely easy to add controls and displays that enable users to control a program and view the results.

However, this book isn't a tutorial on Visual Basic. It assumes you have a basic understanding of the language and how to create and debug a Visual-Basic program.

I developed the examples originally using Visual Basic Version 3, then ported them to Version 4. As much as possible, the programs are designed to be compatible with both versions, including both 16- and 32-bit Version-4 programs. The companion disk includes two versions of each program, one for Version 3 and one for 16- and 32-bit Version 4 programs.

One reason I decided to maintain compatibility with Version 3 is that the standard edition of Version 4 creates 32-bit programs only. Because Windows 3.1 can't run these programs, many users haven't upgraded to Version 4. Also, many parallel-port programs run on older systems that are put to use as dedicated controllers or data loggers. Running the latest version of Windows isn't practical or necessary on these computers.

Of course, in the software world, nothing stays the same for long. Hopefully, the program code will remain compatible in most respects with later versions of Visual Basic.

Compatibility with Version 3 does involve some tradeoffs. For example, Version 3 doesn't support the Byte variable type, so my examples use Integer variables even where Byte variables would be appropriate (as in reading and writing to a byte-wide port). In a few areas, such as some Windows API calls, I've provided two versions, one for use with 16-bit programs, Version 3 or 4, and the other for use with Version 4 programs, 16- or 32-bit.

In the program listings printed in this book, I use Visual Basic 4's line-continuation character (_) to extend program lines that don't fit on one line on the page. In other words, this:

```
PortType = _
Left$(ReturnBuffer, NumberOfCharacters)
```

is the same as this:

```
PortType = Left$(ReturnBuffer, NumberOfCharacters)
```

To remain compatible with Version 3, the code on the disk doesn't use this feature.

Most of the program examples are based on a general-purpose Visual-Basic form and routines introduced early in the book. The listings for the examples in each chapter include only the application-specific code added to the listings presented earlier. The routines within a listing are arranged alphabetically, in the same order that Visual Basic displays and prints them.

Of course, the concepts behind the programs can be programmed with any language and for any operating system. In spite of Windows' popularity, MS-DOS programs still have uses, especially for the type of control and monitoring programs that often use the parallel port. Throughout, I've tried to document the code completely enough so that you can translate it easily into whatever programming language and operating system you prefer.

Several of the examples include a parallel-port interface to a microcontroller circuit. The companion disk has the listings for the microcontroller programs.

About the Example Circuits

This book includes schematic diagrams of circuits that you can use or adapt in parallel-port projects. In designing the examples, I looked for circuits that are as easy as possible to put together and program. All use inexpensive, off-the-shelf components that are available from many sources.

The circuit diagrams are complete, with these exceptions:

Power-supply and ground pins are omitted when they are in standard locations on the package (bottom left for ground, top right for power, assuming pin 1 is top left).

Power-supply decoupling capacitors are omitted. (This book explains when and how to add these to your circuits.)

Some chips may have additional, unused gates or other elements that aren't shown.

The manufacturers' data sheets have additional information on the components.

Conventions

These are the typographic conventions used in this book:

Item	Convention	Example
Signal name	italics	*Busy, D0*
Active-low signal	leading *n*	*nAck, nStrobe*
Signal complement	overbar	$\overline{C0}$, $\overline{S7}$ (equivalent to -C0, -S7 or /C0, /S7)
Program code	monospace font	`DoEvents, End Sub`
File name	italics	*win.ini, inpout16.dll*
Hexadecimal number	trailing *h*	3BCh (same as &h3BC in Visual Basic)

Corrections and Updates

In researching and putting together this book, I've done my best to ensure that the information is complete and correct. I built and tested every circuit and tested all of the program code, most of it multiple times. But I know from experience that on the way from test to publication, errors and omissions do occur.

Any corrections or updates to this book will be available at Lakeview Research's World Wide Web site on the Internet at *http://www.lvr.com.* This is also the place to come for links to other parallel-port information on the Web, including data sheets for parallel-port controllers and software tools for parallel-port programming.

Thanks!

Finally, I want to say thanks to everyone who helped make this book possible. I credit the readers of my articles in *The Microcomputer Journal* for first turning me on to this topic with their questions, comments, and article requests. The series I wrote for the magazine in 1994 was the beginning of this book.

Others deserving thanks are product vendors, who answered many questions, and the Usenet participants who asked some thought-provoking questions that often sent me off exploring areas I wouldn't have thought of otherwise.

Special thanks to SoftCircuits (PO Box 16262, Irvine, CA 92713, Compuserve 72134,263, WWW: http://www.softcircuits.com) for the use of Vbasm.

1

Essentials

A first step in exploring the parallel port is learning how to get the most from a port with your everyday applications and peripherals. Things to know include how to find, configure, and install a port, how and when to use the new bidirectional, EPP, and ECP modes, and how to handle a system with multiple parallel-port peripherals. This chapter presents essential information and tips relating to these topics.

Defining the Port

What is the "parallel port"? In the computer world, a *port* is a set of signal lines that the microprocessor, or CPU, uses to exchange data with other components. Typical uses for ports are communicating with printers, modems, keyboards, and displays, or just about any component or device except system memory. Most computer ports are digital, where each signal, or bit, is 0 or 1. A parallel port transfers multiple bits at once, while a serial port transfers a bit at a time (though it may transfer in both directions at once).

This book is about a specific type of parallel port: the one found on just about every PC, or IBM-compatible personal computer. Along with the RS-232 serial port, the parallel port is a workhorse of PC communications. On newer PCs, you may find other ports such as SCSI, USB, and IrDA, but the parallel port remains popular because it's capable, flexible, and every PC has one.

The term *PC-compatible,* or *PC* for short, refers to the IBM PC and any of the many, many personal computers derived from it. From another angle, a PC is any computer that can run Microsoft's MS-DOS operating system and whose expansion bus is compatible with the ISA bus in the original IBM PC. The category includes the PC, XT, AT, PS/2, and most computers with 80x86, Pentium, and compatible CPUs. It does not include the Macintosh, Amiga, or IBM mainframes, though these and other computer types may have ports that are similar to the parallel port on the PC.

The original PC's parallel port had eight outputs, five inputs, and four bidirectional lines. These are enough for communicating with many types of peripherals. On many newer PCs, the eight outputs can also serve as inputs, for faster communications with scanners, drives, and other devices that send data to the PC.

The parallel port was designed as a printer port, and many of the original names for the port's signals (*PaperEnd, AutoLineFeed*) reflect that use. But these days, you can find all kinds of things besides printers connected to the port. The term *peripheral*, or *peripheral device* is a catch-all category that includes printers, scanners, modems, and other devices that connect to a PC.

Port Types

As the design of the PC evolved, several manufacturers introduced improved versions of the parallel port. The new port types are compatible with the original design, but add new abilities, mainly for increased speed.

Speed is important because as computers and peripherals have gotten faster, the jobs they do have become more complicated, and the amount of information they need to exchange has increased. The original parallel port was plenty fast enough for sending bytes representing ASCII text characters to a dot-matrix or daisy-wheel printer. But modern printers need to receive much more information to print a page with multiple fonts and detailed graphics, often in color. The faster the computer can transmit the information, the faster the printer can begin processing and printing the result.

A fast interface also makes it feasible to use portable, external versions of peripherals that you would otherwise have to install inside the computer. A parallel-port tape or disk drive is easy to move from system to system, and for occasional use, such as making back-ups, you can use one unit for several systems. Because a backup may involve copying hundreds of Megabytes, the interface has to be fast to be worthwhile.

This book covers the new port types in detail, but for now, here is a summary of the available types:

Original (SPP)

The parallel port in the original IBM PC, and any port that emulates the original port's design, is sometimes called the *SPP*, for standard parallel port, even though the original port had no written standard beyond the schematic diagrams and documentation for the IBM PC. Other names used are *AT-type* or *ISA-compatible*.

The port in the original PC was based on an existing Centronics printer interface. However, the PC introduced a few differences, which other systems have continued.

SPPs can transfer eight bits at once to a peripheral, using a protocol similar to that used by the original Centronics interface. The SPP doesn't have a byte-wide input port, but for PC-to-peripheral transfers, SPPs can use a Nibble mode that transfers each byte 4 bits at a time. Nibble mode is slow, but has become popular as a way to use the parallel port for input.

PS/2-type (Simple Bidirectional)

An early improvement to the parallel port was the bidirectional data port introduced on IBM's model PS/2. The bidirectional port enables a peripheral to transfer eight bits at once to a PC. The term *PS/2-type* has come to refer to any parallel port that has a bidirectional data port but doesn't support the EPP or ECP modes described below. Byte mode is an 8-bit data-transfer protocol that PS/2-type ports can use to transfer data from the peripheral to the PC.

EPP

The EPP (enhanced parallel port) was originally developed by chip maker Intel, PC manufacturer Zenith, and Xircom, a maker of parallel-port networking products. As on the PS/2-type port, the data lines are bidirectional. An EPP can read or write a byte of data in one cycle of the ISA expansion bus, or about 1 microsecond, including handshaking, compared to four cycles for an SPP or PS/2-type port. An EPP can switch directions quickly, so it's very efficient when used with disk and tape drives and other devices that transfer data in both directions. An EPP can also emulate an SPP, and some EPPs can emulate a PS/2-type port.

ECP

The ECP (extended capabilities port) was first proposed by Hewlett Packard and Microsoft. Like the EPP, the ECP is bidirectional and can transfer data at ISA-bus speeds. ECPs have buffers and support for DMA (direct memory access) transfers and data compression. ECP transfers are useful for printers, scanners, and other peripherals that transfer large blocks of data. An ECP can also emulate an SPP or PS/2-type port, and many ECPs can emulate an EPP as well.

Multi-mode Ports

Many newer ports are multi-mode ports that can emulate some or all of the above types. They often include configuration options that can make all of the port types available, or allow certain modes while locking out the others.

System Resources

The parallel port uses a variety of the computer's resources. Every port uses a range of addresses, though the number and location of addresses varies. Many ports have an assigned IRQ (interrupt request) level, and ECPs may have an assigned DMA channel. The resources assigned to a port can't conflict with those used by other system components, including other parallel ports

Addressing

The standard parallel port uses three contiguous addresses, usually in one of these ranges:

```
3BCh, 3BDh, 3BEh
378h, 379h, 37Ah
278h, 279h, 27Ah
```

The first address in the range is the port's base address, also called the Data register or just the port address. The second address is the port's Status register, and the third is the Control register. (See Appendix C for a review of hexadecimal numbers.)

EPPs and ECPs reserve additional addresses for each port. An EPP adds five registers at *base address + 3* through *base address + 7*, and an ECP adds three registers at *base address + 400h* through *base address + 402h*. For a base address of 378h, the EPP registers are at 37Bh through 37Fh, and the ECP registers are at 778h through 77Ah.

On early PCs, the parallel port had a base address of 3BCh. On newer systems, the parallel port is most often at 378h. But all three addresses are reserved for parallel ports, and if the port's hardware allows it, you can configure a port at any of the addresses. However, you normally can't have an EPP at base address 3BCh, because the added EPP registers at this address may be used by the video display.

IBM's Type 3 PS/2 port also had three additional registers, at *base address +3* through *base address + 5*, and allowed a base address of 1278h or 1378h.

Most often, DOS and Windows refer to the first port in numerical order as *LPT1*, the second, *LPT2*, and the third, *LPT3*. So on bootup, LPT1 is most often at 378h, but it may be at any of the three addresses. LPT2, if it exists, may be at 378h or 278h, and LPT3 can only be at 278h. Various configuration techniques can change these assignments, however, so not all systems will follow this convention. LPT stands for line printer, reflecting the port's original intended use.

If your port's hardware allows it, you can add a port at any unused port address in the system. Not all software will recognize these non-standard ports as LPT ports, but you can access them with software that writes directly to the port registers.

Interrupts

Most parallel ports are capable of detecting interrupt signals from a peripheral. The peripheral may use an interrupt to announce that it's ready to receive a byte, or that it has a byte to send. To use interrupts, a parallel port must have an assigned interrupt-request level (IRQ).

Conventionally, LPT1 uses IRQ7 and LPT2 uses IRQ5. But IRQ5 is used by many sound cards, and because free IRQ levels can be scarce on a system, even IRQ7 may be reserved by another device. Some ports allow choosing other IRQ levels besides these two.

Many printer drivers and many other applications and drivers that access the parallel port don't require parallel-port interrupts. If you select no IRQ level for a port, the port will still work in most cases, though sometimes not as efficiently, and you can use the IRQ level for something else.

DMA Channels

ECPs can use direct memory access (DMA) for data transfers at the parallel port. During the DMA transfers, the CPU is free to do other things, so DMA transfers can result in faster performance overall. In order to use DMA, the port must have an assigned DMA channel, in the range 0 to 3.

Finding Existing Ports

DOS and Windows include utilities for finding existing ports and examining other system resources. In Windows 95, click on *Control Panel, System, Devices, Ports*, and click on a port to see its assigned address and (optional) IRQ level and DMA channel. In Windows 3.1 or DOS, you can use Microsoft's Diagnostic (*msd.exe*) to view ports, assigned IRQ levels, and other system details.

Configuring

The parallel port that comes with a PC will have an assigned address and possibly an IRQ level and DMA channel. Multi-mode ports may also be configured with specific modes enabled. You can change some or all of these assignments to match your needs. If you're adding a new port, you need to configure it, making sure that it doesn't conflict with existing ports and other resources.

Port Options

There is no standard method for configuring a port. Some ports, especially older ones, use jumper blocks or switches to select different options. Others allow configuring in software, using a utility provided on disk. A port on a system motherboard may have configuration options in the system setup screens (the CMOS setup) that you can access on bootup. On ports that meet Microsoft's Plug and Play standard, Windows 95 can automatically assign an available port address and IRQ level to a port.

Check your system or port's documentation for specifics on how to configure a port. Some ports allow a choice of just one or two of the three conventional base addresses. A few allow you to choose any uncommitted address, including nonstandard ones. On some boards, the jumpers or switches are labeled, which is extremely handy when you don't have other documentation (or can't find it).

If your port supports ECP transfers, assign it an IRQ level and DMA channel if possible. Most ECP drivers do use these, and if they're not available, the driver will revert to a slower mode.

Multi-mode Ports

Configuring a multi-mode port needs special consideration. A multi-mode port's controller chip supports a variety of modes that emulate different port types. In addition to the configuration options described above, on most multi-mode ports, you also have to select a port type to emulate.

The problem is that there is no single standard for the basic setup on the controller chips, and there are many different chips! Usually the setup involves writing to configuration registers in the chip, but the location and means of accessing the registers varies.

For this reason, every port *should* come with a simple way to configure the port. If the port is on the motherboard, look in the CMOS setup screens that you can access on bootup. Other ports may use jumpers to enable the modes, or have configuration software on disk.

The provided setup routines don't always offer all of the available options or explain the meaning of each option clearly. For example, one CMOS setup I've seen allows only the choice of *AT* or *PS/2-type* port. The PS/2 option actually configures the port as an ECP, with the ECP's PS/2 mode selected, but there is no documentation explaining this. The only way to find out what mode is actually selected is to read the chip's configuration registers. And although the port also supports EPP, the CMOS setup includes no way to enable it, so again, accessing the configuration registers is the only option.

If your port is EPP- or ECP-capable but the setup utility doesn't offer these as choices, a last resort is to identify the controller chip, obtain and study its data sheet, and write your own program to configure the port.

The exact terminology and the number of available options can vary, but these are typical configuration options for a multi-mode port:

SPP. Emulates the original port. Also called *AT-type* or *ISA-compatible*.

PS/2, or simple bidirectional. Like an SPP, except that the data port is bidirectional.

EPP. Can do EPP transfers. Also emulates an SPP. Some EPPs can emulate a PS/2-type port.

ECP. Can do ECP transfers. The ECP's internal modes enable the port to emulate an SPP or PS/2-type port. An additional internal mode, *Fast Centronics*, or *Parallel-Port FIFO*, uses the ECP's buffer for faster data transfers with many old-style (SPP) peripherals.

ECP + EPP. An ECP that supports the ECP's internal mode 100, which emulates an EPP. The most flexible port type, because it can emulate all of the others.

Drivers

After setting up the port's hardware, you may need to configure your operating system and applications to use the new port.

For DOS and Windows 3.1 systems, on bootup the operating system looks for ports at the three conventional addresses and assigns each an LPT number.

In Windows 3.1, to assign a printer to an LPT port, click on *Control Panel*, then *Printers*. If the printer model isn't displayed, click *Add* and follow the prompts.

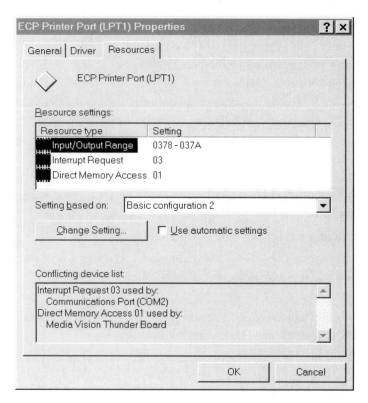

Figure 1-1: In Windows 95, you can select a port configuration in the Device Manager's Resources Window. A message warns if Windows detects any system conflicts with the selected configuration.

Select the desired printer model, then click *Connect* to view the available ports. Select a port and click *OK*, or *Cancel* to make no changes.

In Windows 95, the Control Panel lists available ports under *System Properties, Device Manager, Ports*. There's also a brief description of the port. *Printer Port* means that Windows treats the port as an ordinary SPP, while *ECP Printer Port* means that Windows will use the abilities of an ECP if possible. To change the driver, select the port, then *Properties, Driver*, and *Show All Drivers*. Select the driver and click *OK*. If an ECP doesn't have an IRQ and DMA channel, the Windows 95 printer driver will use the ECP's Fast Centronics mode, which transfers data faster than an SPP, but not as fast as ECP.

The Device Manager also shows the port's configuration. Select the port, then click *Resources*. Figure 1-1 shows an example. Windows attempts to detect these settings automatically. If the configuration shown doesn't match your hardware setup, de-select the *Use Automatic Settings* check box and select a different configuration. If none matches, you can change a setting by double-clicking on the resource type and entering a new value. Windows displays a message if it detects any conflicts with the selected settings. To assign a printer to a port, click on *Control Panel, Printers,* and select the printer to assign.

Parallel-port devices that don't use the Windows printer drivers should come with their own configuration utilities. DOS programs generally have their own printer drivers and methods for selecting a port as well.

Adding a Port

Most PCs come with one parallel port. If there's a spare expansion slot, it's easy to add one or two more. Expansion cards with parallel ports are widely available.

Cards with support for bidirectional, EPP, and ECP modes are the best choice unless you're sure that you won't need the new modes, or you want to spend as little as possible. Cards with just an SPP are available for as little as $15. A card salvaged from an old computer may cost you nothing at all.

You can get more use from a slot by buying a card with more than a parallel port. Because the port circuits are quite simple, many multi-function cards include a parallel port. Some have serial and game ports, while others combine a disk controller or other circuits with the parallel port. On older systems, the parallel port is on an expansion card with the video adapter. These should include a way to disable the video adapter, so you can use the parallel port in any system.

When buying a multi-mode port, it's especially important to be sure the port comes with utilities or documentation that shows you how to configure the port in all of its modes. Some multi-mode ports default to an SPP configuration, where all of the advanced modes are locked out. Before you can use the advanced modes, you have to enable them. Because the configuration methods vary from port to port, you need documentation.

Also, because the configuration procedures and other port details vary from chip to chip, manufacturers of ECP and EPP devices may guarantee compatibility with specific chips, computers, or expansion cards. If you're in the market for a new parallel port or peripheral, it's worth trying to find out if the peripheral supports using EPP or ECP mode with your port.

Port Hardware

The parallel port's hardware includes the back-panel connector and the circuits and cabling between the connector and the system's expansion bus. The PC's microprocessor uses the expansion bus's data, address, and control lines to trans-

Figure 1-2: The photo on the left shows the back panel of an expansion card, with a parallel port's 25-pin female D-sub connector on the left side of the panel. (The other connector is for a video monitor.) The photo on the right shows the 36-pin female Centronics connector used on most printers.

fer information between the parallel port and the CPU, memory, and other system components.

Connectors

The PC's back panel has the connector for plugging in a cable to a printer or other device with a parallel-port interface. Most parallel ports use the 25-contact D-sub connector shown in Figure 1-2. The shell (the enclosure that surrounds the contacts) is roughly in the shape of an upper-case D. Other names for this connector are the subminiature D, DB25, D-shell, or just D connector. The IEEE 1284 standard for the parallel port calls it the IEEE 1284-A connector.

Newer parallel ports may use the new, compact, 36-contact IEEE 1284-C connector described in Chapter 6.

The connector on the computer is female, where the individual contacts are sockets, or receptacles. The cable has a mating male connector, whose contacts are pins, or plugs.

The parallel-port connector is usually the only female 25-pin D-sub on the back panel, so there should be little confusion with other connectors. Some serial ports use a 25-contact D-sub, but with few exceptions, a 25-pin serial D-sub on a PC is male, with the female connector on the cable—the reverse of the parallel-port convention. (Other serial ports use 9-pin D-subs instead.)

SCSI is another interface whose connector might occasionally be confused with the parallel port's. The SCSI interface used by disk drives, scanners, and other devices usually has a 50-contact connector, but some SCSI devices use a 25-contact D-sub that is identical to the parallel-port's connector.

If you're unsure about which is the parallel-port connector, check your system documentation. When all else fails, opening up the enclosure and tracing the cable from the connector to an expansion board may offer clues.

The Circuits Inside

Inside the computer, the parallel-port circuits may be on the motherboard or on a card that plugs into the expansion bus.

The motherboard is the main circuit board that holds the computer's microprocessor chip as well as other circuits and slots for expansion cards. Because just about all computers have a parallel port, the port circuits are often right on the motherboard, freeing the expansion slot for other uses. Notebook and laptop computers don't have expansion slots, so the port circuits in these computers must reside on the system's main circuit board.

The port circuits connect to address, data, and control lines on the expansion bus, and these in turn interface to the microprocessor and other system components.

Cables

Most printer cables have a 25-pin male D-sub connector on one end and a male 36-contact connector on the other. Many refer to the 36-contact connector as the Centronics connector, because it's the same type formerly used on Centronics printers. Other names are parallel-interface connector or just printer connector. IEEE 1284 calls it the 1284-B connector.

Peripherals other than printers may use different connectors and require different cables. Some use a 25-pin D-sub like the one on the PC. A device that uses only a few of the port's signals may use a telephone connector, either a 4-wire RJ11 or an 8-wire RJ45. Newer peripherals may have the 36-contact 1284-C connector.

In any case, because the parallel-port's outputs aren't designed for transmitting over long distances, it's best to keep the cable short: 6 to 10 feet, or 33 feet for an IEEE-1284-compliant cable. Chapter 6 has more on cable choices.

Multiple Uses for One Port

If you have more than one parallel-port peripheral, the easiest solution is to add a port for each. But there may be times when multiple ports aren't an option. In this case, the alternatives are to swap cables as needed, use a switch box, or daisy-chain multiple devices to one port.

If you use only one device at a time and switch only occasionally, it's easy enough to move the cable when you want to use a different device.

For frequent swapping, a more convenient solution is a switch box. A typical manual switch box has three female D-sub connectors. A switch enables you route the contacts of one connector to either of the others. To use the switch box to access two peripherals on one port, you'll need a cable with two male D-subs to connect the PC to the switch box, plus an appropriate cable from the switch box to each peripheral.

You can also use a switch box to enable two PCs to share one printer or other peripheral. This requires two cables with two male D-subs on each, and one peripheral cable. Switch boxes with many other connector types are also available.

Manual switches are inexpensive, though some printer manufacturers warn that using them may damage the devices they connect to. A safer choice is a switch that uses active electronic circuits to route the signals. Some auto-sensing switches enable you to connect multiple computers to one printer, with first-come, first-served access. When a printer is idle, any computer can access it. When the printer is in use, the switch prevents the other computers from accessing it. However, these switches may not work properly if the peripherals use bidirectional communications, or if the peripheral uses the control or status signals in an unconventional way.

The parallel ports on some newer peripherals support a daisy-chain protocol that allows up to eight devices to connect to a single port. The PC assigns a unique address to each peripheral, which then ignores communications intended for the other devices in the chain. The software drivers for these devices must use the protocol when they access the port. The last device in the chain can be daisy-chain-unaware; it doesn't have to support the protocol. Chapter 11 has more on daisy chains.

Security Keys

Security keys, or dongles, are a form of copy protection that often uses the parallel port. Some software—usually expensive, specialized applications—includes a security key that you must plug into the parallel port in order to run the software. If you don't have the key installed, the software won't run.

The key is a small device with a male D-sub connector on one end and a female D-sub on the other. You plug the key into the parallel-port connector, then plug your regular cable into the security key. When the software runs, it attempts to find and communicate with the key, which contains a code that the software recognizes. The key usually doesn't use any conventional handshaking signals, so it should be able to live in harmony with other devices connected to the port.

The keys do require power, however. If you have a key that draws more than a small amount of current, and if your parallel port has weak outputs, you may have problems in using other devices on the same port as the key.

Alternatives to the Parallel Port

The parallel port is just one of many ways to interface inputs and outputs to a computer. In spite of its many virtues, the parallel port isn't the best solution for every project. These are some of the alternatives:

Serial Interfaces

One large group of parallel-port alternatives is serial interfaces, where data bits travel on a single wire or pair of wires (or in the case of wireless links, a single transmission path.) Both ends of the link require hardware or software to translate between serial and parallel data. There are many types of serial interfaces available for PCs, ranging from the ubiquitous RS-232 port to the newer RS-485, USB, IEEE-1394, and IrDA interfaces.

RS-232

Just about every PC has at least one RS-232 serial port. This interface is especially useful when the PC and the circuits that you want to connect are physically far apart.

As a rule, parallel-port cables should be no longer than 10 to 15 feet, though the IEEE-1284 standard describes an improved interface and cable that can be 10 meters (33 feet). In contrast, RS-232 links can be 80 feet or more, with the exact limit depending on the cable specifications and the speed of data transfers.

RS-232 links are slow, however. Along with each byte, the transmitting device normally adds a start and stop bit. Even at 115,200 bits per second, which is a typical maximum rate for a serial port, the data-transfer rate with one start and stop bit per byte is just 11,520 bytes per second.

RS-485

Another useful serial interface is RS-485, which can use cables as long as 4000 feet and allows up to 32 devices to connect to a single pair of wires. You can add an expansion card that contains an RS-485 port, or add external circuits that convert an existing RS-232 interface to RS-485. Other interfaces similar to RS-232 and RS-485 are RS-422 and RS-423.

Universal Serial Bus

A new option for I/O interfacing is the Universal Serial Bus (USB), a project of a group that includes Intel and Microsoft. A single USB port can have up to 127 devices communicating at either 1.5 Megabits/second or 12 Megabits/second over a 4-wire cable. The USB standard also describes both the hardware interface and software protocols. Newer PCs may have a USB port built-in, but because it's so new, most existing computers can't use it without added hardware and software drivers.

IEEE 1394

The IEEE-1394 high-performance serial bus, also known as Firewire, is another new interface. It allows up to 63 devices to connect to a PC, with transmission rates of up to 400 Megabits per second. The 6-wire cables can be as long as 15 feet, with daisy chains extending to over 200 feet. The interface is especially popular for connecting digital audio and video devices. IEEE-1394 expansion cards are available for PCs.

IrDA

The IrDA (Infrared Data Association) interface allows wireless serial communications over distances of 3 to 6 feet. The link transmits infrared energy at up to 115,200 bits/second. It's intended for convenient (no cables or connectors) transmitting of files between a desktop and laptop computer, or any short-range communications where a cabled interface is inconvenient. Some computers and peripherals now have IrDA interfaces built-in.

Other Parallel Interfaces

SCSI and IEEE-488 are two other parallel interfaces used by some PCs.

SCSI

SCSI (small computer system interface) is a parallel interface that allows up to seven devices to connect to a PC along a single cable, with each device having a unique address. Many computers use SCSI for interfacing to internal or external hard drives, tape back-ups, and CD-ROMs. SCSI interfaces are fast, and the cable can be as long as 19 feet (6 meters). But the parallel-port interface is simpler, cheaper, and much more common.

IEEE 488

The IEEE-488 interface began as Hewlett Packard's GPIB (general-purpose interface bus). It's a parallel interface that enables up to 15 devices to communicate at speeds of up to 1 Megabyte per second. This interface has long been popular for interfacing to lab instruments. Expansion cards with IEEE-488 interfaces are available.

Custom I/O Cards

Many other types of input and output circuits are available on custom expansion cards. An advantage of these is that you're not limited by an existing interface design. The card may contain just about any combination of analog and digital inputs and outputs. In addition, the card may hold timing or clock circuits, function generators, relay drivers, filters, or just about any type of component related to the external circuits. With the standard parallel port, you can add these components externally, but a custom I/O card allows you to place them inside the computer.

To use an expansion card, you of course need an empty expansion slot, which isn't available in portable computers and some desktop systems. And the custom hardware requires custom software.

PC Cards

Finally, instead of using the expansion bus, some I/O cards plug into a PC Card slot, which accepts slim circuit cards about the size of a playing card. An earlier name for these was PCMCIA cards, which stands for *Personal Computer Memory Card International Association,* whose members developed the standard. Many portable computers and some desktop models have PC-Card slots. Popular uses include modems and data acquisition circuits. There are even PC Cards that function as parallel ports. You don't need an internal expansion slot, and you don't have to open up the computer to plug the card in. But again, the standard parallel-port interface is cheaper and more widely available.

Chapter 1

2

Accessing Ports

Windows, DOS, and Visual Basic provide several ways to read and write to parallel ports. The most direct way is reading and writing to the port registers. Most programming languages include this ability, or at least allow you to add it. Visual Basic includes other options, including the *Printer* object, the *PrintForm* method, and *Open LPTx*. Windows also has API calls for accessing LPT ports, and 16-bit programs can use BIOS and DOS software interrupts for LPT access.

This chapter introduces the parallel port's signals and ways of accessing them in the programs you write.

The Signals

Table 2-1 shows the functions of each of the 25 contacts at the parallel port's connector, along with additional information about the signals and their corresponding register bits. Table 2-2 shows the information arranged by register rather than by pin number, and including register bits that don't appear at the connector. Most of the signal names and functions are based on a convention established by the Centronics Data Computer Corporation, an early manufacturer of dot-matrix printers. Although Centronics no longer makes printers, its interface lives on.

Table 2-1: Parallel Port Signals, arranged by pin number.

Pin: D-sub	Signal	Function	Source	Register Name	Register Bit #	Inverted at con- nector?	Pin: Centron- ics
1	nStrobe	Strobe D0-D7	PC[1]	Control	0	Y	1
2	D0	Data Bit 0	PC[2]	Data	0	N	2
3	D1	Data Bit 1	PC[2]	Data	1	N	3
4	D2	Data Bit 2	PC[2]	Data	2	N	4
5	D3	Data Bit 3	PC[2]	Data	3	N	5
6	D4	Data Bit 4	PC[2]	Data	4	N	6
7	D5	Data Bit 5	PC[2]	Data	5	N	7
8	D6	Data Bit 6	PC[2]	Data	6	N	8
9	D7	Data Bit 7	PC[2]	Data	7	N	9
10	nAck	Acknowledge (may trigger interrupt)	Printer	Status	6	N	10
11	Busy	Printer busy	Printer	Status	7	Y	11
12	PaperEnd	Paper end, empty (out of paper)	Printer	Status	5	N	12
13	Select	Printer selected (on line)	Printer	Status	4	N	13
14	nAutoLF	Generate automatic line feeds after carriage returns	PC[1]	Control	1	Y	14
15	nError (nFault)	Error	Printer	Status	3	N	32
16	nInit	Initialize printer (Reset)	PC[1]	Control	2	N	31
17	nSelectIn	Select printer (Place on line)	PC[1]	Control	3	Y	36
18	Gnd	Ground return for nStrobe, D0					19,20
19	Gnd	Ground return for D1, D2					21,22
20	Gnd	Ground return for D3, D4					23,24
21	Gnd	Ground return for D5, D6					25,26
22	Gnd	Ground return for D7, nAck					27,28
23	Gnd	Ground return for nSelectIn					33
24	Gnd	Ground return for Busy					29
25	Gnd	Ground return for nInit					30
	Chassis	Chassis ground					17
	NC	No connection					15,18,34
	NC	Signal ground					16
	NC	+5V	Printer				35

[1]Setting this bit high allows it to be used as an input (SPP only).　　　　[2]Some Data ports are bidirectional.

The signal names in the tables are those used by the parallel port in the original IBM PC. The names describe the signals' functions in PC-to-peripheral transfers. In other modes, the functions and names of many of the signals change.

Table 2-2: Parallel port bits, arranged by register.

Data Register (Base Address)

Bit	Pin: D-sub	Signal Name	Source	Inverted at connector?	Pin: Centronics
0	2	Data bit 0	PC	no	2
1	3	Data bit 1	PC	no	3
2	4	Data bit 2	PC	no	4
3	5	Data bit 3	PC	no	5
4	6	Data bit 4	PC	no	6
5	7	Data bit 5	PC	no	7
6	8	Data bit 6	PC	no	8
7	9	Data bit 7	PC	no	9

Some Data ports are bidirectional. (See Control register, bit 5 below.)

Status Register (Base Address +1)

Bit	Pin: D-sub	Signal Name	Source	Inverted at connector?	Pin: Centronics
3	15	nError (nFault)	Peripheral	no	32
4	13	Select	Peripheral	no	13
5	12	PaperEnd	Peripheral	no	12
6	10	nAck	Peripheral	no	10
7	11	Busy	Peripheral	yes	11

Additional bits not available at the connector:
0: may indicate timeout (1=timeout).
1, 2: unused.

Control Register (Base Address +2)

Bit	Pin: D-sub	Signal Name	Source	Inverted at connector?	Pin: Centronics
0	1	nStrobe	PC[1]	yes	1
1	14	nAutoLF	PC[1]	yes	14
2	16	nInit	PC[1]	no	31
3	17	nSelectIn	PC[1]	yes	36

[1]When high, PC can read external input (SPP only).
Additional bits not available at the connector:
4: Interrupt enable. 1=IRQs pass from *nAck* to system's interrupt controller. 0=IRQs do not pass to interrupt controller.
5: Direction control for bidirectional Data ports. 0=outputs enabled. 1=outputs disabled; Data port can read external logic voltages.
6,7: unused

Centronics Roots

The original Centronics interface had 36 lines, and most printers still use the same 36-contact connector that Centronics printers had. The PC, however, has a 25-pin connector, probably chosen because it was small enough to allow room for another connector on the back of an expansion card.

The 25-pin connector obviously can't include all of the original 36 contacts. Some non-essential control signals are sacrificed, along with some ground pins. The PC also assigns new functions to a couple of the contacts. Table 2-3 summarizes the differences between the signals on the original Centronics and PC interfaces.

Naming Conventions

The standard parallel port uses three 8-bit port registers in the PC. The PC accesses the parallel-port signals by reading and writing to these registers, commonly called the Data, Status, and Control registers.

Each of the signals has a name that suggests its function in a printer interface. In interfaces to other types of peripherals, you don't have to use the signals for their original purposes. For example, if you're not interfacing to a printer, you don't need a paper-end signal, and you can use the input for something else.

Because this book concentrates on uses other than the standard printer interface, I often use more generic names to refer to the parallel-port signals. The eight Data bits are *D0-D7*, the five Status bits are *S3-S7*, and the four Control bits are *C0-C3*. The letter identifies the port register, and the number identifies the signal's bit position in the register.

To complicate things, the port's hardware inverts four of the signals between the connector and the corresponding register bits. For *S7, C0, C1,* and *C3,* the logic state at the connector is the complement, or inverse, of the logic state of the corresponding register bit. *When you write to any of these bits, you have to remember to write the inverse of the bit you want at the connector. When you read these bits, you have to remember that you're reading the inverse of what's at the connector.*

In this book, when I refer to the signals by their register bits, an overbar indicates a connector signal that is the inverse of its register bit. For example, register bit *C0* becomes $\overline{C0}$ at the connector. The descriptive names (*nStrobe, Busy*) always refer to the signals at the connector, with a leading *n* indicating that a signal is active-low. For example, *nStrobe* and $\overline{C0}$ are the same signal. *nStrobe* tells you that the signal is a low-going pulse whose function is to strobe data into a peripheral, but the name tells you nothing about which register bit controls the signal. $\overline{C0}$ tells you that you that the signal is controlled by bit 0 in the Control register, and

Table 2-3: Differences between original Centronics interface and PC interface

Pin (Centronics)	Original Function	New (PC) Function
14	signal ground	nAutoLF
15	oscillator out	no connection
16	signal ground	no connection
17	chassis ground	no connection
18	+5V	no connection
33	light detect	Ground return for nSelectIn
34	line count	no connection
35	Ground return for line count	no connection
36	Reserved	nSelectIn

The PC's D-sub connector has just 25 contacts, compared to the Centronics connector's 36. Six of the original Centronics signals have no connection at the PC, and the PC has five fewer ground-return pins.

The PC interface also redefines three signals. Pin 14 (*Signal Ground*) is *nAutoLF* on the PC, pin 36 (*Reserved*) is nSelectIn, and pin 33 (*Light Detect*) is the ground return for *nSelectIn*.

that the register bit is the inverse of the signal at the connector, but the name says nothing about the signal's purpose. Whether to use *nStrobe* or $\overline{C0}$ depends on which type of information is more relevant to the topic at hand.

The Data Register

The Data port, or Data register, (*D0-D7*) holds the byte written to the Data outputs. In bidirectional Data ports, when the port is configured as input, the Data register holds the byte read at the connector's Data pins. Although the Centronics interface and the IEEE-1284 standard refer to the Data lines as *D1* through *D8,* in this book, I use *D0-D7* throughout, to correspond to the register bits.

The Status Register

The Status port, or Status register, holds the logic states of five inputs, *S3* through $\overline{S7}$. Bits *S0–S2* don't appear at the connector. The Status register is read-only, except for *S0*, which is a timeout flag on ports that support EPP transfers, and can be cleared by software. On many ports, the Status inputs have pull-up resistors. In their conventional uses, the Status bits have the following functions:

S0: Timeout. In EPP mode, this bit may go high to indicate a timeout of an EPP data transfer. Otherwise unused. This bit doesn't appear on the connector.

S1: Unused.

S2: Unused, except for a few ports where this bit indicates parallel port interrupt status (PIRQ). 0 = parallel-port interrupt has occurred; 1 = no interrupt has occurred. On these ports, reading the Status register sets PIRQ = 1.

S3: nError or *nFault.* Low when the printer detects an error or fault. (Don't confuse this one with *PError (S5).* below.)

S4: Select. High when the printer is on-line (when the printer's Data inputs are enabled).

S5: PaperEnd, PaperEmpty, or *PError.* High when the printer is out of paper.

S6: nAck or *nAcknowledge.* Pulses low when the printer receives a byte. When interrupts are enabled, a transition (usually the rising edge) on this pin triggers an interrupt.

S7 Busy. Low when the printer isn't able to accept new data. Inverted at the connector.

The Control Register

The Control port, or Control register, holds the states of four bits, $\overline{C0}$ through $\overline{C3}$. Conventionally, the bits are used as outputs. On most SPPs, however, the Control bits are open-collector or open-drain type, which means that they may also function as inputs. To read an external logic signal at a Control bit, you write *1* to the corresponding output, then read the register bit. However, in most ports that support EPP and ECP modes, to improve switching speed, the Control outputs are push-pull type and can't be used as inputs. On some multi-mode ports, the Control bits have push-pull outputs in the advanced modes, and for compatibility they switch to open-collector/open-drain outputs when emulating an SPP. (Chapter 5 has more on output types.) Bits *C4* through *C7* don't appear at the connector. In conventional use, the Control bits have the following functions:

C0: nStrobe. The rising edge of this low-going pulse signals the printer to read *D0-D7.* Inverted at the connector. After bootup, normally high at the connector.

C1: AutoLF or *Automatic line feed.* A low tells the printer to automatically generate a line feed (ASCII code *0Ah*) after each Carriage Return (ASCII *0Dh*). Inverted at the connector. After bootup, normally high at the connector.

C2: nInit or *nInitialize.* Pulses low to reset the printer and clear its buffer. Minimum pulse width: 50 microseconds. After bootup, normally high at the connector.

C3: nSelectIn. High to tell the printer to enable its Data inputs. Inverted at the connector. After bootup, normally low at the connector.

C4: Enable interrupt requests. High to allow interrupt requests to pass from *nAck* (*S6*) to the computer's interrupt-control circuits. If *C4* is high and the port's *IRQ* level is enabled at the interrupt controller, transitions at *nAck* will cause a hardware interrupt request. Does not appear at the connector.

C5: Direction control. In bidirectional ports, sets the direction of the Data port. Set to *0* for output (Data outputs enabled), *1* for input (Data outputs disabled). Usually you must first configure the port for bidirectional use (PS/2 mode) in order for this bit to have an effect. Does not appear at the connector. Unused in SPPs.

C6: Unused.

C7: Unused, except for a few ports where this bit performs the direction-setting function normally done by *C5.*

Bidirectional Ports

On the original parallel port, the Data port was designed as an output-only port. The Status port does have five inputs, and on some ports the Control port's four bits may be used as inputs, but reading eight bits of data requires reading two bytes, either the Status and Control ports, or reading one port twice, then forming a byte of data from the values read. For many projects it would be more convenient to use the Data port as an 8-bit input, and sometimes you can do just this.

In the original PC's parallel port, a 74LS374 octal flip-flop drives the Data outputs (*D0-D7*). The Data-port pins also connect to an input buffer, which stores the last value written to the port. Reading the port's Data register returns this value.

If there were a way to disable the Data-port's outputs, you could connect external signals to the Data pins and read these signals at the Data port's input buffer. The 74LS374 even has an output-enable ($\overline{OE}$) pin. When $\overline{OE}$ is low, the outputs are enabled, and when it's high, the outputs are *tri-stated,* or in a high-impedance state that effectively disables them. On the original PC's port, $\overline{OE}$ is wired directly to ground, so the outputs are permanently enabled.

Beginning with its PS/2 model in 1987, IBM included a bidirectional parallel port whose Data lines can function as inputs as well as outputs. Other computer makers followed with their own bidirectional ports. EPPs and ECPs have other, high-speed modes for reading the Data port with handshaking, but these ports can also emulate the PS/2's simple bidirectional ability.

Configuring for Bidirectional Operation

Most bidirectional ports have two or more modes of operation. To remain compatible with the original port, most have an SPP mode, where the Data port is output-only. This is often the default mode, because it's the safest—it's impossible to disable the Data outputs accidentally. To use a bidirectional Data port for input, you must first configure the port as bidirectional. The configuration may be in a software utility, or in the system's CMOS setup screen that you can access on bootup, or it may be a jumper on the port's circuit board.

After the port is configured as bidirectional, you can use the Data lines as inputs or outputs by setting and clearing bit 5 in the port's Control register, as described earlier. A *0* selects output, or write (the default), and a *1* selects input, or read. (Just remember that *1* looks like *I* for input, and *0* looks like *O* for output.) Chapter 4 includes program code to test for the presence of a bidirectional port.

A few ports use bit 7 instead of bit 5 as a direction control. To ensure compatibility with all ports, software can toggle both bits 5 and 7 to set the direction.

In an SPP or a port that hasn't been configured as bidirectional, bit C5 may read as 1 or 0. It's also possible, though rare, to have a bidirectional port whose direction bit is write-only, so you can set and clear the bit, but you can't read the bit to determine its current state. This is especially important to be aware of if you use the technique of reading the Control port, altering selected bits, then writing the value back to the Control port. If bit 5 always reads 1, you'll end up always writing 1 back to the bit, even when you don't want to disable the Data-port outputs! To avoid this problem, keep track of the desired state of bit 5 and always be sure to set or clear it as appropriate when you write to the Control port.

If you have an older output-only parallel port with a 74LS374 driving the Data port, it's possible to modify the circuits so that you can use the Data port for input. Chapter 5 shows how.

On some output-only ports, you may be able to bring the Data outputs high and drive the input buffer with external signals, with no modifications at all. But in doing so, you run the risk of damaging the port circuits. The outputs on non-bidirectional ports aren't designed to be used in this way, and connecting logic outputs to Data lines with enabled outputs can cause damaging currents in both devices. Even if the circuits don't fail right away, the added stress may cause them to fail over time. If the circuit does work, the voltages will be marginal and susceptible to noise, and performance will be slow. So, although some have used this method without problems, I don't recommend it.

Addressing

There are many ways to access a parallel port in software, but all ultimately read or write to the port's registers. The registers are in a special area dedicated to accessing input and output (I/O) devices, including printers as well as the keyboard, disk drives, display, and other components. To distinguish between I/O ports and system memory, the microprocessor uses different instructions and control signals for each. You can read and write to the ports using assembly language or higher-level languages like Basic, Pascal, and C.

On the original PC, port addresses could range from 0 to 3FFh (decimal 1024). Many newer parallel ports decode an eleventh address line to extend the range to 7FFh (decimal 2048). The number of available ports may seem like a lot, but existing devices use or reserve many of these, so only a few areas are free for other uses. Each address stores 8 bits.

Finding Ports

The PC has some parallel-port support built into its BIOS (Basic Input/Output Services), a set of program routines that perform many common tasks. The BIOS routines are normally stored in a ROM or Flash-memory chip in the computer.

When a PC boots, a BIOS routine automatically tests for parallel ports at each of three addresses: 3BCh, 378h, and 278h, in that order. To determine whether or not a port exists, the BIOS writes to the port, then reads back what it wrote. If the read is successful, the port exists. (This write/read operation doesn't require anything connected to the port; it just reads the port's internal buffer.)

The BIOS routine stores the port addresses in the BIOS data area, a section of memory reserved for storing system information. The port addresses are in a table from 40:08h to 40:0Dh in memory, beginning with LPT1. Each address uses two bytes. An unused address should read 0000.

In rare cases, the next two addresses in the BIOS data area (40:0Eh and 40:0Fh) hold an address for LPT4. But few computers have four parallel ports and not all software supports a fourth port. Some systems use 40:0Eh to store the starting address of an extended BIOS area, so in these systems, the location isn't available for a fourth port. Windows 95 doesn't depend on the BIOS table for storing port addresses, and does allow a fourth LPT port.

Many programs that access the parallel port use this table to get a port's address. This way, users only have to select LPT1, LPT2, or LPT3, and the program can find the address. By changing the values in the BIOS table, you can swap printer addresses or even enter a nonstandard address. This enables you to vary from the port assignments that were stored on boot-up. For example, some older DOS software supported only LPT1. If you want to use a printer assigned to LPT2, you can do so by swapping the two printers' addresses in the table. However, Windows and most DOS programs now allow selecting of any available port, so the need to swap addresses in the BIOS table has become rare. Windows 95's Control Panel allows you to assign any address to an LPT port.

Direct Port I/O

Reading and writing directly to the port registers gives you the most complete control over the parallel-port signals. Unlike other methods, direct I/O doesn't automatically add handshaking or control signals; it just reads or writes a byte to the specified port. (In EPP and ECP modes, however, a simple port read or write will cause an automatic handshake.)

To write directly to a port, you specify a port register and the data to write, and instruct the CPU to write the data to the requested port. To read a port, you specify a port register and where to store the data read, and instruct the CPU to read the data into the requested location.

You can use direct port reads and writes under DOS, Windows 3.1, and Windows 95. Under Windows NT, the ports are protected from direct access by applications. You can access ports under NT by using a kernel-mode device driver, such as WinRT's, described in Chapter 10.

Programming in Basic

Basic has long been popular as a programming language, partly because many have found it easy to learn and use. Although the Basic language has evolved hugely over the years, a major focus of Basic has always been to make it as simple as possible to get programs up and running quickly. The latest version of Visual Basic is much more complicated and powerful than the *BasicA* interpreter that shipped with the original PC, yet many of the keywords and syntax rules are still familiar to anyone who's programmed in any dialect of Basic.

Basic under DOS

For creating DOS programs, two popular Basics are Microsoft's QuickBasic and the QBasic interpreter included with MS-DOS. PowerBasic is another DOS Basic that evolved from Borland's TurboBasic. In all of these, you use `Inp` and `Out` to access I/O ports.

This statement writes *AAh* to a Data port at 378h:

```
OUT(&h378,&hAA)
```

This statement displays the value of a Status port at 379h, using hexadecimal notation:

```
PRINT HEX$(INP(&h379))
```

Visual Basic for Windows

Microsoft's Visual Basic has been the most popular choice for Basic programmers developing Windows programs. Unlike other Basics, however, Visual Basic for Windows doesn't include `Inp` and `Out` for port access. However, you can add `Inp` and `Out` to the language in a dynamic linked library (DLL).

A DLL contains code that any Windows program can access, including the programs you write in Visual Basic. This book includes two DLLs for port access: *inpout16.dll*, for use with 16-bit programs, including all Visual Basic 3 programs and 16-bit Visual Basic 4 programs, and *inpout32.dll*, for use with 32-bit Visual Basic 4 programs.

The *Inpout16* files include these:

Inpout16.dll. This is the DLL itself, containing the routines that your programs will access.

Inpout16.bas. This file (Listing 2-1) contains the declarations you must add to any program that uses the new subroutine and function added by the *inpout* DLL. Each `Declare` statement names a subroutine or function, the argument(s) passed to it, and the name of the DLL that contains the subroutine or function.

The use of `Alias` in the Declares enables Visual Basic to use alternate names for the routines. This feature is handy any time that you don't want to, or can't, use the routines' actual names. In this case, the inp and out routines were compiled with PowerBasic's DLL compiler. Because `Inp` and `Out` are reserved words in PowerBasic, and a routine can't have the same name as a reserved word, I named the routines `Inp16` and `Out16`. Using `Alias` enables you to call them in Visual Basic with the conventional `Inp` and `Out`.

On the user's system, the file *Inpout16.dll* should be copied to one of these locations: the default Windows directory (usually *Windows*), the default System directory (usually *Windows\\System*), or the application's working directory. These are the locations that Windows automatically searches when it loads a DLL. If for some reason the DLL is in a different directory, you'll need to add its path to the filename in the Declare statements.

With `Inp` and `Out` declared in your program, you can use them much like `Inp` and `Out` in QuickBasic. This statement writes AAh to a Data port at 378h:

```
Out(&h378,&hAA)
```

This statement displays the value of a Status port at 379h, using hexadecimal notation:

```
Debug.Print HEX$(Inp(&h379))
```

Inpout16 is a 16-bit DLL, which means that you can call it from any 16-bit Visual-Basic program.

```
Declare Function Inp% Lib "InpOut.Dll" Alias "Inp16" _
(ByVal PortAddress%)
Declare Sub Out Lib "InpOut.Dll" Alias "Out16" _
(ByVal PortAddress%, ByVal ByteToWrite%)
```

Listing 2-1: Declarations for Inp and Out in 16-bit programs.

Calling a 16-bit DLL from a 32-bit program will result in the error message *Bad DLL Calling Convention.* A 32-bit program needs a 32-bit DLL, and this book provides *inout32* for this purpose. As with *inout16*, you copy the DLL to a directory where Windows can find it, and declare Inp and Out in a *.bas* module.

Listing 2-2 shows a single declaration file that you can use in both 16-bit and 32-bit Visual Basic 4 programs. It uses Version 4's conditional compiling ability to decide which routines to declare. In a 32-bit program, Win32 is True, and the program declares the Inp32 and Out32 contained in *inout32*. In a 16-bit program, Visual Basic ignores the Win32 section and declares the Inp16 and Out16 contained in *inout16*.

Visual Basic 3 doesn't support the conditional-compile directives, so version 3 programs have to use the 16-bit-only Declares in Listing 2-1.

The Declares for *inout32* also use Aliases, but for a different reason. *Inout32* is compiled with Borland's Delphi. Inp and Out aren't reserved words in Delphi, so the compiler doesn't object to these names. However, in Win32, DLLs' declared procedure names are case-sensitive. If the procedures had the names Inp and Out you would have to be very careful to call them exactly that, not INP, out, or any other variation. The Alias enables Visual Basic to define Inp and Out without regard to case, so if you type INP or inp, Visual Basic will know that you're referring to the Inp32 function.

Why did Microsoft leave Inp, Out (and other direct memory-access functions) out of Visual Basic? Direct writes to ports and memory have always held the possibility of crashing the system if a critical memory or port address is overwritten by mistake. Under Windows, where multiple applications may be running at the same time, the dangers are greater. A program that writes directly to a parallel port has no way of knowing whether another application is already using the port.

Under Windows 95, a more sophisticated way to handle port I/O is to use a virtual device driver (*VxD*). The VxD can ensure that only applications with permission to access a port are able to do so, and it can inform other applications when a port isn't available to them.

```
Attribute VB_Name = "inpout"
'Declare Inp and Out for port I/O
'Two versions, for 16-bit and 32-bit programs.

#If Win32 Then
'DLL procedure names are case-sensitive in VB4.
'Use Alias so Inp and Out don't have to have matching case in VB.
Public Declare Function Inp Lib "inpout32.dll" _
Alias "Inp32" (ByVal PortAddress As Integer) As Integer
Public Declare Sub Out Lib "inpout32.dll" _
Alias "Out32" (ByVal PortAddress As Integer, ByVal Value _
As Integer)

#Else
Public Declare Function Inp Lib "inpout16.Dll" _
Alias "Inp16" (ByVal PortAddress As Integer) As Integer
Public Declare Sub Out Lib "inpout16.Dll" _
Alias "Out16" (ByVal PortAddress As Integer, ByVal Value As _
Integer)
#End If
```

Listing 2-2: Declarations for Inp and Out in version 4 programs, 16-bit or 32-bit.

But sometimes a port is intended just for use with a single application. For example, an application may communicate with instrumentation, control circuits, or other custom hardware. If other applications have no reason to access the port, direct I/O with Inp and Out should cause no problems, and is much simpler than writing a VxD. (Chapter 3 has more on VxDs.)

Other Programming Languages

Other programming languages, including C, Pascal/Delphi, and of course assembly language, include the ability to access I/O ports. Briefly, here's how to do it:

C

In C, you can access a parallel port with the inp and outp functions, which are much like Basic's inp and out.

This writes *AAh* to a Data port at 378h:

```
unsigned DataAddress=0x378;
int DataPort;
DataPort=outp(DataAddress,0xAA);
return 0;
```

This displays the value of a Status port at 379h:

```
unsigned StatusAddress=0x379;
int StatusPort;
StatusPort=inp(StatusAddress);
printf ("Status port = %Xh\n",StatusPort);
return 0;
```

Pascal

Pascal programmers can use the `port` function to access parallel ports.

To write *AAh* to a Data port at 378h:

```
port[378h]:=AAh
```

To read a Status port at 379h:

```
value:=port[379h]
```

Delphi 2.0

The 32-bit version of Borland's Delphi Object Pascal compiler has no port function, but you can access ports by using the in-line assembler.

To write *AAh* to a Data port at 378h:

```
asm
 push dx
 mov dx,$378
 mov al, $AA
 out dx,al
 pop dx
end;
```

To read a Status port at 379h into the variable `ByteValue`:

```
var
   ByteValue:byte;
asm
   push dx
   mov dx, $379
   in al,dx
   mov ByteValue,al
   pop dx
end;
```

Assembly Language

In assembly language, you use the microprocessor's `In` and `Out` instructions for port access.

To write *AAh* to a Data port at 378h:

```
mov dx,378h    ;store port address in dx
```

```
mov al,AAh      ;store data to write in al
out dx,al       ;write data in al to port address in dx
```

To read a Status port at 379h into register al:

```
mov dx,379h     ;store port address in dx
in al,dx        ;read data at port address into al
```

Other Ways to Access Ports

Visual Basic, Windows, and DOS include other ways to access ports that have been assigned an LPT number. These options are intended for use with printers and other devices with similar interfaces. They write bytes to the parallel port's Data port, and automatically check the Status inputs and send a strobe pulse with each byte. Because this book focuses on uses other than printer drivers, most of the examples use direct port reads and writes rather than LPT functions. But the other options do have uses. This section describes these alternate ways to access ports.

LPT Access in Visual Basic

Although Visual Basic has no built-in ability for simple port I/O, it does include ways to access LPT ports, including the `Printer` object, the `PrintForm` method, and the `Open  LPTx` statement. Their main advantage is that they're built into Visual Basic, so you don't have to declare a DLL to use them. The main limitation is that these techniques perform only a few common functions. For example, there's no way to write a specific value to the Control port, or to read the Data port.

Each of the options for accessing LPT ports automates some of the steps used in accessing a device. This can be a benefit or a hindrance, depending on the application. When using these methods to write to a port, instead of having to include code to toggle the strobe line and check the Status port, these details are taken care of automatically. And instead of having to know a port's address, you can select an LPT port by number.

But if your application doesn't need the control signals or error-checking, using these techniques adds things you don't need, and will cause problems if you're using any of the Status and Control signals in unique ways. For example, if you're using the *nStrobe* output for another purpose, you won't want your program toggling the bit every time it writes to the Data port.

These methods won't write to the Data port if the Status port's *Busy* input is high. Of course, if the *Busy* line indicates that the peripheral is busy, this is exactly what you want, but it won't work if you're using the bit for something else.

The Printer Object

Visual Basic's `Printer` object sends output to the default printer. (In Version 4 you can change the printer with a `Set` statement.) Sending the output requires two steps. First, use the `Print` method to place the data to write on the Printer object, then use the `NewPage` or `EndDoc` method to send the data to the printer.

The Printer Object isn't very useful for writing to devices other than printers or other peripherals that expect to receive ASCII text, because `NewPage` and `End-Doc` send a form-feed character (*0Ch*) after the data. The device has to be able to recognize the form feed as an end-of-data character rather than as a data byte.

A possible non-printer use for the Printer object would be to send ASCII text to an input port on a microcontroller. Plain ASCII text uses only the characters 21h to 7Eh, so it's easy to identify the form feeds and other control codes. For sending numeric data, ASCII hex format provides a way to send values from 0 to 255 using only the characters 0-9 and A-F. Appendix C has more on this format.

For writing simple data to the parallel port, select Windows' printer driver for the *Generic Line Printer* driver.

To send data to the Printer object, Status bit *S3* must be high, and *S5* and $\overline{S7}$ must be low. If not, the program will wait.

Here's an example of using the Printer object.

```
'place the byte AAh on the printer object
Printer.Print Chr$(&hAA)
'place the byte 1Fh on the printer object
Printer.Print Chr$(&h1F)
'or use this format to send text
Printer.Print "hello"
'send the bytes to the printer
Printer.NewPage
```

PrintForm

The `PrintForm` method sends an image of a form to the default printer. Because the form is sent as an image, or pattern of dots, rather than as a byte to represent each character, it's useful mainly for sending data to printers and other devices that can print or display the images.

Here's an example of the PrintForm method:

```
'First, print "hello" on Form1.
Form1.Print "hello"
```

```
'Then send the form's image to the printer.
Form1.PrintForm
```

Open "LPT1"

The documentation for Visual Basic's Open statement refers only to using it to open a file, but you can also use it to allow access to a parallel (or serial) port.

Here's an example:

```
ByteToWrite=&h55
Open "LPT1" for Output as #1
Print #1, Chr$(ByteToWrite);
```

"LPT1" selects the port to write to, and #1 is the unique file number, or in this case the device number, assigned to the port. The semicolon after the value to print suppresses the line-feed or space character that Visual Basic would otherwise add after each write. At the Status port, *nError (S3)* must be high, and *PaperEnd (S5)* and Busy $(\overline{S7})$ must be low. If *Busy* is high, the program will wait, while incorrect levels at *nError* or *PaperEnd* will cause an error message.

Windows API Calls

The Windows API offers yet another way to access parallel ports. The API, or *Application Programming Interface,* contains functions that give programs a simple and consistent way to perform many common tasks in Windows. The API's purpose is much like that of the BIOS and DOS functions under DOS, except that Windows and its API are much more complicated (and capable). To perform a task, a program calls an appropriate API function. Although Windows has no API calls for generic port I/O, it does have extensive support for printer access. If Visual Basic doesn't offer the printer control you need, you can probably find a solution in the API.

Windows uses printer-driver DLLs to handle the details of communicating with different models of printers. Under Windows 3.1, there are dozens of printer drivers, with each driver supporting just one model or a set of similar models. Under Windows 95, most printers use the universal driver *unidrv.dll*, which in turn accesses a data file that holds printer-specific information. The Windows API includes functions for sending documents and commands to a printer, controlling and querying the print spooler, adding and deleting available printers, and getting information about a printer's abilities.

The API's OpenComm and WriteComm functions offer another way to write to parallel ports.

This book concentrates on port uses other than the printer interface, so it doesn't include detail on the API's printer functions. Appendix A lists sources with more on the Windows API.

DOS and BIOS Interrupts

In 16-bit programs, MS-DOS and BIOS software interrupts provide another way to write to parallel ports. For DOS programs, QuickBasic has `Call Interrupt` and `Call Interruptx`. The QBasic interpreter included with DOS doesn't have these, however.

In 16-bit Visual-Basic programs, you can use the VBasm DLL on this book's companion disk. Vbasm includes three interrupt functions: `VbInterrupt`, `VbInterruptX`, and `VbRealModeIntX`. Each is useful in certain situations. (`VbInterrupt` doesn't pass microprocessor registers `ds` and `es`, while `VbInterruptX` and `VbRealModeIntX` do. `VbRealModeIntX` switches the CPU to real mode before calling the interrupt, while the others execute under Windows protected mode. `VbRealModeIntX` is slower, but sometimes necessary.) Vbasm includes many other subroutines and functions, such as `VbInp` and `VbOut` for port access (similar to *inpout16*), and `Vbpeek` and `Vbpoke` for reading and writing to memory locations.

The *Vbasm.txt* file includes the declarations for Vbasm's subroutines and functions. You declare and call the DLL's routines in the same way as the `Inp` and `Out` examples above. Vbasm is for use with 16-bit programs only. There is no equivalent for 32-bit programs.

BIOS Functions

The PC's BIOS includes three parallel-port functions. You call each with software interrupt 17h.

The BIOS functions are intended for printer operations, but you can use them with other devices with compatible interfaces. Before calling interrupt 17h of the BIOS, you place information (such as the function number, port number, and data to write) in specified registers in the microprocessor.

When you call the interrupt, the BIOS routine performs the action requested and writes the printer status information to the microprocessor's `ah` register, where your program can read it or perform other operations on it.

Just to keep things confusing, when the BIOS routine returns the Status register, it inverts bits 3 and 6. Bit 7 is already inverted in hardware, so the result is that bits 3, 6, and 7 in ah are the complements of the logic states at the connector. (In contrast, if you read the Status register directly, only bit 7 will be inverted from the logic states at the connector.)

These are the details of each of the BIOS functions at INT 17h:

Function 00
Sends a byte to the printer.
Called with:
ah=0 (function number)
al=the byte to print
dx=0 for LPT1, dx=1 for LPT2, dx=2 for LPT3
Returns:
ah=printer status

When a program calls function 0, the routine first verifies that *Busy* ($\overline{S7}$) is low. If it's high, the routine waits for it to go low. When *Busy* is low, the routine writes the value in `al` to the LPT port specified in `dx`. *nStrobe* ($\overline{C0}$) pulses low after each write. The function returns with the value of the Status port in `ah`.

Listing 2-3 is an example of how to use interrupt 17, function 0 to write a byte to a parallel port in Visual Basic:

Function 01
Initializes the printer.
Called with:
ah=1 (function number)
dx=0 for LPT1, 1 for LPT2, or 2 for LPT3
Returns:
ah=printer status

Calling function 01 brings *nInit* (*C2*) of the specified port low for at least 50 microseconds. It also stores the value read from the Status port in `ah`.

Function 02
Gets printer status.
Called with:
ah=2 (function number)
dx=0 for LPT1, 1 for LPT2, or 2 for LPT3
Returns:
ah=printer status

Function 02 is a subset of Function 0. It reads the Status port and stores the value read in `ah`, but doesn't write to the port.

MS-DOS Functions

In addition to the BIOS interrupt functions, MS-DOS has functions for parallel-port access. Both use interrupt 21h. Like the BIOS functions, these pulse *nStrobe* ($\overline{C0}$) low on each write. These functions won't write to the port unless

```
Dim InRegs As VbRegs
Dim OutRegs As VbRegs
Dim LPT%
Dim TestData%
Dim Status%

'Change to 1 for LPT2, or 2 for LPT3
LPT = 0
TestData = &h55

'Place the data to write in al, place the function# (0) in ah.
InRegs.ax = TestData
'Place (LPT# - 1) in dl.
InRegs.dx = LPT

'Write TestData to the port.
Call VbInterruptX(&H17, InRegs, OutRegs)

'Status is returned in high byte of OutRegs.ax
Status = (OutRegs.ax And &HFF00) / &H100 - &HFF00
'Reinvert bits 3, 6, & 7 so they match the logic states at the
'connector.
Status = Hex$(Status Xor &HC8)
```

Listing 2-3: Using Bios Interrupt 17h, Function 0 to write to a parallel port.

Busy ($\overline{S7}$) and *Paper End* (*S5*) are low and *nError* (*S3*) is high. If *Busy* is high, the routine will wait for it to go low. Unlike the BIOS functions, the MS-DOS functions don't return the Status-port information in a register.

Both of the following functions write to the PRN device, which is normally LPT1. MS-DOS's MODE command can redirect PRN to another LPT port or a serial port.

Function 05
Writes a byte to the printer.
Called with:
ah=5 (function number)
dl=the byte to write

Listing 2-4 is an example of using Interrupt 21h, Function 5 with Vbasm in Visual Basic.

Function 40h
Writes a block of data to a file or device:
Called with:
ah=40h (function number)
bx=file handle (4 for printer port)

```
Dim InRegs As Vbregs
Dim OutRegs As Vbregs
Dim I%
Dim LPT%
'Change to 1 for LPT2, or 2 for LPT3:
LPT = 0
TestData = &h55
InRegs.dx = TestData   'place the byte to write in dl
InRegs.ax = &H500          'place LPT#-1 in ah
I = VbRealModeIntX(&H21, InRegs, OutRegs)
```

Listing 2-4: Using DOS Interrupt 21h, Function 5, to write to the parallel port.

cx= number of bytes to be written

dx=offset of first byte of buffer to write

ds=segment of first byte in buffer to write

Returns:

ax=number of bytes read, or error code if carry flag (cf)=1:

5 (access denied), 6 (invalid handle).

Listing 2-5 is an example of using Interrupt 21h, Function 40h in Visual Basic.

Two additional DOS functions provide other options for accessing ports. **Function 3Fh** accesses files and devices (including the printer port) using a handle assigned by DOS. The standard handle for the LPT or PRN device is 4. **Function 44h** reads and writes to disk drives and other devices, including devices that connect to the parallel port.

```
Dim ArrayByte%
Dim BytesWritten%
'array containing data to write:
Dim A(0 To 127)
Dim DataWritten as String
LPT = 0          'Change to 1 for LPT2, or 2 for LPT3
NL = Chr(13) + Chr(10) 'new line
'create an array that stores 128 bytes
For ArrayByte = 0 To 127
    A(ArrayByte) = ArrayByte
Next ArrayByte
'get the segment and offset of the array
ArraySegment = VbVarSeg(A(0))
ArrayOffset = VbVarPtr(A(0))
InRegs.bx = 4 'file handle for PRN device
InRegs.cx = 128 'number of bytes to write
InRegs.dx = ArrayOffset 'array's starting address in segment
InRegs.ax = &H4000  'function # (40h) stored in ah
'write 128 bytes to the parallel port
BytesWritten = VbRealModeIntX(&H21, InRegs, OutRegs)
```

Listing 2-5: Using DOS Interrupt 21h, Function 40h, to write a block of data to the parallel port.

3

Programming Issues

In many ways, writing a program that accesses a parallel port is much like writing any application. Two programming topics that are especially relevant to parallel-port programming are where to place the code that communicates with the port and how to transfer data as quickly as possible. This chapter discusses options and issues related to these.

Options for Device Drivers

For communicating with printers and other peripherals, many programs isolate the code that controls the port in a separate file or set of routines called a *device driver*. The driver may be as simple as a set of subroutines within an application, or as complex as a Windows virtual device driver that controls accesses to a port by all applications.

The device driver translates between the specific commands that control a device's hardware and more general commands used by an application program or operating system. Using a driver isolates the application from the hardware details. For example, a device driver may translate commands like *Print a character* or *Read a block of data* to code that causes these actions to occur in a specific device. Instead of reading and writing directly to the device, the application or operating system communicates with the driver, which in turn accesses the device.

To access a different device, the application or operating system uses a different driver.

Under MS-DOS, some drivers, such as the mouse driver, install on bootup and any program may access the driver. Other drivers are specific to an application. For example, DOS applications typically ship with dozens of printer drivers. When you select a different printer, the application uses a different driver. Under Windows, the operating system handles the printer drivers, and individual applications use Windows API calls to communicate with the drivers. Individual applications can also install their own device drivers under Windows.

There are several ways to implement a device driver in software. You can include the driver code directly in an application. You can write a separate program and assemble or compile it as a DOS device driver or as a terminate-and-stay-resident program (TSR). You can use any of these methods under MS-DOS and—with some cautions—under Windows. Windows also has the additional options of placing the device-driver code in a dynamic link library (DLL) or a virtual device driver (VxD). Each of these has its pluses and minuses.

Simple Application Routines

For simple port input and output with a device that a single application accesses, you can include the driver code right in the application. This method is fine when the application and driver code are short and simple. If the code is in an isolated subroutine or set of subroutines, it's easy to reuse it in other applications if the need arises. Most of the examples in this book use this technique for the code that handles port accesses.

DOS Drivers

A driver installed as an MS-DOS device driver is accessible to all programs, so it's useful if multiple programs will access the same device. The code has a special format and header that identifies it as a device driver. MS-DOS drivers may have an extension of *.sys*, *.exe*, or *.com*. A *.sys* driver is listed in MS-DOS's *config.sys* file, with the form `device=driver.sys`, with `device` being the device name, and `driver.sys` being the filename of the driver. The driver then installs automatically on bootup. An *.exe* or *.com* file is an executable file that users can run anytime. To install this type of driver on bootup, include it in the system's *autoexec.bat* file. A common use for DOS drivers is the mouse driver (*mouse.sys, mouse.com*).

DOS Drivers under Windows

DOS device drivers are usable under Windows, with some limitations and drawbacks. Although this book concentrates on Windows programming and won't go into detail about how to write a DOS device driver, some background about using DOS device drivers under Windows is helpful in understanding the alternatives.

The 80286 and higher microprocessors used in PCs can run in either of two modes, *real* or *protected.* In real mode, only one application runs at a time and the application has complete control over memory and other system resources. MS-DOS runs in real mode. Although early versions of Windows could run in real mode, Windows 3.1 and higher require protected mode, which enables multiple applications to run at the same time. To ensure that applications don't interfere with each other, Windows has more sophisticated ways of managing memory and other system resources.

In real mode, reading or writing to a specific memory address will access a particular location in physical memory. In protected mode, Windows uses a descriptor table to translate between an address and the physical memory it points to.

When the microprocessor is in protected mode, Windows can run in either *standard* or *enhanced* mode. Most systems use enhanced mode because the operating system can access more memory—up to 4 Gigabytes—and swap between memory and disk to create a virtual memory space that is much larger than the installed physical memory. Systems with 80286 CPUs must use standard mode, however.

In enhanced mode, Windows divides memory into pages, and the operating system may move the information on a page to a different location in physical memory or to disk. If a program bypasses the operating system and accesses memory directly, there's no guarantee that a value written to a particular address will be at that same physical address later.

MS-DOS device drivers must run in real mode. When a Windows program calls a DOS driver, Windows has to translate between the real and protected-mode addresses. Each time it executes the driver code, Windows switches from protected mode to real mode, then switches back when the driver returns control of the system. All of this takes time, and while the MS-DOS driver has control of the system, other programs can't access the operating system. In a single-tasking operating system like MS-DOS, this isn't a problem. But under Windows, where multiple applications may need to perform actions without delay, an MS-DOS device driver may not be the best choice.

TSRs

Another option is a driver written as a TSR (terminate and stay resident) program. A TSR can reside in memory while other DOS programs run, and users can load

TSRs as needed. You can create TSRs with many DOS programming languages, including C, Turbo Pascal, and PowerBasic, but not QuickBasic.

Like DOS device drivers, TSRs run in real mode, with the same drawbacks. An added complication under Windows is that in a TSR, the program, rather than the operating system, must translate between real- and protected-mode addresses.

Windows Drivers

Windows has other options for device drivers, including DLLs and VxDs. A Visual-Basic program can call a DLL directly or use a Vbx or Ocx to access a DLL or VxD.

DLLs

A DLL (dynamic linked library) is a set of procedures that Windows applications can call. When an application runs, it links to the DLLs declared in its program code, and the corresponding DLLs load into memory. Multiple applications can access the same DLL. The application calls DLL procedures much like any other subroutine or function.

Many programming languages enable you to write and compile DLLs. Creating a DLL can be as simple as writing the code and choosing to compile it as a DLL rather than as an executable (.*exe*) file. Basic programmers can use products like PowerBasic's DLL Compiler to write DLLs in Basic. Visual-Basic programs can call any DLL, whether it was originally written in Basic or another language.

As Chapter 2 showed, a DLL is also a simple way to add the Inp and Out that Visual Basic lacks.

VxDs

A VxD (virtual device driver) is the most sophisticated way of implementing a device driver under Windows 3.1 or Windows 95. A VxD can trap any access to a port, whether it's from a Windows or DOS program, and whether it uses a direct port read or write or a BIOS or API call. When a program tries to access a port, the VxD can determine whether or not the program has permission to do so. If it does, the port access is allowed, and if not, the VxD can pass a message to the virtual machine that requested it. A VxD also can respond quickly to hardware interrupts, including interrupts caused by transitions at the parallel port's *nAck* input.

Creating a VxD isn't a simple process. It requires a wealth of knowledge about Windows, the system hardware, and how they interact. Most VxD developers use Microsoft's Device Developers Kit, which includes an assembler and other tools-for use in developing VxDs. Some C compilers also support VxD development.

Because how to write VxDs is a book-length topic in itself, this book won't go into detail on it. Appendix A lists resources on VxD writing. But because Visual-Basic programs can make use of VxDs, some background on how they work is useful.

VxDs require Windows to be in enhanced mode, where a supervisor process called the Virtual Machine Manager (VMM) controls access to system resources. Instead of allowing Windows and DOS programs complete access to the system hardware, the VMM creates one or more Virtual Machines, with each application belonging to a Virtual Machine. The VMM creates a single System Virtual Machine for the Windows operating system and its applications, and a separate virtual machine for each DOS program.

To an application, the Virtual Machine that owns the application appears to be a complete computer system. In reality, many hardware accesses first go through the VMM. The VMM also ensures that each Virtual Machine gets its share of CPU time. This arrangement allows DOS programs, which know nothing about multitasking or Windows, to co-exist with Windows programs.

A process called *port trapping* can control conflicts between DOS applications, or between a DOS and Windows application. For example, if a Windows program is using the printer port, the VMM will be aware of this, and can prevent a DOS program from accessing the same port.

The VMM is able to control port accesses from any program because it has a higher level of privilege than the applications it's controlling. The 80386 and higher CPUs allow four levels of privilege, though most systems use just two. Ring 3 is the lowest (least powerful), and Ring 0 is the highest. The Virtual Machines run under Ring 3, and the VMM runs under Ring 0.

VxDs run under Ring 0, and this is why they're powerful. A VxD can have complete control over port accesses from any Virtual Machine, and can respond quickly to parallel-port events.

Printer accesses in Windows 95 use two VxDs. *Vcomm.vxd* is the Windows 95 communications driver, which controls accesses to a variety of devices, including the Windows print spooler. *Vcomm* in turn accesses a printer driver called *lpt.vxd*, which handles functions that are specific to parallel ports. And *lpt.vxd* in turn accesses data files that contain printer-specific information.

A Virtual Printer Device (VPD) handles contentions when a Windows program requests to use a printer port that is already in use by another Windows program. Windows may display a dialog box that asks the user to decide which application gets to use the port.

Under Windows NT, a kernel-mode driver can control port accesses much like VxDs do under Windows 95.

Hardware Interrupts

Interrupt service routines, like VxDs, run under Ring 0, in protected mode. When a hardware interrupt occurs, the VMM switches to Ring 0 and passes the interrupt request to a special VxD, called the VPICD, that acts as an interrupt controller.

A VxD that wants to service a hardware interrupt must first register the interrupt-service routine (ISR) with the VPICD. When the interrupt occurs, the VPICD calls the VxD.

If no VxD has registered the interrupt, the ISR belongs to one of the Virtual Machines. The VPICD must determine which Virtual Machine owns the interrupt, and then schedule that Virtual Machine so it can service the interrupt. If the interrupt was enabled when Windows started, the interrupt is global and any of the Virtual Machines can execute the ISR. If the interrupt was enabled after Windows started, the interrupt is local, and the VPICD considers the owner of the interrupt to be the Virtual Machine that enabled it.

Custom Controls

Visual-Basic programs can access a special type of software component called the Custom Control. A common use for Custom Controls is to add abilities and features that Visual Basic lacks, such as port I/O or hardware interrupt detecting. Other Custom Controls don't do anything that you couldn't do in Visual Basic alone, but they offer a quick and easy way to add needed functions to an application, often with better performance. Visual Basic includes some Custom Controls, and many more are available from other vendors. Visual Basic supports two types of Custom Controls: the Vbx and the Ocx. Either of these may handle parallel-port accesses.

Vbx

A Vbx is a Custom Control that Visual-Basic 3 and 16-bit Visual-Basic 4 programs can use. A Vbx is a form of DLL that includes properties, events, and methods, much like Visual-Basic's Toolbox controls. The Grid control is an example of a custom control included with Visual Basic. To use a Grid control, you add the file *Grid.vbx* to your project. A Grid item then appears in the Toolbox, and you can add a grid to your project and configure it much as you do with the standard controls.

Ocx

Visual Basic 4 introduced a new form of Custom Control: the Ocx. Like a Vbx, an Ocx has properties and can respond to events. In addition, Ocx's use Object Linking and Embedding (OLE) technology, which enables applications to display and alter data from other applications. An Ocx may be 16-bit or 32-bit. Ocx's aren't limited to Visual Basic; other programming languages can use them as well. Visual Basic 3 programs can't use Ocx's, however. Chapter 10 shows an example of an Ocx that handles port accesses and interrupts in 32-bit programs.

Speed

How fast can you transfer data at the parallel port? The answer depends on many factors, both hardware- and software-related.

Hardware Limits

The circuits in the PC and peripheral are one limiting factor for port accesses.

Bus speed

The clock rate on the PC's expansion bus limits the speed of parallel-port accesses. This is true even if the port's circuits are located on the motherboard, because the CPU still uses the expansion bus's clock and control signals to access the parallel port.

Figure 3-1 shows the timing of the signals on the ISA expansion bus for reading and writing to a parallel port. The signal that controls the timing is *BCLK*. One *BCLK* cycle equals one T-cycle, and a normal read or write to a port takes six T-cycles. During T1, the CPU places the port address on *SA0-SA19*. These lines connect to the port's address-decoding circuits. (The port hardware usually decodes only the lower 10 or 11 address lines.) On the falling edge of $\overline{IOR}$ (read I/O port) or $\overline{IOW}$ (write to I/O port), the port latches the address.

For a write operation, the CPU places the data on *SD0-SD7*, and on the rising edge of $\overline{IOW}$, the data is written to the port register. A normal write allows four wait states (T2-T5) before $\overline{IOW}$ goes high.

A read operation is similar, except that after four wait states, the data from a port register is available on *SD0-SD7*, and the CPU reads the data on the rising edge of $\overline{IOR}$.

In most modern PC's, *BCLK* runs at about 8 Mhz, so a read or write to a port takes at least 750 nanoseconds, for a maximum transfer rate of 1.33 Megabytes/second.

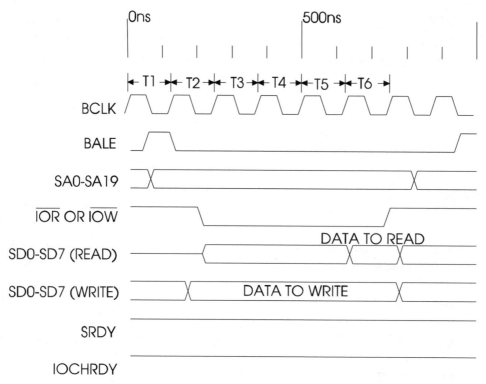

Figure 3-1: Timing diagram for port I/O cycles.

According to the IEEE's ISA-bus standard, *BCLK* may actually vary from 4 to 8.33 Mhz, so you can't assume it will be a particular value. The clock speed of the bus and microprocessor in the original IBM PC was 4.77 Mhz. The 8.33 Mhz rate is the result of dividing a 50-Mhz clock by 6.

For faster access, there is a shortened, or zero-wait-state memory-access cycle achieved by eliminating three of the wait states on the bus. This occurs if the port circuits bring $\overline{NOWS}$ (no wait states) on the ISA bus low during T2. The data to be read or written must be available by the end of T2. This doubles the speed of port accesses, to 2.67 Megabytes per second on an 8-Mhz bus. Using the shortened cycles requires both hardware and software support. Some of the newer parallel-port controllers support the shortened cycles.

CPU Speed

Because all applications do more than just read and write to ports, the CPU (microprocessor) speed also affects the speed at which a program can transfer data at the parallel port. The speed of a microprocessor's internal operations depends on the clock rate of the timing crystal that controls the chip's operations; a faster clock means faster processing.

The internal architecture of the microprocessor chip also affects how fast it can execute instructions. For example, the Pentium supports pipelining of instructions, which enables new instructions to begin feeding into the chip before previous instructions have finished. Older 80x86 chips don't have this ability.

EPP and ECP Support

A port that supports EPP or ECP modes of data transfer has the best chance for fast parallel-port transfers. An SPP requires four port writes to read the Status port, write a byte to the port, and bring *nStrobe* low, then high. With this handshaking, the fastest that you can write to the port is the time it takes for four port writes, or around 300,000 data bytes per second. If you use the DOS or BIOS software interrupts to write to a port, the speed will be much less because these routines stretch the strobe pulse.

In EPP and ECP modes, the port's hardware takes care of the handshaking automatically, within a single read or write operation. When the PC and peripheral both support one of these modes, you can transfer data at the speed of port writes on the ISA bus, typically 1.3 Mbytes/sec, or 2.7 Mbytes/sec with the shortened cycles. ECPs also support DMA transfers and data compression, discussed below.

For faster switching, a port's Control outputs often switch from open-collector to push-pull type when the port is in ECP or EPP mode.

Cables and Terminations

Cable design and the line-terminating circuits for the cable signals may also affect the maximum speed of data transfers. Chapter 6 has more on this topic.

Software Limits

Software issues that affect access speed include the choice of programming language as well as the program code itself.

Language Choices

Three basic categories of programming languages are assemblers, compilers, and interpreters.

Assemblers

With an assembler, you write programs in an assembly language whose instructions correspond directly to each of the instructions in the microprocessor's instruction set. The assembler translates the program code into machine-level, binary instructions that the microprocessor executes.

Because assembly language gives intimate control over the microprocessor, assembly-language programs can be very fast. But assembly language is a very low-level language that requires detailed knowledge of the microprocessor's architecture. Even the simplest operation requires specifying particular registers in the chip. For example, for the simple task of reading a port, you first store the port address in the *dx* register, then read the port register into the *al* register. Then you can perform calculations on the value or move the data to another memory location.

Higher-Level Languages

Higher-level languages make things easier by providing functions, operators, and other language tools that help you perform these and other complex operations more easily.

For example, in Basic, this statement reads a port into a variable:

```
DataRead = INP(PortAddress)
```

You can then use the `DataRead` variable in any way you wish, without concerning yourself with the specific registers or memory locations where the data is stored.

Higher-level languages also include tools that make it easy to display information, read keyboard input, send text and graphics to a printer, store information in files, perform complex calculations, and do other common tasks. Most higher-level languages also have programming environments with tools for easier testing, debugging, and compiling of programs.

Higher-level languages are also somewhat portable. If you learn to program in Basic on a PC, you don't have to learn an entirely new language in order to write Basic programs for a Macintosh, or even a microcontroller like the 8052-Basic.

Two types of higher-level languages are compilers and interpreters.

Compilers

With a compiled language, you create one or more source files that hold your program code. From the source files, the compiler program creates an executable file that runs on its own. Like assembled programs, a compiled program consists of machine code that the microprocessor executes. Examples of compiled languages include the C/C++ compilers from Microsoft, Borland, and others, and Borland's Delphi.

Interpreters

With an interpreted language, you also create source files, but there is no stand-alone executable file. Instead, each time you want to run a program, you run an interpreter program that translates the source file line by line into machine code.

An advantage to interpreters is that while you're developing a program, you can run the program immediately without having to compile the code first. But because the interpreter has to translate the code each time the program runs, interpreted programs tend to be much slower than compiled ones.

Although future versions may include a compiler, as of Version 4, Visual Basic is an interpreted language. Visual-Basic does create executable (*.exe*) files, but the *.exe* file must have access to a Vbrun DLL, which performs the function of an interpreter on it. QBasic is also an interpreted language. QuickBasic's programming environment includes an interpreter, and you can also compile QuickBasic programs into *.exe* files.

Choices

Different vendors' implementations of the same language will also vary in execution speed. Some compilers allow in-line assembly code, so you can have the best of both worlds by writing the most time-critical code in assembler. An optimizing compiler examines the source files and uses various techniques to make the compiled program as fast as possible. Some compilers claim to produce programs that are as fast as assembled programs, so there's no need to use assembly language at all.

In an interpreted language like Visual Basic, how you write programs has an especially big effect on execution speed. Visual Basic's documentation includes tips for optimizing your code for faster performance, such as using integer variables for calculations and assigning frequently-used object properties to variables. You can also speed execution by eliminating subroutine and function calls in favor of fewer, longer routines. But there's a tradeoff with this technique, because it also tends to make the code less readable, less portable, and harder to maintain.

Programmers endlessly debate the merits of different languages and products, and the products themselves change frequently. Visual Basic's strength is its ease of use, rather than the performance, or speed, of its programs. When speed is essential, a Visual-Basic program can call a DLL that contains the critical code in compiled form. Power Basic's DLL Compiler offers an easy way to place code in a compiled DLL, while still programming in a dialect of Basic.

Windows versus DOS

For the fastest data transfers, and especially for the fastest response to hardware interrupts, DOS beats Windows. A DOS system runs just one program at a time, while a Windows application has to share system time with whatever other applications a user decides to run. When a hardware interrupt occurs, a DOS program can jump quickly to an interrupt-service routine. Under Windows, the operating system has to decide which driver or virtual machine should service the interrupt and pass control to it, all the while handling the demands of whatever other applications are running. All of that takes time, so under Windows, the interrupt latency, or the time before an interrupt is serviced, is much longer than under DOS, and isn't as predictable.

Code Efficiency

In addition to the programming language you use, how you write your programs can affect execution speed. A complete discussion on how to write efficient program code is well beyond the scope of this book, but a simple example illustrates the issues involved:

You can generate a sine wave or other waveform by connecting a parallel port's outputs to the inputs of a digital-to-analog converter (DAC), and writing a repeating series of bytes to the port. One way to generate the series of bytes would be to use a Sine function to calculate the value for each point in the waveform before writing it. Another, usually faster way is to calculate the values just once, store them, and write the stored values in sequence to the port.

Data Compression

For the fastest data transfers, compressing the data in software can reduce the number of bytes to write. Even though the number of port writes per second doesn't change, the effective transmission rate (the amount of uncompressed data sent per second) is greater. To use this method, you of course have to have software on the receiving end that knows how to decompress what it receives. Parallel ports in ECP mode can automatically decompress incoming data that uses ECP mode's protocol for data compression.

Application-related Limits

The simplest I/O operations just write data from a register to the port, or read the port into a register. But all programs have to do more than just this, and the extra time required for processing and moving data will also limit the rate at which you can access a port in an application.

For example, a program might read an analog-to-digital converter's output in two nibbles, combine the nibbles into a byte, store the byte along with time and date information, display the information, and use the information to decide if the system needs to take an action such as sounding an alarm or adjusting a temperature control. All of this takes time!

Ports that support ECP mode can use direct memory access (DMA), where data can transfer between memory and a port without intervention by the CPU. The DMA transfers use the system's expansion bus, but the CPU is free to perform other tasks during the DMA transfers, and this can speed up the overall performance of some applications.

Chapter 3

4

Programming Tools

Many programs that access the parallel port do many of the same things, including reading and writing to the port registers and finding and testing ports on a system. Another common task is reading, setting, clearing, and toggling individual bits in a byte. This chapter introduces tools to perform these functions in any Visual-Basic program.

Routines for Port Access

Listing 4-1 is a set of subroutines and functions that simplify the tasks of reading and writing to the port registers and performing bit operations. You can add the file as a *.bas* module in your parallel-port programs (use *Add Module*) and call the routines as needed in your code.

The individual routines are very short. The reason to use them is convenience. For the port-write subroutines, you pass the base address of a port and a value to write to the port. The routines automatically calculate the register address from the base address and invert the appropriate bits, so the value passed matches the value that appears at the connector. You don't have to worry about calculating an address and inverting the bits every time you write to a port. For the port-read functions, you pass a base address and the function returns the value at the port connector. For the bit operations, you pass a variable and bit number, and the routine auto-

```
Function BitRead% (Variable%, BitNumber%)
'Returns the value (0 or 1) of the requested bit in a Variable.
Dim BitValue%
'the value of the requested bit
BitValue = 2 ^ BitNumber
BitRead = (Variable And BitValue) \ BitValue
End Function
```

```
Sub BitReset (Variable%, BitNumber%)
'Resets (clears) the requested bit in a Variable.
Dim BitValue, CurrentValue%
'the value of the requested bit
BitValue = 2 ^ BitNumber
Variable = Variable And (&HFFFF - BitValue)
End Sub
```

```
Sub BitSet (Variable%, BitNumber%)
'Sets the requested bit in a Variable.
Dim BitValue, CurrentValue%
'the value of the requested bit
BitValue = 2 ^ BitNumber
Variable = Variable Or BitValue
End Sub
```

```
Sub BitToggle (Variable%, BitNumber%)
'Toggles the requested bit in a Variable.
Dim BitValue, CurrentValue%
'the value of the requested bit
BitValue = 2 ^ BitNumber
'Is the current value 0 or 1?
CurrentValue = Variable And BitValue
Select Case CurrentValue
    Case 0
        'If current value = 0, set it
        Variable = Variable Or BitValue
    Case Else
        'If current value = 1, reset it
        Variable = Variable And (&HFFFF - BitValue)
End Select
End Sub
```

Listing 4-1: Routines for reading and writing to the parallel port registers and for reading, setting, clearing, and toggling individual bits in a byte. (Sheet 1 of 2)

```
Function ControlPortRead% (BaseAddress%)
'Reads a parallel port's Control port.
'Calculates the Control-port address from the port's
'base address, and inverts bits 0, 1, & 3 of the byte read.
'The Control-port hardware reinverts these bits,
'so the value read matches the value at the connector.
ControlPortRead = (Inp(BaseAddress + 2) Xor &HB)
End Function
```

```
Sub ControlPortWrite (BaseAddress%, ByteToWrite%)
'Writes a byte to a parallel port's Control port.
'Calculates the Control-port address from the port's
'base address, and inverts bits 0, 1, & 3.
'The Control-port hardware reinverts these bits,
'so Byte is written to the port connector.
Out BaseAddress + 2, ByteToWrite Xor &HB
End Sub
```

```
Function DataPortRead% (BaseAddress%)
'Reads a parallel port's Data port.
DataPortRead = Inp(BaseAddress)
End Function
```

```
Sub DataPortWrite (BaseAddress%, ByteToWrite%)
'Writes a byte to a parallel port's Data port.
Out BaseAddress, ByteToWrite
End Sub
```

```
Function StatusPortRead% (BaseAddress%)
'Reads a parallel port's Status port.
'Calculates the Status-port address from the port's
'base address, and inverts bit 7 of the byte read.
'The Status-port hardware reinverts these bits,
'so the value read matches the value at the connector.
StatusPortRead = (Inp(BaseAddress + 1) Xor &H80)
End Function
```

Listing 4-1: Routines for reading and writing to the parallel port registers and for reading, setting, clearing, and toggling individual bits in a byte. (Sheet 2 of 2)

matically sets, resets, toggles, or returns the value of the requested bit in the variable.

Most of the example programs in this book use these routines. The routines require the *Inpout* DLL described in Chapter 2. Because the routines are fundamental to accessing the parallel port, I'll explain them in detail.

Data Port Access

`DataPortWrite` and `DataPortRead` access a port's Data register (*D0-D7*), which controls the eight Data outputs (pins 2-9). In a printer interface, these lines hold the data to be printed. For other applications, you can use the Data lines for anything you want. If you have a bidirectional port, you can use the Data lines as inputs.

To control the states of pins 2-9 on the parallel connector, you write the desired byte to the Data register. The address of the Data register is the base address of the port. `DataPortWrite` has just one line of code, which calls `Out` to write the requested byte to the selected address. `DataPortRead` calls `Inp`. On an SPP or a bidirectional Data port configured as output, it returns the last value written to the port. On a bidirectional port configured as input, it returns the byte read on the Data lines at the connector.

Status Port Access

`StatusPortRead` reads a port's Status register (*S0-S7*). Bits 3-7 show the states of the five Status inputs at pins 15, 13, 12, 10, and 11. Bit 0 may be used as a time-out flag, but isn't routed to the connector, and bits 1 and 2 are usually unused.

The Status register is at *base address +1*, or 379h for a port at 378h. However, as Chapter 2 explained, the value that you read doesn't exactly match the logic states at the connector. Bits 3-6 read normally—the bits in the Status register match the logic states of their corresponding pins. But bit 7 is inverted between the pin and its register bit, so the logic state of bit 7 in the register is the complement of the logic state at its connector pin. To match the connector, you have to complement, or re-invert, bit 7.

Using Xor to Invert Bits

The Boolean Exclusive-Or (Xor) operator is an easy way to invert one or more bits in a byte, while leaving the other bits unchanged. This is the truth table for an Exclusive-OR operation:

A	B	A Xor B
0	0	0
0	1	1
1	0	1
1	1	0

The result is 1 only when the inputs consist of one 1 and one 0. Xoring a bit with 1 has the result of inverting, or complementing, the bit.

If the bit is 0:

```
0 Xor 1 = 1
```

and if the bit is 1:

```
1 Xor 1 = 0.
```

To invert selected bits in a byte, you first create a mask byte, where the bits to invert are 1s, and the bits to ignore are 0s. For example, to invert bit 7, the mask byte is 10000000 (binary) or 80h. If you Xor this byte with the byte read from the Status register, the result is the value at the connector. The zeros mask, or hide, the bits that you don't want to change. The StatusPortRead subroutine uses this technique to return the value at the connector.

Here's an example:

`10101XXX`	Status port, bits 3-7, at the connector. (X=don't care)
`00101XXX`	Result when you read the Status register. (Bit 7 is inverted.)
`10000000`	Mask byte to make bit 7 match the connector
`10101XXX`	The result of Xoring the previous two bytes (matches the byte at the connector)

StatusPortRead also automatically adds 1 to the base address passed to it. This way, the calling program doesn't have to remember the Status-port address. Because the Status port is read-only (except for the timeout bit in EPPs), there is no StatusPortWrite subroutine.

Control Port Access

`ControlPortRead` and `ControlPortWrite` access a port's Control register ($C0$-$C7$). Bits 0-3 show the states of the four Control lines at pins 1, 14, 16, and 17. On an SPP, the Control port is bidirectional and you can use the four lines as inputs or outputs, in any combination. The Control register's address is *base address + 2,* or 37Ah for a port with a base address of 378h.

Bits 4-7 aren't routed to the connector. When bit 4 = 1, interrupt requests pass from the parallel-port circuits to the interrupt controller. When bit 4 = 0, the interrupt controller doesn't see the interrupt requests.

If you don't want to use interrupts, bit 4 should remain low. However, in most cases just bringing bit 4 high has no effect because the interrupt isn't enabled at the interrupt controller or at the interrupt-enable jumper or configuration routine, if used. Chapter 10 has more on interrupt programming.

In ports with bidirectional Data lines, bit 5 (or rarely, bit 7) may configure the Data port as input (1) or output (0). Usually, you must enable bidirectional ability on the port before setting pin 5 will have an effect. But to be safe, you should take care not to change bit 5 in your programs unless you intend to change the direction of the Data port.

As on the Status port, the Control port has inverted bits. In fact, only bit 2 at the connector matches the logic state of its bit in the Control register. The circuits between the connector and the register invert bits 0, 1, and 3. In other words, if you write *1111* (Fh) to the lower four bits in the Control register, the bits at the connector will read *0100* (4h).

As with the Status port, you can make the bits match what you read or write by re-inverting the inverted bits. To make the value you write match the bits at the connector, Xor the value you want to write with 0Bh (00001011 binary). The Control-port routines use this technique so that the values passed to or read from the Control port match the logic states at the connector.

Keeping Bits Unchanged

In writing to the Control port, you can use logic operators to keep the upper bits from changing. (You can use the same technique anytime you want to change some bits in a byte, but keep others unchanged.)

These are the steps to changing selected bits:

1. XXXX1010   Determine the bits to write. (X=don't change)
2. 11001100   Read the port's current value.
3. 11111010   Create a byte containing all 1s except the bits desired to be 0.
4. 11001000   AND the bytes in steps 2 and 3.
5. 00001010   Create a byte containing all 0s except the bits desired to be 1.
6. 11001010   OR the bytes in steps 4 and 5. Bits 0-3 now match the desired logic states from step 1 and bits 4-7 are unchanged from the original byte read in step 2.

Reading External Signals

To read an external input at a Control bit, you must first bring the corresponding output high. You can use the Control-port bits as inputs or outputs in any combination. Because of this, the ControlPortRead routine doesn't bring the bits high automatically; the application program is responsible for doing it. (To bring all four outputs high, call `ControlPortWrite` with `ByteToWrite=&h0F`.)

As with the outputs, the value read at the Control port has bits 0, 1, and 3 inverted from their logic states at the connector. To re-invert bits 0, 1, and 3 and return the value at the connector, `ControlPortRead` Xors the byte read with 0Bh.

Optimizing for Speed

These routines are designed for ease of use, rather than fast execution. These techniques will increase the speed of the routines:

Eliminate subroutine and function calls by placing the code directly in the routine that would otherwise make the calls. The routines are short, and easily copied.

Assign the Status and Control-port addresses to variables instead of calculating them from the base address each time. You then need to specify the appropriate address instead of using the base address. To use this technique, do the following:

Eliminate this line from StatusPortRead:

```
StatusPortAddress=BaseAddress+1
```

Eliminate this line from ControlPortWrite and ControlPortRead:

```
ControlPortAddress=BaseAddress+2
```

In your application:

Assign the Status and Control port's addresses to variables:

```
StatusPortAddress=BaseAddress+1
ControlPortAddress=BaseAddress+2
```

And use these calls:

```
StatusPortData = Inp(StatusPortAddress)
ControlPortWrite Value, ControlPortAddress
ControlPortData = Inp(ControlPortAddress)
```

Instead of re-inverting the inverted Status and Control bits each time you read or write to them, you can just take the inverted bits into account in the program. For example, if a 1 at Control bit 0 switches on a relay, have the software write 0 to the bit when it wants the relay to switch on. Keeping track of which bits are inverted can be difficult however! One way to keep the program readable is to assign the values to constants:

```
Const Relay3On% = 0
Const Relay3Off% = 1
```

Often, while you're developing an application, you don't have to be concerned about speed. When the code is working properly, you can do some or all of the above to speed it up.

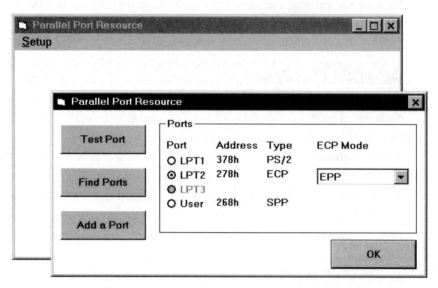

Figure 4-1: A form with a setup menu that enables uses to select and test ports.

Bit Operations

Sometimes you just want to set, reset, or toggle one bit in a byte, toggle a control signal, or set or read a switch. The `BitSet`, `BitReset`, `BitToggle`, and `BitRead` routines perform these operations, which you can use any time you want to read or write to a bit in an integer variable. Each routine is passed a variable and a bit number. The routine calculates the value of the selected bit and uses logic operators to perform the requested action on the individual bit.

For example, to set bit 4 in the variable PortData:

```
BitSet PortData, 4
```

and to read back this bit's value:

```
Bit4 = BitRead(PortData, 4)
```

A Form Template

Figure 4-1 shows a second tool for parallel-port programs: a set of Visual-Basic forms that you can use as a template, or starting point, for programs. The startup form is blank except for a Setup menu with a Port submenu, which displays a form that enables users to select a port, find the ports on a system, and test the ports. (You can add other items to the Setup menu.)

Most of the programs in this book use these elements as a base, with command buttons, text boxes, other controls and application-specific code added to the main form or in other modules.

Listing 4-2 contains the code for the form that displays the Ports. Listing 4-3 has the startup form's small amount of code. Most of the code is in a separate *.bas* module, Listing 4-4. In Visual Basic 3, procedures in a form module are local to the form, but all forms can access procedures in a *.bas* module. Version 4 is more flexible, with the ability to declare procedures Public or Private. Still, grouping the general routines in one module is useful for keeping the code organized.

The listings show the Visual Basic 4 version of the program. The Version-3 code differs in just a few areas, such as the calls for getting and saving initialization data. The companion disk includes both Version 3 and Version 4 code.

Saving Initialization Data

Each time the program runs, Listing 4-4's GetIniData subroutine retrieves information about the system's ports. When the program ends, WriteInidata stores the information to be retrieved the next time the program runs. This way, the program can remember what ports a system has, which port is selected, and any other information the program wants to store. Remembering these isn't essential, but it's a convenience that users will appreciate.

Ini Files

One way to access initialization data is to use Visual Basic's file I/O statements to read and write to a file. Under Windows, however, there are other options. Windows defines a standard method for storing data in *ini* files, which are text files normally found in the Windows directory. The best-known *ini* file is *win.ini,* which holds information used by Windows and may also contain data sections for individual applications. An application may also have its own *ini* file. This is the method used by Listing 4-4, which accesses a file called *Lptprogs.ini.* Listing 4-5 shows an example *ini* file. *Ini* files must follow a standard format consisting of one or more section names in square brackets [lptdata], with each section name followed by data assignments.

Although you can use ordinary file I/O statements to read and write to an *ini* file, Windows provides API functions for this purpose. Calling an API function in a Visual-Basic program is much like calling other functions. As when calling a DLL, the program must declare the API function before it can call it. The listing includes the Declare statements for the API functions GetPrivatePro-

```
Private Sub cboEcpMode_Click(Index As Integer)
SetEcpMode (cboEcpMode(Index).ListIndex)
End Sub
```

```
Private Sub cmdAddPort_Click()
'Display a text box to enable user to add a port
'at a nonstandard address.
frmNewPortAddress.Show
End Sub
```

Listing 4-2: Code for Figure 4-1's form that enables users to find, test, and select ports. (Sheet 1 of 4)

```
Private Sub cmdFindPorts_Click()
'Test the port at each of the standard addresses,
'and at the non-standard address, if the user has entered one.
Dim Index%
Dim PortExists%
Dim Count%
Index = 0
'First, test address 3BCh
Port(Index).Address = &H3BC
PortExists = TestPort(Index)
'If the port exists, increment the index.
If Not (Port(Index).Address) = 0 Then
    Index = Index + 1
End If
'Test address 378h
Port(Index).Address = &H378
PortExists = TestPort(Index)
'If the port exists, increment the index.
If Not (Port(Index).Address) = 0 Then
    Index = Index + 1
End If
'Test address 278h
Port(Index).Address = &H278
PortExists = TestPort(Index)
'Disable option buttons of unused LPT ports
For Count = Index + 1 To 2
    optPortName(Count).Enabled = False
    Port(Count).Enabled = False
Next Count
If Not (Port(3).Address = 0) Then
    PortExists = TestPort(Index)
Else
    optPortName(3).Enabled = False
End If
End Sub
```

```
Private Sub cmdOK_Click()
frmSelectPort.Hide
End Sub
```

Listing 4-2: Code for Figure 4-1's form that enables users to find, test, and select ports. (Sheet 2 of 4)

```
Private Sub cmdTestPort_Click()
Dim PortExists%
Dim Index%
'Get the address of the selected port
Index = -1
Do
    Index = Index + 1
Loop Until optPortName(Index).Value = True
PortExists = TestPort(Index)
Select Case PortExists
    Case True
        MsgBox "Passed: Port " + Hex$(BaseAddress) + _
        "h is " + Port(Index).PortType + ".", 0
    Case False
        MsgBox "Failed port test. ", 0
End Select

End Sub
```

Listing 4-2: Code for Figure 4-1's form that enables users to find, test, and select ports. (Sheet 3 of 4)

```
Private Sub Form_Load()
Dim Index%
Left = (Screen.Width - Width) / 2
Top = (Screen.Height - Height) / 2

'Load the combo boxes with the ECP modes.
For Index = 0 To 3
    cboEcpMode(Index).AddItem "SPP (original)"
Next Index
For Index = 0 To 3
    cboEcpMode(Index).AddItem "bidirectional"
Next Index
For Index = 0 To 3
    cboEcpMode(Index).AddItem "Fast Centronics"
Next Index
For Index = 0 To 3
    cboEcpMode(Index).AddItem "ECP"
Next Index
For Index = 0 To 3
    cboEcpMode(Index).AddItem "EPP"
Next Index

'Enable the option buttons for existing ports.
For Index = 0 To 3
    optPortName(Index).Enabled = Port(Index).Enabled
Next Index
UpdateLabels
End Sub
```

```
Private Sub optPortName_Click(Index As Integer)
'Store the address and index of the selected port.
Dim Count%
BaseAddress = Port(Index).Address
IndexOfSelectedPort = Index
EcpDataPortAddress = BaseAddress + &H400
EcrAddress = BaseAddress + &H402
For Count = 0 To 3
    cboEcpMode(Count).Enabled = False
Next Count
cboEcpMode(Index).Enabled = True
End Sub
```

Listing 4-2: Code for Figure 4-1's form that enables users to find, test, and select ports. (Sheet 4 of 4)

```
Private Sub Form_Load()
StartUp
End Sub
```

```
Private Sub Form_Unload(Cancel%)
ShutDown
End
End Sub
```

```
Private Sub mnuPort_Click(Index%)
frmSelectPort.Show
End Sub
```

Listing 4-3: The startup form for the sample project is blank except for a menu. You can add whatever controls you need for a specific application.

fileString and WritePrivateProfileString. The API calls differ slightly under Windows 3.1 and Windows 95. The Version-4 code uses Visual Basic's conditional compile ability to decide which calls to declare. You can add these statements to any *.bas* module in a program. In Version 3, you use only the declares following #Else.

GetIniData uses GetPrivateProfileString to retrieve several values, including the address and type of each existing port, and a value that indicates the port that was selected the last time the program ran. WriteIniData uses WritePrivateProfileString to save these values when the program ends.

System Registry

Windows' System Registry offers another way to store program information. Visual Basic 4's SaveSetting and GetSetting are a simple way to store and retrieve information related to Visual Basic programs, and you can use these in a similar way to save port information.

Under Windows 95, two API functions enable programs to find and add system ports. EnumPorts returns the LPT number and a brief description of each parallel port that Windows is aware of, and AddPort displays a dialog box that enables users to add a port to the list.

Finding, Selecting, and Testing Ports

Because the parallel-port's address can vary, programs must have a way of selecting a port to use. There are several ways to accomplish this.

```
#If Win32 Then
Declare Function GetPrivateProfileStringByKeyName& Lib _
"Kernel32" Alias "GetPrivateProfileStringA" _
(ByVal lpApplicationName$, ByVal lpszKey$, ByVal lpszDefault$, _
ByVal lpszReturnBuffer$, ByVal cchReturnBuffer&, ByVal lpszFile$)

Declare Function WritePrivateProfileString& Lib _
"Kernel32" Alias "WritePrivateProfileStringA" _
(ByVal lpApplicationName$, ByVal lpKeyName$, ByVal lpString$, _
ByVal lpFileName$)

Declare Function GetWindowsDirectory& Lib "Kernel32" _
Alias "GetWindowsDirectoryA" (ByVal lpBuffer$, ByVal nSize%)

#Else

Declare Function GetPrivateProfileStringByKeyName% Lib "Kernel" _
Alias "GetPrivateProfileString" _
(ByVal lpApplicationName$, ByVal lpKeyName$, ByVal lpDefault$, _
ByVal lpReturnedString$, ByVal nSize%, ByVal lpFileName$)

Declare Function WritePrivateProfileString% Lib "Kernel" _
(ByVal lpApplicationName$, ByVal lpKeyName$, _
ByVal lpString$, ByVal lpFileName$)

Declare Function GetWindowsDirectory% Lib "Kernel" _
(ByVal lpBuffer$, ByVal nSize%)

#End If
```

Listing 4-4: Code for finding and testing ports, and getting and saving initialization data from an *ini* file. (Sheet 1 of 14)

```
Type PortData
    Name As String
    Address As Integer
    PortType As String
    EcpModeDescription As String
    EcpModeValue As Integer
    Enabled As Integer
End Type
Global Port(0 To 3) As PortData
Global BaseAddress%
Global PortType$
Global IniFile$

Global EcrAddress%
Global EcrData%
Global EcpDataPortAddress%
Global EppDataPort0Address%
Global IndexOfSelectedPort%
Global PortDescription$

Global EcpExists%
Global SppExists%
Global PS2Exists%
Global EppExists%
```

```
Function GetEcpModeDescription$(EcpModeValue%)
Select Case EcpModeValue
    Case 0
        GetEcpModeDescription = "SPP"
    Case 1
        GetEcpModeDescription = "PS/2"
    Case 2
        GetEcpModeDescription = "Fast Centronics"
    Case 3
        GetEcpModeDescription = "ECP"
    Case 4
        GetEcpModeDescription = "EPP"
    Case 6
        GetEcpModeDescription = "Test"
    Case 7
        GetEcpModeDescription = "Configuration"
End Select
End Function
```

Listing 4-4: Code for finding and testing ports, and getting and saving initialization data from an *ini* file. (Sheet 2 of 14)

```
Sub GetIniData()
'Use the Windows API call GetPrivateProfileString to read
'user information from an ini file.
Dim NumberOfCharacters
Dim ReturnBuffer As String * 128
Dim Index%
Dim WindowsDirectory$
'Get the Windows directory, where the ini file is stored.
NumberOfCharacters = GetWindowsDirectory(ReturnBuffer, 127)
WindowsDirectory = Left$(ReturnBuffer, NumberOfCharacters)
IniFile = WindowsDirectory + "\lptprogs.ini"

'If the ini file doesn't exist, don't try to read it.
If Not Dir$(IniFile) = "" Then
    'The port addresses:
    Port(0).Address = _
CInt(VbGetPrivateProfileString("lptdata","Port0Address",
 IniFile))
    Port(1).Address = _
CInt(VbGetPrivateProfileString("lptdata","Port1Address",
 IniFile))
    Port(2).Address = _
CInt(VbGetPrivateProfileString("lptdata","Port2Address",
 IniFile))
    Port(3).Address = _
CInt(VbGetPrivateProfileString("lptdata","Port3Address",
 IniFile))

    'The port types:
    Port(0).PortType = _
VbGetPrivateProfileString("lptdata", "Port0Type", IniFile)
    Port(1).PortType = _
VbGetPrivateProfileString("lptdata", "Port1Type", IniFile)
    Port(2).PortType = _
VbGetPrivateProfileString("lptdata", "Port2Type", IniFile)
    Port(3).PortType = _
VbGetPrivateProfileString("lptdata", "Port3Type", IniFile)
```

Listing 4-4: Code for finding and testing ports, and getting and saving initialization data from an *ini* file. (Sheet 3 of 14)

```
'Port enabled?
    Port(0).Enabled = _
CInt(VbGetPrivateProfileString("lptdata",
 "Port0Enabled",IniFile))
    Port(1).Enabled = _
CInt(VbGetPrivateProfileString("lptdata",
 "Port1Enabled",IniFile))
    Port(2).Enabled = _
CInt(VbGetPrivateProfileString("lptdata",
 "Port2Enabled",IniFile))
    Port(3).Enabled = _
CInt(VbGetPrivateProfileString("lptdata",
 "Port3Enabled",IniFile))

'The selected port
    IndexOfSelectedPort = _
Int(VbGetPrivateProfileString("lptdata", _
"IndexOfSelectedPort", IniFile))
End If
End Sub
```

```
Function ReadEcpMode%(TestAddress%)
'The Ecr mode is in bits 5, 6, and 7 of the ECR.
EcrAddress = TestAddress + &H402
EcrData = Inp(EcrAddress)
ReadEcpMode = (EcrData And &HE0) \ &H20
End Function
```

```
Function ReadEppTimeoutBit%(BaseAddress%)
'Reads and clears the EPP timeout bit (Status port bit 0).
'Should be done after each EPP operation.
'The method for clearing the bit varies, so try 3 ways:
'1. Write 1 to Status port bit 0.
'2. Write 0 to Status port, bit 0.
'3. Read the Status port again.
Dim StatusPortAddress%
StatusPortAddress = BaseAddress + 1
ReadEppTimeoutBit = BitRead(StatusPortRead(BaseAddress), 0)
Out StatusPortAddress, 1
Out StatusPortAddress, 0
ReadEppTimeoutBit = BitRead(StatusPortRead(BaseAddress), 0)
End Function
```

Listing 4-4: Code for finding and testing ports, and getting and saving initialization data from an *ini* file. (Sheet 4 of 14)

```
Sub SetEcpMode(EcpModeValue%)
'Store the Ecp mode's value and description in the Port array.
Port(IndexOfSelectedPort).EcpModeValue = EcpModeValue
Port(IndexOfSelectedPort).EcpModeDescription = _
GetEcpModeDescription(EcpModeValue)
EcrAddress = BaseAddress + &H402
'Read the ECR & clear bits 5, 6, 7.
EcrData = Inp(EcrAddress) And &H1F
'Write the selected value to bits 5, 6, 7.
EcrData = EcrData + EcpModeValue * &H20
Out EcrAddress, EcrData
End Sub
```

```
Sub ShutDown()
WriteIniData
End
End Sub
```

```
Sub StartUp()
Dim PortExists%
Dim Index%
'Get information from the ini file.
GetIniData

'Load the forms.
frmMain.Left = (Screen.Width - frmMain.Width) / 2
frmMain.Top = (Screen.Height - frmMain.Height) / 2
Load frmSelectPort
frmSelectPort.optPortName(IndexOfSelectedPort).Value = True
frmMain.Show
End Sub
```

Listing 4-4: Code for finding and testing ports, and getting and saving initialization data from an *ini* file. (Sheet 5 of 14)

```
Function TestForEcp%(TestAddress%)
'Test for the presence of an ECP.
'If the ECP is idle and the FIFO empty,
'in the ECP's Ecr (at Base Address+402h),
'bit 1(Fifo full)=0, and bit 0(Fifo empty)=1.
'The first test is to see if these bits differ from the
'corresponding bits in the Control port (at Base Address+2).
'If so, a further test is to write 34h to the Ecr,
'then read it back. Bit 1 is read/write, and bit 0 is read-only.
'If the value read is 35h, the port is an ECP.
Dim EcrBit0%, EcrBit1%
Dim ControlBit0%, ControlBit1%
Dim ControlPortData%
Dim TestEcrAddress%
Dim OriginalEcrData%
TestForEcp = False
EcrAddress = TestAddress + &H402
'Read ECR bits 0 & 1 and Control Port bit 1.
EcrData = Inp(EcrAddress)
EcrBit0 = BitRead(EcrData, 0)
EcrBit1 = BitRead(EcrData, 1)
ControlPortData = ControlPortRead(TestAddress)
ControlBit1 = BitRead(ControlPortData, 1)
If EcrBit0 = 1 And EcrBit1 = 0 Then
    'Compare Control bit 1 to ECR bit 1.
    'Toggle the Control bit if necessary,
    'to be sure the two registers are different.
    If ControlBit1 = 0 Then
        ControlPortWrite TestAddress, &HF
        ControlPortData = ControlPortRead(TestAddress)
        ControlBit1 = BitRead(ControlPortData, 1)
    End If
    If EcrBit1 <> ControlBit1 Then
        OriginalEcrData = EcrData
        Out EcrAddress, &H34
        EcrData = Inp(EcrAddress)
        If EcrData = &H35 Then
            TestForEcp = True
        End If
        'Restore the ECR to its original value.
        Out EcrAddress, OriginalEcrData
    End If
End If
End Function
```

Listing 4-4: Code for finding and testing ports, and getting and saving initialization data from an *ini* file. (Sheet 6 of 14)

Parallel Port Complete

```
Function TestForEpp%(TestAddress%)
'Write to an Epp register, then read it back.
'If the reads match the writes, it's probably an Epp.
'Skip this test if TestAddress = 3BCh.
Dim ByteRead%
Dim StatusPortData%
Dim EppAddressPort%
Dim TimeoutBit%
Dim StatusPortAddress%
StatusPortAddress = TestAddress + 1
TestForEpp = False
'Use EppAddressPort for testing.
'SPPs, ECPs, and PS/2 ports don't have this register.
EppAddressPort = TestAddress + 3
Out EppAddressPort, &H55
'Clear the timeout bit after each EPP operation.
TimeoutBit = ReadEppTimeoutBit%(TestAddress%)
ByteRead = Inp(EppAddressPort)
TimeoutBit = ReadEppTimeoutBit%(TestAddress%)
If ByteRead = &H55 Then
    Out EppAddressPort, &HAA
    TimeoutBit = ReadEppTimeoutBit%(TestAddress%)
    ByteRead = Inp(EppAddressPort)
    TimeoutBit = ReadEppTimeoutBit%(TestAddress%)
    If ByteRead = &HAA Then
        TestForEpp = True
    End If
End If
End Function
```

Listing 4-4: Code for finding and testing ports, and getting and saving initialization data from an *ini* file. (Sheet 7 of 14)

```
Function TestForPS2%(TestAddress%)
'Tests a parallel port's Data port for bidirectional ability.
'First, try to tri-state (disable) the Data outputs by
'setting bit 5 of the Control port.
'Then write 2 values to the Data port and read each back
'If the values match, the Data outputs are not disabled,
'and the port is not bidirectional.
'If the values don't match,
'the Data outputs are disabled and the port is bidirectional.
Dim DataInput%
Dim ControlPortData%
Dim OriginalControlPortData%
Dim OriginalDataPortData%

'Set Control port bit 5.
ControlPortWrite TestAddress, &H2F
TestForPS2 = False
'Write the first byte and read it back:
DataPortWrite TestAddress, &H55
DataInput = DataPortRead(TestAddress)
'If it doesn't match, the port is bidirectional.
If Not DataInput = &H55 Then TestForPS2 = True
'If it matches, write another and read it back.
If DataInput = &H55 Then
    DataPortWrite TestAddress, &HAA
    DataInput = DataPortRead(TestAddress)
    'If it doesn't match, the port is bidirectional
    If Not DataInput = &HAA Then
        TestForPS2 = True
    End If
End If
'Reset Control port bit 5
ControlPortWrite TestAddress, &HF
End Function
```

Listing 4-4: Code for finding and testing ports, and getting and saving initialization data from an *ini* file. (Sheet 8 of 14)

```
Function TestForSpp%(TestAddress%)
'Write two bytes and read them back.
'If the reads match the writes, the port exists.
Dim ByteRead%
'Be sure that Control port bit 5 = 0 (Data outputs enabled).
ControlPortWrite TestAddress, &HF
TestForSpp = False
DataPortWrite TestAddress, &H55
ByteRead = DataPortRead(TestAddress)
If ByteRead = &H55 Then
    DataPortWrite TestAddress, &HAA
    ByteRead = DataPortRead(TestAddress)
    If ByteRead = &HAA Then
        TestForSpp = True
    End If
End If
End Function
```

Listing 4-4: Code for finding and testing ports, and getting and saving initialization data from an *ini* file. (Sheet 9 of 14)

```
Function TestPort%(PortIndex%)
'Test for a port's presence, and if it exists, the type of port.
'In order, check for presence of ECP, EPP, SPP, and PS/2 port.
'Update the information in the Port array and the display.
Dim EcpModeDescription$
Dim EcpModeValue%
Dim TestAddress%
TestPort = False
EcpExists = False
EppExists = False
SppExists = False
PS2Exists = False
PortType = ""
TestAddress = Port(PortIndex).Address
'Begin by hiding all port details.
frmSelectPort.lblAddress(PortIndex).Visible = False
frmSelectPort.lblType(PortIndex).Visible = False
frmSelectPort.cboEcpMode(PortIndex).Visible = False
EcpExists = TestForEcp(TestAddress)
If EcpExists Then
    PortType = "ECP"
    'Read the current Ecp mode.
    EcpModeValue = ReadEcpMode(TestAddress)
Else
    'If it's not an ECP, look for an EPP.
    'If TestAddress = 3BCh, skip the EPP test.
    'EPPs aren't allowed at 3BCh due to possible conflict
    'with video memory.
    frmSelectPort.cboEcpMode(PortIndex).Visible = False
    If TestAddress = &H3BC Then
        EppExists = False
    Else
        EppExists = TestForEpp(TestAddress)
    End If
    frmSelectPort.cboEcpMode(PortIndex).Visible = False
    EppExists = TestForEpp(TestAddress)
    If EppExists Then
        PortType = "EPP"
```

Listing 4-4: Code for finding and testing ports, and getting and saving initialization data from an *ini* file. (Sheet 10 of 14)

```
     Else
         'If it's not an EPP, look for an SPP.
         SppExists = TestForSpp(TestAddress)
         If SppExists Then
             'Test for a PS/2 port only if the SPP exists
             '(because if the port doesn't exist,
             'it will pass the PS/2 test!)
             PS2Exists = TestForPS2(TestAddress)
             If PS2Exists Then
                 PortType = "PS/2"
             Else
                 PortType = "SPP"
             End If
         Else
             PortType = ""
         End If
     End If
End If

If PortType = "" Then
    frmSelectPort.optPortName(PortIndex).Enabled = False
    Port(PortIndex).PortType = ""
    Port(PortIndex).Address = 0
    Port(PortIndex).Enabled = False
Else
    TestPort = True
    Port(PortIndex).Enabled = True
    Port(PortIndex).PortType = PortType
    Port(PortIndex).Enabled = True
    If EcpExists Then
        Port(PortIndex).EcpModeValue = EcpModeValue
        Port(PortIndex).EcpModeDescription = _
          GetEcpModeDescription(EcpModeValue)
    End If
End If
UpdateLabels
End Function
```

Listing 4-4: Code for finding and testing ports, and getting and saving initialization data from an *ini* file. (Sheet 11 of 14)

```
Sub UpdateLabels()
'Use the information in the Port array to update the display.
Dim Index%
Dim EcpModeValue%
For Index = 0 To 3
    frmSelectPort.lblAddress(Index).Caption = _
      Hex$(Port(Index).Address) + "h"
    If Port(Index).Enabled = True Then
        frmSelectPort.optPortName(Index).Enabled = True
        frmSelectPort.lblAddress(Index).Visible = True
        frmSelectPort.lblType(Index).Caption = _
          Port(Index).PortType
        frmSelectPort.lblType(Index).Visible = True
        If Port(Index).PortType = "ECP" Then
            EcpModeValue = ReadEcpMode(Port(Index).Address)
            frmSelectPort.cboEcpMode(Index).ListIndex = _
            EcpModeValue
            Port(Index).EcpModeValue = EcpModeValue
            Port(Index).EcpModeDescription = _
            GetEcpModeDescription(EcpModeValue)
            frmSelectPort.cboEcpMode(Index).Visible = True
        Else
            frmSelectPort.cboEcpMode(Index).Visible = False
        End If
    Else
        frmSelectPort.optPortName(Index).Enabled = False
        frmSelectPort.lblAddress(Index).Visible = False
        frmSelectPort.lblType(Index).Visible = False
        frmSelectPort.cboEcpMode(Index).Visible = False

    End If
Next Index
End Sub
```

Listing 4-4: Code for finding and testing ports, and getting and saving initialization data from an *ini* file. (Sheet 12 of 14)

Parallel Port Complete

```
Sub WriteIniData()
Dim BaseAddressWrite%
Dim PortTypeWrite%
Dim Index%
Dim IniWrite

'Use Windows API call WritePrivateProfileString to save
'initialization information.
'If the ini file doesn't exist, it will be created and stored in
'the Windows directory.

'The port addresses:
IniWrite = WritePrivateProfileString _
("lptdata", "Port0Address", CStr(Port(0).Address), IniFile)
IniWrite = WritePrivateProfileString _
("lptdata", "Port1Address", CStr(Port(1).Address), IniFile)
IniWrite = WritePrivateProfileString _
("lptdata", "Port2Address", CStr(Port(2).Address), IniFile)
IniWrite = WritePrivateProfileString _
("lptdata", "Port3Address", CStr(Port(3).Address), IniFile)

'The port types:
IniWrite = WritePrivateProfileString _
("lptdata", "Port0Type", Port(0).PortType, IniFile)
IniWrite = WritePrivateProfileString _
("lptdata", "Port1Type", Port(1).PortType, IniFile)
IniWrite = WritePrivateProfileString _
("lptdata", "Port2Type", Port(2).PortType, IniFile)
IniWrite = WritePrivateProfileString _
("lptdata", "Port3Type", Port(3).PortType, IniFile)

'Port enabled?
IniWrite = WritePrivateProfileString _
("lptdata", "Port0Enabled", CStr(Port(0).Enabled), IniFile)
IniWrite = WritePrivateProfileString _
("lptdata", "Port1Enabled", CStr(Port(1).Enabled), IniFile)
IniWrite = WritePrivateProfileString _
("lptdata", "Port2Enabled", CStr(Port(2).Enabled), IniFile)
IniWrite = WritePrivateProfileString _
("lptdata", "Port3Enabled", CStr(Port(3).Enabled), IniFile)
```

Listing 4-4: Code for finding and testing ports, and getting and saving initialization data from an *ini* file. (Sheet 13 of 14)

```
'Find the selected port and save it:
Index = 4
Do
Index = Index - 1
Loop Until (frmSelectPort.optPortName(Index).Value = True) _
Or Index = 0
IniWrite = WritePrivateProfileString("lptdata", _
  "IndexOfSelectedPort", CStr(Index), IniFile)
End Sub
```

```
Function VbGetPrivateProfileString$(section$, key$, file$)
    Dim KeyValue$
    'Characters returned as integer in 16-bit, long in 32-bit.
    Dim Characters
    KeyValue = String$(128, 0)
    Characters = GetPrivateProfileStringByKeyName _
    (section, key, "", KeyValue, 127, file)
    KeyValue = Left$(KeyValue, Characters)
    VbGetPrivateProfileString = KeyValue
End Function
```

Listing 4-4: Code for finding and testing ports, and getting and saving initialization data from an *ini* file. (Sheet 14 of 14)

For a short test routine, you can just place the port address in the code:

```
Out &H378, &HAA
```

Or, you can set a variable equal to the port's address, and use the variable name in the program code:

```
BaseAddress = &H378
Out BaseAddress, &HAA
```

Using a variable has advantages. If the port address changes, you need to change the code in just one place. And for anyone reading the code, a descriptive variable name is usually more meaningful than a number.

Most programs will run on a variety of computers, and even on a single computer, the port that a program accesses may change. In this case, it's best to allow the software or user to select a port address while the program is running.

The Port Menu

In Figure 4-1, the startup form contains a *Port* item in the *Setup* menu. Clicking on *Port* brings up a form that enables users to find, test, and select ports. Clicking on *Find Ports* causes the program to look for a port at each of the three standard port addresses. If a port exists, the program tests it to find out whether it's an SPP,

```
[lptdata]
Port0Address=888
Port1Address=632
Port2Address=0
Port3Address=256
Port0Type=ECP
Port1Type=SPP
Port2Type=
Port3Type=SPP
Port0Enabled=-1
Port1Enabled=-1
Port2Enabled=0
Port3Enabled=-1
IndexOfSelectedPort=1
```

Listing 4-5: The contents of an ini file that stores information about the system ports.

PS/2-type, EPP, or ECP. If it's ECP, the program displays a combo box that shows the currently selected ECP mode, which the user can change.

To select a port, you click its option button. The *Test Port* command button tests an individual port and displays the result.

You can also use the routines to test a port under program control. For example, if you're writing a program that will run on many different computers, you may want the software to detect the port type so it can choose the best communications mode available.

Adding a Non-standard Port

The *Add A Port* command button brings up a form that allows you to enter an address of a user port with a non-standard address. You can then use Test Port to determine its type.

Detecting an ECP

In testing a port, you might think that the first step would be to test for an SPP, and work your way up from there. But if the port is an ECP, and it happens to be in its internal SPP mode, the port will fail the PS/2 (bidirectional) test. For this reason, the TestPort routine in Listing 4-4 begins by testing for an ECP.

An ECP has several additional registers. One of these, the extended control register (ECR) at *base address + 402h*, is useful in detecting an ECP.

Microsoft's ECP document (see Appendix A) recommends a test for detecting an ECP. First, read the port's ECR at and verify that bit 0 (FIFO empty) =1 and bit 1 (FIFO full) =0. These bits should be distinct from bits 0 and 1 in the port's Control register (at *base address + 2*). You can verify this by toggling one of the bits in the Control register, and verifying that the corresponding bit in the ECR doesn't change. A further test is to write 34h to the ECR and read it back. Bits 0 and 1 in the ECR are read-only, so if you read 35h, you almost certainly have an ECP.

If an ECP exists, you can read and set the port's internal ECP mode in bits 5, 6, and 7 of the ECR. In Listing 4-4, a combo box enables users to select an ECP mode when a port is ECP. Chapter 15 has more on reading, setting, and using the ECP's modes.

Detecting an EPP

If the port fails the ECP test, the program looks for an EPP. Like the ECP, an EPP has additional registers. In the EPP, they're at *base address + 3* through *base address + 6*. These additional registers, and the EPP's timeout bit, provide a couple of ways to test for the presence of an EPP.

One test is to write two values to one of the EPP registers and read them back, much as you would test for an SPP. If there is no EPP-compatible peripheral attached, the port won't be able to complete the EPP handshake. When the transfer times out, the state of the Data port and the EPP register are undefined. However, in my experiments, I was able to read back values written to an EPP register, while other port types failed the test. This is the method used in Listing 4-4. If the reads aren't successful, either the port isn't an EPP or it is an EPP but doesn't pass this test.

If the port's base address is 3BCh, the routine skips the EPP test. This address isn't used for EPPs because the added EPP registers (3BFh–3C3) may conflict with video memory. One such conflict is register 3C3h, which may contain a bit that enables the system's video adapter. Writes to this register can blank the screen and require rebooting!

Another possible test is to detect the EPP's timeout bit, at bit 0 of the Status port (*base address + 1*). On ports that aren't EPPs, this bit is unused. On an EPP, if a peripheral doesn't respond to an EPP handshake, the timeout bit is set to 1. If you can detect the setting of the timeout bit, then clear the bit and can read back the result, you almost certainly have an EPP.

The problem with using the timeout bit to detect an EPP is that ports vary in how they implement the bit. On some EPPs (type 1.9), the timeout bit is set if you attempt an EPP transfer with nothing attached to the port. On others (type 1.7), to force a timeout you must tie *nWait* (*Busy*, or Status port bit 7) low. Ports also vary in the method required to clear the timeout bit. On some ports, you clear the bit to 0 by writing 1 to it. On others, reading the Status port twice clears the bit. And it's possible that on still other ports, you clear the bit in the conventional way, by writing 0 to it.

So, to use the timeout bit to detect an EPP, you need to bring Status bit 7 low (in case it's type 1.7), then attempt an EPP read or write cycle, by writing a byte to *base address + 3,* for example. Then read the timeout bit. If it's set to 1, write both 1 and 0 to the bit to attempt to clear it, then read the bit. If it's zero, you have an EPP. (You can also use this difference to detect whether an EPP is type 1.7 or 1.9.) Some controller chips, such as Intel's 82091, don't seem to implement the timeout bit at all, or at least don't document it. (The chip's data sheet doesn't mention the timeout bit.)

Detecting an SPP

If a port fails both the ECP and EPP tests, it's time to test for an SPP. To do this the program writes two values to the Data port and reads them back. If the values match, the port exists. Otherwise, the port doesn't exist, or it's not working properly. Also note that the port-test routine only verifies the existence of the Data port. It doesn't test the Status and Control lines. The other port types should also pass this test.

Detecting a PS/2-type Port

If the port passes the SPP test, the final test is for simple bidirectional ability (PS/2-type). The program first tries to put the port in input mode by writing 1 to bit 5 in the port's Control register *(base address + 2)*. If the port is bidirectional, this tri-states the Data port's outputs. Then the test writes two values to the Data port and reads each back. If the outputs have been tri-stated, the reads won't match what was written, and the port is almost certainly bidirectional. If the reads do match the values written, the program is reading back what it wrote, which tells you that the Data-port outputs weren't disabled and the port isn't bidirectional.

An ECP set to its internal PS/2 mode should also pass this bidirectional test. Some EPPs support PS/2 mode, while other don't. You should test for a PS/2-type port only after you've verified that a port exists at the address. Because the PS/2 test uses the failure of a port read to determine that a port is bidirectional, a non-existent port will pass the test!

Using the Port Information

The program stores information about the ports in a user-defined array. For each port, the array stores the base address, port type, and whether or not it's the selected port. For ECPs, the array also stores two values: an integer equal to the ECP's currently selected internal mode (as stored in the ECR) and a string that describes the mode ("SPP", "ECP", etc.). The port's array index ranges from 0 to 2, or *Lpt number - 1*, with the user port, if available, having an index of 3.

Applications can use the information in the port array to determine which port is selected, and what its abilities are.

When the program ends, the *ini* file stores the port information. When the program runs again, it reads the stored information into the port array. This way, the program remembers what ports are available and which port the program used last. If you add, remove, or change the configuration of any ports in the system, you'll need to click *Find Ports* to update the information.

Automatic Port Selection

Rather than testing each of the standard addresses to find existing ports, another approach is to read the port addresses stored in the BIOS data area beginning at 40:00. In 16-bit programs, you can use VbAsm's VbPeekW (See Chapter 2) to read these addresses:

```
Dim PortAddress(1 to 3)%
Dim Segment%
Dim LptNumber%
'memory segment of BIOS table
Segment = &H40
For LptNumber = 1 to 3
    Offset = LptNumber * 2 + 6
    PortAddress(LptNumber) = vbPeekw(Segment, Offset)
Next LptNumber
```

Autodetecting a Peripheral

An intelligent peripheral can enable an application to detect its presence automatically. For example, on power-up, the peripheral might write a value to its Status lines. The PC's software can read each of the standard port addresses, looking for this value, and on detecting it, the PC's software can write a response to the Data lines. When the peripheral detects the response, it can send a confirming value that the PC's software recognizes as "Here I am!" The program can then select this port automatically, without the user's having to know which port the peripheral connects to.

5

Experiments

You can learn a lot about the parallel port by doing some simple experiments with it. This chapter presents a program that enables you to read and control each of the port's 17 bits, and an example circuit that uses switches and LEDs for port experiments and tests.

Viewing and Controlling the Bits

Figure 5-1 shows the form for a program that enables you to view and control the bits in a port's Data, Status, and Control registers. The program is based on the form template described in Chapter 4. Listing 5-1 shows the code added to the template for this project.

The screen shows the Data, Status, and Control registers for the port selected in the *Setup* menu. Clicking the *Read All* button causes the program to read the three registers and display the results. Clicking a Data or Control bit's command button toggles the corresponding bit and rereads all three registers. The Status port is read-only, so it has no command buttons. On the Control port, bits 6 and 7 have no function and can't be written to. These bits do have command buttons, and you can verify that the values don't change when you attempt to toggle them. On an SPP, Control port bit 5 is read-only, and its state is undefined. In other modes, set-

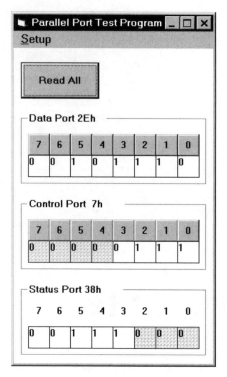

Figure 5-1: The form for the port-test program.

ting bit 5 to 1 disables the Data outputs, so if this bit is 1, you won't be able to tog-gle the Data-port bits.

Circuits for Testing

Figure 5-2 Figure 5-3, and Figure 5-4 show circuits you can use to test the opera-tion of a parallel port, using Figure 5-1's program or your own programs.

In Figure 5-2, the port's Data outputs each control a pair of LEDs. As you click on a Data button, the LEDs should match the display: red for 1 and green for 0. Instead of using LEDs, you can monitor the bits with a voltmeter, logic probe, or oscilloscope.

In Figure 5-3, switches determine the logic states at the Status inputs. Opening a switch brings an input high, and closing it brings the input low. After clicking *Read Ports*, the display should match the switch states.

Figure 5-4 shows the Control port. As with the Data port, a pair of LEDs shows the states of the Control outputs. On an SPP, writing 1 to a Control bit enables you to read the state of the switch connected to that bit. If you have an ECP, EPP, or PS/2-type port, the Control bits may be open-collector type only when in SPP

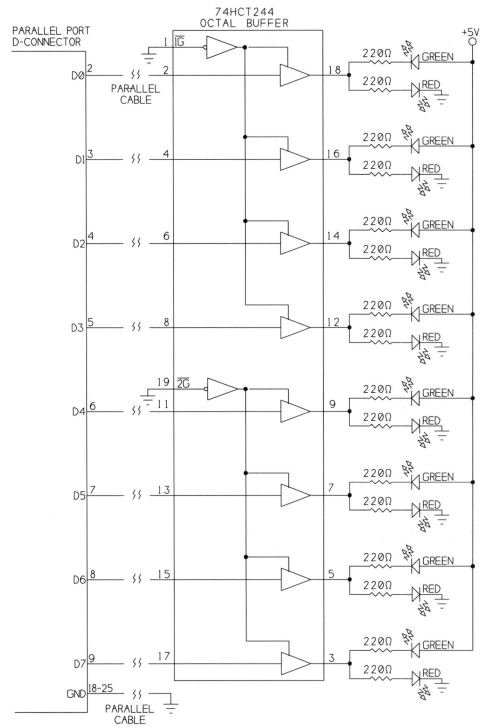

Figure 5-2: Buffer and LEDs for monitoring Data outputs.

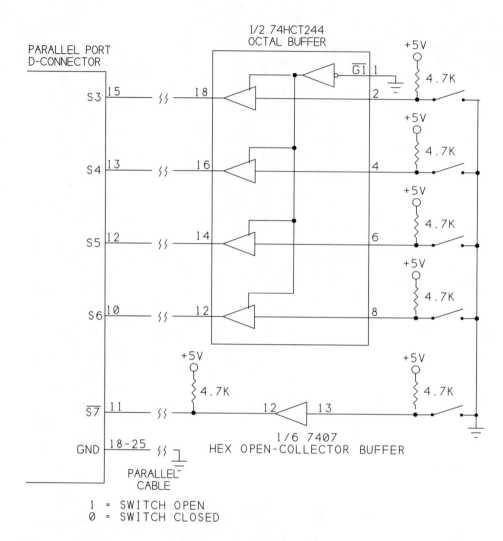

Figure 5-3: Driver and switches for testing Status port.

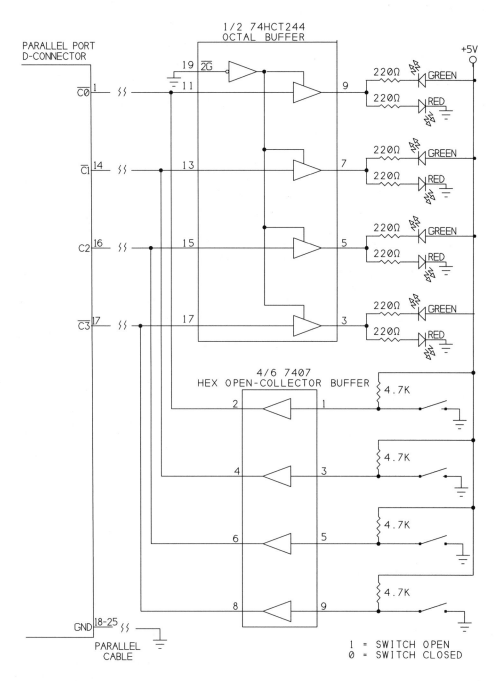

Figure 5-4: Buffer/driver, LEDs, and switches for Control-port testing.

```
Sub cmdControlBitToggle_Click (Index As Integer)
'toggle a bit at the Control port
Dim ControlPortData As Integer
ControlPortData = ControlPortRead(BaseAddress)
BitToggle ControlPortData, Index
ControlPortWrite BaseAddress, ControlPortData
ReadPorts (BaseAddress)
End Sub
```

```
Sub cmdDataBitToggle_Click (Index As Integer)
'toggle a bit at the Data port
Dim DataPortData As Integer
DataPortData = DataPortRead(BaseAddress)
BitToggle DataPortData, Index
DataPortWrite BaseAddress, DataPortData
ReadPorts (BaseAddress)
End Sub
```

```
Sub cmdReadAll_Click ()
ReadPorts (BaseAddress)
End Sub
```

Listing 5-1: Code for Figure 5-1's program. (Sheet 1 of 2)

```
Sub ReadPorts (BaseAddress As Integer)
'Read the Data, Status, and Control ports of selected port.
'Display the byte read and each bit in the byte.
Dim ByteRead%
Dim BitNumber%
Dim BitValue%

ByteRead = DataPortRead(BaseAddress)
frmMain.lblDataPortByte(0).Caption = Hex$(ByteRead) + "h"
For BitNumber = 0 To 7
    BitValue = BitRead(ByteRead, BitNumber)
    frmMain.lblDataBit(BitNumber).Caption = BitValue
Next BitNumber

ByteRead = StatusPortRead(BaseAddress)
frmMain.lblStatusPortByte(0).Caption = Hex$(ByteRead) + "h"
For BitNumber = 0 To 7
    BitValue = BitRead(ByteRead, BitNumber)
    frmMain.lblStatusBit(BitNumber).Caption = BitValue
Next BitNumber

ByteRead = ControlPortRead(BaseAddress)
frmMain.lblControlPortByte(0).Caption = Hex$(ByteRead) + "h"
For BitNumber = 0 To 7
    BitValue = BitRead(ByteRead, BitNumber)
    frmMain.lblControlBit(BitNumber).Caption = BitValue
Next BitNumber
End Sub
```

Listing 5-1: Code for Figure 5-1's program. (Sheet 2 of 2)

mode, or not at all. If in doubt, don't connect the 7407's buffer outputs in Figure 5-4.

If you have a bidirectional port, you can use Figure 5-5's circuit. It has a buffer and switches that you can connect to bidirectional Data lines when you're using the lines for input. To prevent the buffer outputs from being enabled when the parallel port's Data outputs are enabled, it's best to have a way to enable and disable the buffers' outputs under program control. In the schematic, a Control line from the parallel port controls the output-enable input of the buffers. Bit $\overline{C3}$ is normally low on bootup. An inverter brings the bit high and disables the buffers. You could also use a manual switch to enable and disable the outputs.

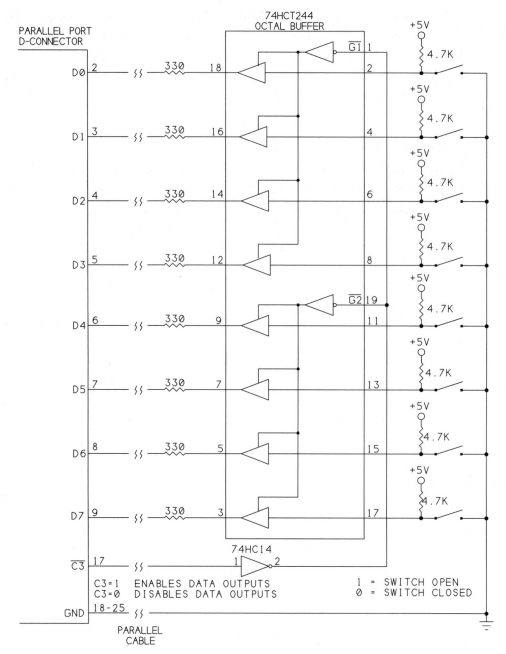

Figure 5-5: Circuit for reading external inputs on a bidirectional Data port.

The 330-ohm resistors protect the circuits on both ends of the link in case the parallel port's outputs and the buffer outputs happen to be enabled at the same time. The resistors limit the current in each line to under 15 milliamperes.

You can connect both Figure 5-2's and Figure 5-5's circuits to the Data port at the same time. Connect the buffer inputs of the '244 (pins, 2, 4, etc.) in Figure 5-2 to the PC (parallel-port D-sub connector) side of the 330-ohm resistors in Figure 5-5.

Buffers and Drivers

The circuit uses HCTMOS-family driver/buffers at inputs $D0$-$D7$ and $\overline{C0}$-$\overline{C3}$ and outputs $S3$-$S6$. Using HCT-family logic has two benefits. HCT devices have TTL-compatible input voltages, which are compatible with the parallel-port's outputs. Plus, unlike TTL logic, HCT-family outputs can both source and sink enough current to power an LED from either a high or low output.

The outputs that drive inputs $\overline{C0}$-$\overline{C3}$ are 7407 open-collector buffers. One of the remaining 7407 buffers drives $\overline{S7}$, only because any other choice would require adding another chip to the circuit. (You could use a 7407 in place of the 'HC14 in Figure 5-5 as well. Just remember to add a pull-up resistor, and be aware that the 7407 doesn't invert like the 'HC14.)

The 7407's open-collector outputs help to protect the Control port's outputs. Each Control output also connects to an input buffer. In early parallel ports, the Control-port outputs were 7405 open-collector inverters with 4.7K pull-up resistors. When an open-collector Control output is high, you can drive its input buffer with another digital output, which you can then read at the Control register. In newer designs, the Control outputs may be push-pull type, so if you want a design to be usable with any port, don't use the Control bits as inputs.

Output Types

To understand how to use the Control lines (and bidirectional Data lines) for input, it helps to understand the circuits that connect to the port pins. Output configurations common to digital logic are open-collector/open-drain, totem-pole, push-pull, and 3-state.

Open Collector and Open Drain

Figure 5-6A shows an open-collector output. The collector of its output transistor is open, or not connected to any circuits on-chip. To use the output, you have to add a pull-up resistor to +5V. When the output transistor switches on, the low resistance from the output pin to ground results in a logic-low output. When the

(A) Open collector outputs:
When two open-collector outputs connect together,
any low output brings the combined output low.

(B) Totem-pole outputs:

Can't be tied together. If one output is high and the other is low,
the logic level is unpredicatable and the resulting high currents
may damage the components.

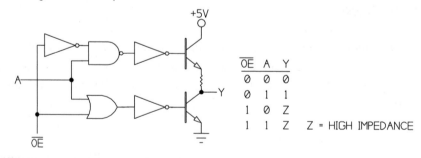

$\overline{OE}$	A	Y	
0	0	0	
0	1	1	
1	0	Z	
1	1	Z	Z = HIGH IMPEDANCE

(C) 3-state outputs:
When $\overline{OE}$ is low, the Y output follows the A input.
When $\overline{OE}$ is high, the output is high impedance.

Figure 5-6: Output types used in digital logic.

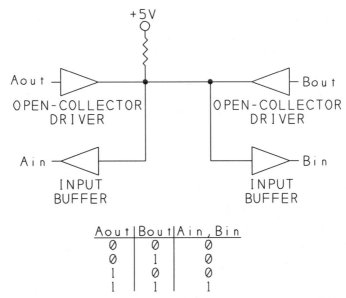

Figure 5-7: A simple way to make a bidirectional link is to use open-collector drivers. When Aout is high, Ain follows Bout. When Bout is high, Bin follows Aout.

output transistor is off, the pull-up resistor brings the output pin to +5V. Another name for the pullup resistor is *passive pullup*.

An advantage to open-collector logic is the ability to tie two or more outputs together. When any of the outputs goes low, the low resistance from the output to ground brings the combined output low.

This arrangement is sometimes called a wired-OR output, though it actually behaves like an OR gate only if you assume negative logic, where a low voltage is a logic 1 and a high voltage is logic 0. Using the more common positive logic, if the individual gates are non-inverting buffers, the circuit behaves like an AND gate: any low input brings the combined output low. If the gates are inverters, the circuit is a NOR gate: any high input brings the combined output low.

You can use the ability to tie outputs together to create a bidirectional data line. Figure 5-7 shows an example of a link with two nodes. Each node has an open-collector output and an input buffer. When 1 is written to Aout, the input buffers follow Bout. When 1 is written to Bout, the input buffers follow Aout. With this arrangement, you can send data in either direction, one way at a time. If both nodes' outputs are low at the same time, the inputs will be low, and the pull-up resistor will limit the current.

In a link with multiple lines like this, you can configure the individual bits at each node to act as inputs or outputs according to the needs of your circuit.

A disadvantage to open-collector logic is its slow switching speed. When an output switches from low to high, the cable's capacitance has to charge through the resistance of the pull-up. The larger the resistance, the more slowly the output voltage changes.

In CMOS components, the equivalent to open-collector is the open-drain output. An example is the 74HCT03, a CMOS quad NAND gate with open-drain outputs. The technology is different, but the operation is much the same.

Some NMOS and CMOS devices have outputs that behave in a way similar to open-collector or open-drain outputs. Instead of an external, passive pull-up, this type of device has an internal transistor with a high resistance that acts as weak, active pull-up. As with open-collector logic, writing 1 to this type of output enables you to read an external logic signal at the bit. The ports on the 8051 and 80C51 microcontrollers are examples of this type of output. Another name for these outputs is *quasi-bidirectional*.

Totem Pole

In contrast to open-collector logic, many LSTTL devices use a type of output called *totem pole,* with two transistors stacked one above the other. Figure 5-6B illustrates. When the output is low, the bottom transistor conducts, creating a low-resistance path from the output to ground, as in an open-collector output. When the output is high, the top transistor conducts, creating a low-resistance path to +5V. The original parallel port used the totem-pole outputs of a 74LS374 to drive the Data lines (*D0-D7*).

In TTL logic, the resistance from a logic-high output to +5V is greater than the resistance of a logic-low output to ground, so a totem-pole output can sink more current to ground than it can source from +5V.

Their lower output resistance means that as a rule, totem-pole outputs can switch faster than open-collector outputs. But it also means that the outputs aren't suitable for bidirectional links. If you tie two totem-pole outputs together, if one is high and the other is low, you have one output with a low resistance to +5V and another with a low resistance to ground. The result is an unpredictable logic level and large currents that may destroy the components involved.

Tying a totem-pole output to an open-collector output is OK as long as the open-collector output stays high. If the open-collector output goes low and the totem-pole output is high, you can end up with the same high current and unpredictable result.

On the parallel port, you can avoid the problem by using only open-collector outputs to drive the Control-port inputs on the parallel port. If you do connect a totem-pole output to an open-collector output, a 330-ohm series resistor in the line will protect the circuits (though it will slow the switching speed).

Push-pull

Outputs on most digital CMOS logic chips have complementary outputs that are similar to totem-pole, except that the current-sourcing and sinking abilities of the outputs are equal. This type of output is called *push-pull*.

3-state

A third type of output is *3-state*, or *tri-state,* which has a control signal that disables the outputs entirely. For all practical purposes, disabling, or tri-stating, an output electrically disconnects it from any circuits it physically connects to. Figure 5-6C illustrates. When the Output Enable line ($\overline{OE}$) is low, the output follows the input. When $\overline{OE}$ is high, both output transistors are off and the output has no effect on external circuits.

Outputs that connect to computer buses are often 3-state, with address-decoding circuits controlling the output-enable pins. This enables memory chips and other components to share a data bus, with each enabled only when the computer selects the component's addresses.

As with totem-pole logic, if two connected 3-state outputs are on at the same time, the result will be unpredictable. If you can't guarantee the behavior of the outputs in your circuit, open-collector is the safest choice.

Three-state logic also requires an extra input to control each set of outputs. One output-enable bit typically controls all of the bits in a data bus. With open-collector logic, you can easily configure individual bits as either inputs or outputs, with no extra control lines required.

Component Substitutions

If you don't have the exact chips on hand for the circuits in this chapter, you can substitute. With some cautions, you can use almost any HC, HCT, or TTL/LSTTL inverters in many simple circuits. The buffer/driver chips are recommended because they have stronger drivers and their inputs have hysteresis, which gives a clean output transition even when an input is noisy or changes slowly. If you use the Control port for input, open-collector drivers will protect the circuits, as described above.

Logic Families

If you use a 74HC-family buffer instead of the 74HCT244 at *D0-D7*, add a 10K pullup resistor from each buffer's input to +5V. The pullup ensures that the port's outputs will go high enough to meet the 74HC-family's minimum for a logic high. If you don't use a pullup, the circuit will probably work. However, a logic-high TTL output is usually guaranteed to be just 2.4V, while 5V HC-family logic requires at least 3.5V for a logic-high input. HCT-family logic is designed to work with TTL logic voltages, so pull-ups aren't needed.

The Control outputs should already be pulled up by the port circuits, so you shouldn't have to add pullups to them.

You can use a 74LS244 buffer instead of the 74HCT244, but because TTL logic can sink, but not source, enough current to drive an LED, remove the red LEDs and their current-limiting resistors. The green LEDs will light when the corresponding outputs are low, and they will be off when the corresponding outputs are high.

If you use 74HCT240 inverting buffers, swap the red and green LEDs. (Be sure to keep the polarity of the LEDs correct. The cathode always connects to the more negative voltage.) With inverters, the switches will read 1 when closed and 0 when open.

Switches and Power Supplies

You can use any SPST (single-pole, single-throw) toggle or slide switches to control the Data, Status, and Control inputs. Power the circuit with any +5V supply that can provide at least 300 milliamperes. (The LEDs use most of the current.)

Inverting Bits in Hardware

One reason you might use inverters for some of the bits is to reinvert the bits that the port's circuits invert between the connector and the register where you read the port. If you use inverting buffers and drivers for just these bits, you don't have to reinvert bits in software when you read or write to the ports.

For example, in Figure 5-3 you could replace bit 7's buffer with an inverting buffer such as a 7405. If the inverter is an ordinary LSTTL or HCMOS logic gate (not a driver), wire the inverter's output to the 7407's input, and let the 7407 drive the line.

You could also invert the signal by replacing the normally open switch with a normally closed one. Or rewire the normally open switch with a pull-down resistor instead of a pull-up, so that an open switch is logic-low rather than logic-high. With TTL and HCTMOS inputs, however, a pull-up resistor gives better noise immunity. (Noise is usually a greater problem when the switch is open. With a pull-up, there's a 3V difference between +5V and the minimum TTL logic-high input of 2V. With a pull-down, there's just 0.8V between 0V and the maximum logic-low input.)

Using any of these approaches to reinvert the inverted signals, the values that you write to a port will match the bits at your outputs, with no software complementing required. But if you use any code that assumes that the bits will be inverted as usual, you'll either have to change the routines or reinvert the bits elsewhere in your program. The examples in this book assume no special inversions in the hardware.

Cables & Connectors for Experimenting

Connecting a printer or another commercial product to a parallel port is usually just a matter of plugging the device's cable into the computer and the printer. But for experimenting, you need a cable that allows access to all of the lines. There are several options, depending on whether you're soldering or wire-wrapping components onto perfboard, or using a solderless breadboard.

One approach is to use a standard printer cable and wire a mating Centronics connector to your circuits. This is probably the best solution because you can use a readily available shielded printer cable for the link from the computer to your device. You can buy PC-board-mountable connectors that solder onto perfboard. Or you can use a solder-cup connector and solder individual wires to the connector, with the other ends of the wires soldered to perfboard or plugged into a solderless breadboard.

Another option is to use a cable with D-sub connectors on both ends. Although there are PC-board-mountable D-subs, the pin spacings on the connector don't match the 0.1" grid used by most perfboards. If you want to use perfboard, you'll need to look for one with a hole pattern that will accept a D-sub. Of course, if you're designing your own printed-circuit board, you can add holes and solder pads for the D-sub. Or use a solder-cup D-sub and solder the individual wires to perfboard or plug them into a breadboard.

Yet another possibility is to use ribbon cable with a dual-row socket connector crimped onto one end, and plug the connector into a dual header soldered onto perfboard.

For solderless breadboards, which typically have two parallel rows of contacts spaced 0.3" apart, a convenient solution is to use a ribbon cable with a D-sub on one end and a ribbon-cable DIP connector on the other. The DIP connector has two rows of pins with the same spacing as a DIP IC: the pins within a row are 0.1" apart, and the rows are 0.3" or 0.5" apart. Use an IDC (insulation-displacement connector) tool or a vise to press the cable onto the contacts. Then plug the connector into a breadboard or perfboard.

It's best to limit cable length to 10 feet if possible, 15 at most. You can try longer cables - even much longer - and you may be able to use them without problems. But if you stretch the limits like this, there are no guarantees. Chapter 6 has more on cables and cable length.

Making an Older Port Bidirectional

If you have one of the older expansion cards that uses a 74LS374 for the Data outputs, a fairly simple modification will enable you to use the Data port for input. Although buying a board with a true bidirectional port is a quick and inexpensive solution, this section describes an alternative for the determined.

Cautions

First of all, be warned that this method works only with parallel-port cards that use the TTL chips described below. Not all cards will follow the exact design of the original port, so unless you happen to have a schematic of your card, you'll need to do some signal tracing with an ohmmeter to find out exactly how the signals on your card are routed. The modification requires cutting one lead on the 74LS374 and adding at least one jumper wire. You've been warned; proceed at your own risk!

Second, there is one difference about cards modified with this method. The modification allows you to use Control bit 5 to enable and disable the Data outputs, as you do on other bidirectional ports. On these other ports, you can read this bit as well as write to it. On a port that's modified to be bidirectional, the bit is write-only, because the early cards have no input buffer for Control bit 5 (unless you can find a spare buffer and wire the connections). Because of this difference, you have to be careful not to inadvertently turn off the Data outputs by writing 1 to Control bit 5.

Reading the bit on a modified port returns a 1. This means that if you read the Control port, then write the same value back to the port, bit 5 will be set to 1, which disables the Data outputs. A program that writes to the Control port of a modified port should always write 0 to Control bit 5 if the Data port is being used for output. If the Data port is being used for input, the program should always write 1 to Control bit 5.

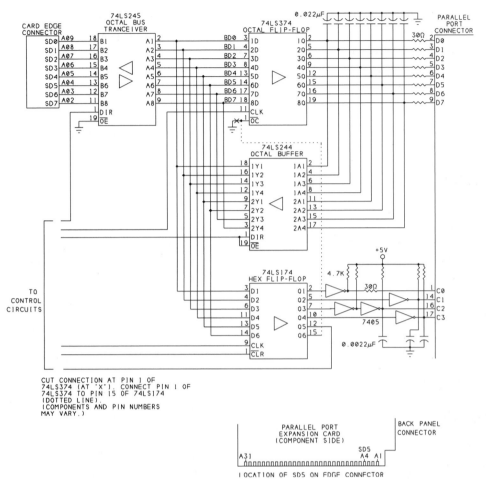

Figure 5-8: On many older parallel ports, you can make the Data port bidirectional by cutting one connection and adding a jumper wire.

On most true bidirectional ports, you don't have to worry about whether the Data port is input or output. You can just read the port and write back the same value for bit 5, and the bit won't change.

The Circuits

Figure 5-8 shows the relevant parts in the design of a typical early parallel port. Not shown are the Control and Status port's input buffers or the address-decoding and other control signals.

Lines *SD0-SD7* on the expansion bus carry Data bits *D0-D7*. On the parallel-port card, a 74LS245 octal transceiver buffers *AD0-AD7*. The lines that connect to

A1-A8 on the transceiver form a bidirectional, buffered Data bus (*BD0-BD7*). When the 74LS245's direction Control input (*DIR*) is low, *B1-B8* are inputs and *A1-A8* are outputs. When *DIR* is high, *A1-A8* are inputs and *B1-B8* are outputs.

(Most of the chips in this circuit use the numbering 1 through 8 for sets of eight bits, but the parallel port's Data and Control bits and the buffered data bus are numbered beginning with 0.)

When the CPU writes to the Data port, *BD0-BD7* drive the inputs of a 74LS374 octal flip-flop. The outputs of the flip-flops connect through 30-ohm resistors to *DC0-DC7* on the parallel-port connector. These lines also connect to the inputs of a 74LS244 octal buffer, and the buffer's outputs connect back to *BD0-BD7*. This buffer is what enables you to read the last byte written to the Data port.

The '374's Output-Control input ($\overline{OC}$) connects to *GND*, so its outputs are always enabled. If you could disable the outputs, external signals at the connector's *D0-D7* could drive the '244's inputs, and reading the Data port would tell you the logic states of *D0-D7* at the connector.

At the Control port, six bits (*C0-C5*) drive the inputs of a 74LS174 hex flip-flop. Outputs *Q1-Q4* connect to 7405 open-collector inverters, whose outputs are wired to *C0-C3* at the connector. Output *Q5* (*C4* in the Control register) controls the interrupt-enable circuits. and output *Q6* (*C5*) connects to nothing at all. This is the bit you can use to enable and disable the Data outputs.

The Changes

To make the modification, you cut the connection from the 74LS374's $\overline{OC}$ (pin 1) to ground and instead wire this pin to *Q6* (pin 15) on the 74LS174.

To break pin 1's connection, use a wire snips to clip pin 1's lead, then bend the stub on the chip so it doesn't touch the bottom of the leg it's cut away from. Then take a short length of insulated wire (#30 wire-wrap wire works well) and trim 1/8" or so of insulation from each end. Solder one end of the wire to the stub of pin 1 on the '374, and solder the other end to pin 15 on the 74LS174.

Bit *C5* will then determine the port's direction. Writing 0 to *C5* enables the Data outputs, for an output port, and writing 1 to *C5* disables the outputs and allows you to use the Data port for input. Because *C5* has no input buffer, you can't read it; all reads of the bit will return 1.

Not all cards will follow the exact wiring of Figure 5-7. To determine the wiring on your card, first use an ohmmeter to find the connection between *SD5* and the 74LS245. The schematic shows the location of *SD5* (at *A4*) on the card connector. The 74LS245 may be wired with either the *A* or *B* lines connected to the expansion bus, so check all 16 signal pins to find the connection.

If you don't find a connection, your card is too different from the original design to speculate on here, so you're out of luck unless you can figure out the connections yourself.

If you do find a connection, you can determine which pin on the 74LS245 is the corresponding I/O pin. For example, in Figure 5-8, pin 13 (*B6*) corresponds to pin 7 (*A6*). (Again, the signal names are numbered from 1 to 8 rather than from 0 to 7.) This pin should connect to one of the *D* inputs on the 74LS174. Use an ohmmeter to find the connection.

On one board that I modified, there was no connection from *BD5* to the '174, but the '174 did have an unused input. If you don't find the connection on your board, you can use the process of elimination to see if you have a spare input. Use an ohmmeter to trace the existing connections from *BD0-BD5* to the 74LS174. Then determine which input remains. If you don't see any pc-board traces connected to this pin (check both sides of the board), chances are that it's unused and you can solder a wire from it to *BD5* (in Figure 5-8, pin 7 of the '245).

When you've found the pin, determine its corresponding *Q* output. For example, in Figure 5-8, pin 14 (*D6*) of the '174 corresponds to pin 15 (*Q6*). Wire this *Q* output to the stub of pin 1 on the 74LS374 and you're done. Reinstall the port card and you're ready to test it. (Chapter 4 has a bidirectional-test program.)

Note that the Data outputs of this port are the totem-pole outputs of a 74LS374. If you intend to use the Data port for input, you must disable the Data outputs before you connect external outputs to the Data lines. Otherwise, you risk damaging the port circuits. To protect the outputs, you can add a 330-ohm series resistor on each Data line, to limit the current in case this situation occurs. This will affect the impedance match on the lines and limit the link's performance at high speeds, however.

Chapter 5

6

Interfacing

Because parallel-port signals may travel over cables of ten feet or more, the cable's design and the circuits that interface to the cable can mean the difference between a circuit that works reliably and one that fails, if not completely and immediately, then intermittently and unpredictably. The cable and interface can also affect the maximum speed of data transfers. This chapter includes tips on designing circuits that connect to the parallel port, and on choosing cables to connect the circuits. There's also a section on how and when you can use the parallel port as a power source for low-power devices.

Port Variations

Many parallel ports use ordinary TTL logic, or at best bus drivers and buffers, as the cable interface. On the original parallel port, a 74LS374 flip-flop drove the eight Data lines, 7405 open-collector inverters drove the Control lines, and the Status lines connected to inputs of LSTTL logic gates. These days there's no way to know exactly what components a PC or peripheral may use for its parallel-port circuits.

Although all parallel ports have the same 17 bits, the bits can differ in characteristics such as output impedance and noise immunity. Although every parallel port's outputs *should* have at least the same current-sourcing and sinking ability as the original port, some ports do have weaker drivers. A symptom of weak drivers is when a port works only with short cables, or at low speeds. Some very low-power devices that connect to the parallel port don't use an external power supply, and draw their current from the port's outputs, and these devices may not work with weak ports.

The outputs of many of the newer port controllers meet the improved Level 2 interface described in IEEE 1284. These ports can use cables of over 30 feet, if they connect to another Level 2 device.

Drivers and Receivers

The IEEE 1284 standard specifies characteristics for parallel-port drivers and receivers. It describes two types of devices: Level 1 devices are similar to the design of the original parallel port, while Level 2 devices give better performance while remaining compatible with the original interface. A port with Level-2 drivers and receivers can connect to a port with Level-1 drivers and receivers without problems, though you won't get the full benefit of using Level 2 devices unless they're present on both ends of the link. Both assume a power supply of +5V.

Level 1 Devices

The specification for Level-1 drivers and receivers are met by off-the-shelf LSTTL, TTL, and HCTMOS components, including those in the original parallel port.

Drivers

These are the characteristics of Level 1 drivers:

Logic-high outputs: +2.4V minimum at 0.32ma source current.

Logic-low outputs: +0.4V maximum at 12ma sink current.

Pullup resistors (if used): 1.8K minimum on Control and Status lines, 1.0K minimum on Data lines.

Not surprisingly, since they were the chips used in the original parallel port, LSTTL drivers are a good choice for the Data outputs, with 7405s or similar TTL gates for the open-collector Control outputs.

LSTTL chips characterized as buffer/drivers easily meet the requirements. These include the 74LS24X series and the 74LS374 octal flip-flop. On the 74LS240, low outputs are guaranteed to sink 12 milliamperes at 0.5V, and high outputs are guaranteed to source 3 milliamperes at 2.4V, compared to 4 and 0.4 milliamperes for ordinary LSTTL. Table 6-1 shows chips you might use:

Table 6-1: Level-1 driver and buffer chips for parallel-port circuits.

Drivers for the Data, Status, and Control inputs:	
74LS244, 74HC(T)244	octal buffer
74LS240, 74HC(T)240	octal inverting buffer
7405, 7406	open-collector hex inverting buffer
7407, 7417	open-collector hex buffer
(Use open-collector drivers for the Control lines.)	
Schmitt-trigger buffers for the Data or Control outputs:	
74LS14, 74HCT14	hex inverter
74LS374	octal buffered flip-flop
74LS244	octal buffer
74LS240	octal inverting buffer

In normal operation, the outputs don't provide their maximum rated currents continuously, but the ability to source and sink high currents means that the output has low impedance, and this in turn implies that the output can switch quickly. As an output switches, the voltage must charge or discharge through the cable's capacitance, and the lower the output impedance, the faster the voltage can change.

Ordinary LSTTL logic gates, like the 74LS14 hex inverter, are guaranteed to sink just 8 milliamperes at 0.4V, so these aren't recommended for driving a parallel cable. Standard TTL, such as the 7405, does meet the requirements. The drawback to using standard TTL is that each chip draws 20–40 milliamperes, compared to 8–12 milliamperes for an equivalent LSTTL chip, or 15–35 milliamperes for an LSTTL octal driver.

The HCMOS family has equivalents to most LSTTL chips. However, the data sheets for the 74HC24X buffer/drivers don't include enough information to guarantee that these chips meet the Level 1 requirements. With a power supply of 4.5V, the outputs are guaranteed to sink 6 milliamperes at 0.33V. The sink current will be greater with a 5V supply and 0.4V output, but the data sheets don't include figures for these conditions. Overall, the outputs of HCMOS driver chips aren't are strong as LSTTL, although in most situations, they'll work without problems.

Receivers

These are the characteristics of Level 1 receivers:

Logic-high inputs: 2.0V maximum at 0.32ma sink current.

Logic-low inputs: 0.8V minimum at 12ma source current.

Pullup resistors (if used): recommended minimum values are 470 ohms on Control and Status lines, 1000 ohms on Data lines.

Rise and fall time (between 0.8V and 2.0V): 120ns maximum.

Input limits: inputs should withstand transient voltages from -2.0V to +7.0V.

Just about any LSTTL or HCTMOS input will meet the above requirements. HCMOS chips aren't a good choice, however, because their minimum voltage guaranteed for a logic-high input is 3.5V, which is 1.5V greater than the 2V (TTL-compatible) requirement. If you do use an HCMOS chip, add a pull-up resistor from the input to +5V. HCTMOS devices have TTL-compatible inputs, so you don't need the pullups.

Although the specification doesn't mention it, Schmitt-trigger inputs will give greater noise immunity. A Schmitt-trigger input has two switching thresholds: one that determines when the gate switches on a low to high transition, and a second, lower, threshold that determines when the input switches on a high to low transition.

For example, the output of a 74LS14 inverter won't go low until the input rises to at least 1.6V. After the output switches low, it won't go high again until the input drops to at least 0.8V. The 0.8V hysteresis, or difference between the two thresholds, means that the input will ignore noise or ringing of up to 0.8V. The hysteresis also prevents the output from oscillating when a slowly changing input reaches the switching threshold.

The inputs of the 74LS24X buffer/driver series have Schmitt-trigger inputs with 0.4V of hysteresis. However, inputs of the 74HC(T)24X equivalents are ordinary, non-Schmitt-trigger type. (But you may decide to use HCT inputs anyway, for lower power consumption or CMOS's greater noise immunity.

Level 2 devices

Level 2 devices have stronger drivers and inputs with hysteresis.

Drivers

These are the characteristics of Level 2 drivers:

Logic-high outputs: +2.4V minimum at 12ma source current. This is much greater than Level 1's requirement of 0.32ma.

Logic-low outputs: +0.4V maximum at 12ma sink current. This is the same as the Level-1 specification.

Driver output impedance: 45-55 ohms at the measured (V_{OH} - V_{OL}).

Driver slew rate: 0.05 to 0.40 V/nsec.

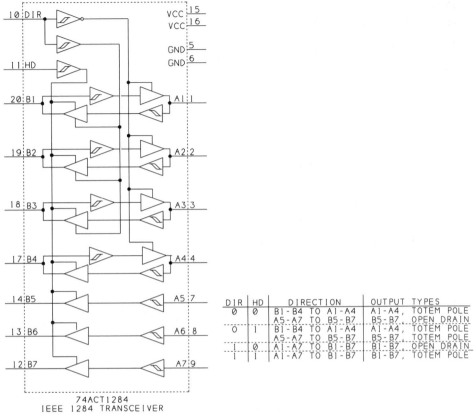

Figure 6-1: National's 74ACT1284 is a transceiver with seven lines that meet IEEE 1284's Level 2 interface standard.

Ordinary LSTTL drivers can't sink enough current to meet the specification. HC(T)MOS devices have equal source and sink currents, but aren't strong enough to meet the standard's minimum. The outputs of many of the new controller chips, including those from SMC and National, do meet the Level-2 requirements.

For simple parallel-port I/O with a Level-2 interface, you can use National's 74ACT1284 IEEE 1284 transceiver, which, as the name suggests, is designed specifically as a parallel-port interface. Figure 6-1 shows the chip and pinout. It includes four bidirectional lines and three one-way buffer/drivers. A Direction input (*DIR*) sets the direction of the bidirectional lines. A high-drive-enable input (*HD*) determines whether the B-side outputs are open-drain or push-pull type.

You can wire the 74ACT1284's in any of a number of ways, depending on your application. For example, using three chips, you could use eight bidirectional bits for the Data lines, four more for the Control lines, and use five of the remaining bits for Status inputs, with four bits left over. For bidirectional use, the Control outputs can emulate the original port's open-collector design. If you don't need bidirectional Control lines, you can use two chips for the Data and Status bits and one Control bit, and use cheaper buffers for the remaining Control bits.

The 74ACT1284 is available in two surface-mount packages: an SOIC with 0.05" lead spacing, and a *very* tiny SSOP with 0.025" lead spacing.

Receivers

These are the characteristics of Level 2 receivers:

Logic-high input: 2.0V maximum at 20µa sink current. (Same voltage as Level 1 devices, but much lower current.)

Logic-low input: 0.8V minimum at 20µa source current. (Same voltage as Level 1 devices, but much lower current.)

Receiver hysteresis: 0.2V minimum. Greater hysteresis, up to 1.2V, will give greater noise immunity.

Again, many new parallel-port controller chips meet the Level-2 requirements for receivers.

For simple I/O applications, you can use 74HCT14 Schmitt-trigger inverters or 74HCT24X series buffer/drivers as receivers. LSTTL inputs draw too much current to meet the requirement. The inputs of the 74ACT1284 are also suitable as Level 2 inputs, with a minimum input hysteresis of 0.35V.

Interfacing Guidelines

When you're designing circuits that connect to the parallel port, following some guidelines will help to ensure that the link between the port and your device works reliably.

General Design

These are general guidelines for interfacing digital logic to a cable:

Use plenty of decoupling capacitors. Connect a capacitor from +5V to ground near each IC that connects to the cable. Use a type with good high-frequency response, such as ceramic, mica, or polystyrene. Keep the wires or traces between the capacitor's leads and the chip's +5V and ground pins as short as possible. A good, general-purpose value is 0.01µF, but the precise value isn't critical. Also connect a 10µF electrolytic capacitor from +5V to ground, near where the 5-volt supply enters the board.

The decoupling capacitors store energy needed by the logic gates as they switch. All logic gates draw current as they respond to changes at their inputs. When the current can be drawn from a nearby capacitor, the gate can switch quickly, without causing voltage spikes in the power-supply or ground lines. The capacitor should be near the chip it supplies, to minimize the inductance of the loop formed by the electrical path connecting the capacitor and the chip. Lower inductance means faster response.

The large electrolytic capacitor stores energy that the smaller capacitors can draw on to recharge.

Buffer all clock and control signals. Add buffers like those in Table 6-1 to help isolate clock and control signals from noise on the cable. Critical signals include inputs and outputs of flip-flops, counters, and shift registers. Some chips, like the 74LS374 octal flip-flop, have buffered outputs on-chip.

Use the slowest logic family possible. LSTTL and HCTMOS chips are fine for many links. Higher-speed logic can cause unwanted transmission-line effects (described below).

Don't leave CMOS inputs open. If you have unused inputs, tie them to +5V or ground. A floating CMOS input can cause the chip to draw large amounts of current. You can leave unused TTL inputs open, or pull them high with a 4.7K pullup resistor. Without the pullup, a TTL input will float at around 1.1 to 1.4V, which is usually treated as a logic high, though it's less than the 2V minimum specification for a logic high input. An open TTL input won't draw large currents like CMOS can, however.

Port Design

These guidelines apply specifically to PC parallel-port interfaces:

Status line cautions. If you're using DOS interrupts or other LPT functions to access the port, tie $S3$ high and $S5$ and $\overline{S7}$ low (unless you're using these bits for their intended purposes). The BIOS interrupt requires only $\overline{S7}$ to be low.

Control line cautions. Use the Control bits as inputs on the PC only on SPPs or ports that emulate the SPP. If you do use the Control lines as inputs, drive them with open-collector outputs. This will protect the port's circuits if a low Control-port output should connect to a high output. If you don't use open collector devices, place a 330-ohm resistor in series with each Control line.

Bidirectional data cautions. Use series resistors to protect the outputs when you use a bidirectional Data port for input. (Some controllers have current-limiting circuits that protect against damaging currents, but this isn't guaranteed.)

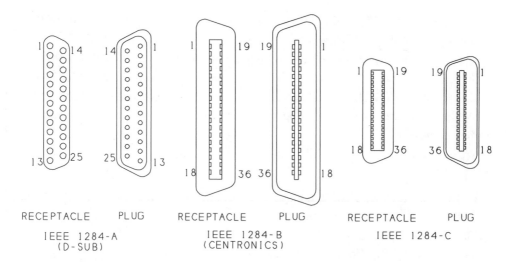

RECEPTACLE   PLUG   RECEPTACLE   PLUG   RECEPTACLE   PLUG

IEEE 1284-A   IEEE 1284-B   IEEE 1284-C
(D-SUB)   (CENTRONICS)

Figure 6-2: Parallel-port devices and cables may use any of these connector types.

Cable Choices

Parallel-port cables may vary in connector type, shielding, the arrangement of the wires in the cable, and the number of ground wires.

Connectors

The IEEE-1284 standard describes both the PC's D-sub connector and the Centronics connector found on many peripherals. It describes the conventional uses for the connectors—a female D-sub on the PC and female Centronics connector on the peripheral—but it doesn't recommend a particular connector for either device. The standard does recommend using connectors with metal shells for shielding continuity.

The standard calls the D-sub the 1284-A connector, and the Centronics connector, the 1284-B. The standard also introduces a new connector, the 1284-C. It's a 36-contact connector similar to the Centronics type, but more compact, with the contacts on 0.05" centers rather than 0.85". With this connector, the standard recommends using female (receptacle) connectors on both the host and peripheral, with male (plug) connectors on the cable. Table 6-2 shows the pin assignments for all of the connectors.

Figure 6-2 shows the pin numbering for the connectors. The pin numbers are labeled on most connectors, but the labeling typically consists of tiny,

Table 6-2: Pin assignments for D-sub, Centronics, and IEEE 1284C connectors.

Signal Name	Register bit	Signal Pin			Ground Return Pin		
		D-sub (IEEE 1284-A)	Centronics (IEEE 1284-B)	IEEE 1284-C	D-sub (IEEE 1284-A)	Centronics (IEEE 1284-B)	IEEE 1284-C
Data bit 0	D0	2	2	6	19	20	24
Data bit 1	D1	3	3	7	19	21	25
Data bit 2	D2	4	4	8	20	22	26
Data bit 3	D3	5	5	9	20	23	27
Data bit 4	D4	6	6	10	21	24	28
Data bit 5	D5	7	7	11	21	25	29
Data bit 6	D6	8	8	12	22	26	30
Data bit 7	D7	9	9	13	22	27	31
nError (nFault)	S3	15	32	4	23	29	22
Select	S4	13	13	2	24	28	20
PaperEnd	S5	12	12	5	24	28	23
nAck	S6	10	10	3	24	28	21
Busy	$\overline{S7}$	11	11	1	23	29	19
nStrobe	$\overline{C0}$	1	1	15	18	19	33
nAutoLF	$\overline{C1}$	14	14	17	25	30	35
nInit	C2	16	31	14	25	30	32
nSelectIn	$\overline{C3}$	17	36	16	25	30	34
HostLogicHigh				18			18
PeriphLogicHigh				36			36

hard-to-read numbers molded into the cable shell. Use bright light and a magnifier!

Cable Types

For a non-critical, low-speed link with a short cable, you can use just about any assortment of wires and connectors without problems. For example, if you're using the parallel port's inputs to read manual switches and using the outputs to light LEDs, it doesn't really matter if the signals change slowly or have a few glitches as they switch.

At other times, especially at higher speeds and over longer cables, cable design may mean the difference between a link that works reliably and one that doesn't.

Some interfaces are designed to be able to carry signals over long cables. In an RS-232 serial link, the drivers use large voltage swings and limited slew rates (the rate at which the output switches) to help provide a good-quality signal at the receiver. The RS-485 serial interface use differential signals, where the transmitting end sends both the signal and its inverse and the receiving end detects the voltage difference between the two. An advantage to this type of transmission is that any noise common to both lines cancels out.

When you're using the PC's parallel port, you have to make do with many of the limits built into the design. IEEE 1284's Level 2 drivers and receivers are improved over the original design, but the improvement isn't dramatic because the Level-2 components are designed to be compatible with the original interface. You still can't use the parallel port for a 100-foot link. There are some things you can do to ensure reliable communications, however.

Ground Returns

Most importantly, even though you might get by with just 18 wires in a parallel-port cable, a full 25-wire cable is better, and a 36-wire twisted-pair cable is better still.

In all circuits, current must flow back to its source. In a cabled link, the ground wires provide the return path for the current. Although you may think of a ground wire as having no voltage, every wire has some impedance, and current in the wire induces a voltage. When multiple signals share a ground return, each of the inputs sees the ground voltages caused by all of the others.

In the original Centronics interface, most signals had their own ground returns, with the signal wire and its return forming a twisted pair in the cable. In a twisted pair, two wires spiral around each other, with a twist every inch or so.

The PC's D-sub connector has room for just eight ground contacts. The reduced number of grounds is a compromise caused by the decision to use a 25-contact connector on the PC, rather than Centronics' 36-contact connector. A few of the contacts are designated as ground returns for a particular signal, while others are the ground return for two signals. Some signals have no designated ground return at all.

If a peripheral uses a 36-contact connector, each of the shared ground wires in a 25-wire cable connects to two or three contacts. For example, the returns for *nStrobe* and *D0* share a wire. Using 1284-C connectors allows the return 36 contacts on both ends.

In reality, ground currents will take the path of least resistance, and there's no way to guarantee that a current will flow in a particular wire. Multiple ground wires do lower the overall impedance of the ground returns, however, and this reduces ground currents.

If you eliminate seven of the ground wires and wire all of the ground contacts to a single wire, the interface will probably work, most of the time, especially at low speeds and over short distances. But a cable with at least 25 wires is preferable.

In a ribbon cable that connects to a dual header, the ground lines (18-25) alternate with signal lines, and this helps to reduce noise in the cable. Although ribbon cables usually aren't shielded, they're acceptable for low-speed, shorter links.

36-wire Cables

IEEE 1284 introduces a new cable for the parallel port. The cable contains 18 twisted pairs, with each signal line paired with its own ground return. Compared to the original parallel cable's 10-foot limit, the new cable may be as long as 10 meters, or 33 feet. A cable that meets the standard's requirements may be labeled *IEEE Std. 1284-1994 compliant.*

The 18th pair (at pins 18 and 36) has the only wires with new functions. The host and peripheral each use this pair to detect the presence of the other device. At the host, pin 18, *HostLogicHigh*, is a logic-high output, and pin 36 is an input with 7.5K impedance to ground. At the peripheral, pin 36, *PeripheralLogicHigh*, is a logic-high output and pin 18 is the 7.5K input. When there is no device connected, or when a device isn't powered, the inputs read logic low. With this arrangement, the host can read pin 36 and the peripheral can read pin 18 to detect whether or not the opposite device is present and powered.

If you use the new cable with 1284-C connectors, each contact connects to one wire, as Table 6-3 shows. You can also use this cable with 1284-A and -B connectors. In these cases, the ground returns for two or more signals connect to a single contact on the connector. (Even though the Centronics connector has 36 contacts, its conventional use doesn't include a ground return for every signal.) Table 6-4 shows the recommended wiring for a link with one D-sub and one Centronics connector. Other combinations of connectors can use similar wiring schemes, with each signal wire twisted with its ground wire.

Table 6-3: Wiring for a 36-wire, twisted-pair cable with two IEEE 1284-C connectors.

Cable Pair	Host		Peripheral	
	Signal	Pin	Pin	Signal
1	$\overline{S7}$ (Busy)	1	1	$\overline{S7}$ (Busy)
	Signal Ground ($\overline{S7}$)	19	19	Signal Ground ($\overline{S7}$)
2	$S4$ (Select)	2	2	$S4$ (Select)
	Signal Ground ($S4$)	20	20	Signal Ground ($S4$)
3	$S6$ (nAck)	3	3	$S6$ (nAck)
	Signal Ground ($S6$)	21	21	Signal Ground ($S6$)
4	$S3$ (nError)	4	4	$S3$ (nError)
	Signal Ground ($S3$)	22	22	Signal Ground ($S3$)
5	$S5$ (PaperEnd)	5	5	$S5$ (PaperEnd)
	Signal Ground ($S5$)	23	23	Signal Ground ($S5$)
6	Data Bit 0 ($D0$)	6	6	Data Bit 0 ($D0$)
	Signal Ground ($D0$)	24	24	Signal Ground ($D0$)
7	Data Bit 1 ($D1$)	7	7	Data Bit 1 ($D1$)
	Signal Ground ($D1$)	25	25	Signal Ground ($D1$)
8	Data Bit 2 ($D2$)	8	8	Data Bit 2 ($D2$)
	Signal Ground ($D2$)	26	26	Signal Ground ($D2$)
9	Data Bit 3 ($D3$)	9	9	Data Bit 3 ($D3$)
	Signal Ground ($D3$)	27	27	Signal Ground ($D3$)
10	Data Bit 4 ($D4$)	10	10	Data Bit 4 ($D4$)
	Signal Ground ($D4$)	28	28	Signal Ground ($D4$)
11	Data Bit 5 ($D5$)	11	11	Data Bit 5 ($D5$)
	Signal Ground ($D5$)	29	29	Signal Ground ($D5$)
12	Data Bit 6 ($D6$)	12	12	Data Bit 6 ($D6$)
	Signal Ground ($D6$)	30	30	Signal Ground ($D6$)
13	Data Bit 7 ($D7$)	13	13	Data Bit 7 ($D7$)
	Signal Ground ($D7$)	31	31	Signal Ground ($D7$)
14	$C2$ (nInit)	14	14	$C2$ (nInit)
	Signal Ground ($C2$)	32	32	Signal Ground ($C2$)
15	($\overline{C0}$) nStrobe	15	15	($\overline{C0}$) nStrobe
	Signal Ground ($\overline{C0}$)	33	33	Signal Ground ($\overline{C0}$)
16	$\overline{C3}$ (nSelectIn)	16	16	$\overline{C3}$ (nSelectIn)
	Signal Ground ($\overline{C3}$)	34	34	Signal Ground ($\overline{C3}$)
17	$\overline{C1}$ (nAutoFd)	17	17	$\overline{C1}$ (nAutoFd)
	Signal Ground ($\overline{C1}$)	35	35	Signal Ground ($\overline{C1}$)
18	Host Logic High	18	18	Host Logic High
	Peripheral Logic High	36	36	Peripheral Logic High
-	Shield			Shield

Table 6-4: Wiring for a 36-wire, twisted-pair cable with one 25-pin D-sub (IEEE 1284-A) and one Centronics (IEEE 1284-B) connector.

Cable Pair	Host (D-sub)		Peripheral (Centronics)	
	Signal	Pin	Pin	Signal
1	$\overline{S7}$ (Busy)	11	11	$\overline{S7}$ (Busy)
	Signal Ground ($\overline{S7}$, S3)	23	29	Signal Ground ($\overline{S7}$)
2	S4 (Select)	13	13	S4 (Select)
	Signal Ground (S4, S5, S6)	24	28	Signal Ground (S4)
3	S6 (nAck)	10	10	S6 (nAck)
	Signal Ground (S4, S5, S6)	24	28	Signal Ground (S6)
4	S3 (nError)	15	32	S3 (nError)
	Signal Ground (S4, S5, S6)	23	29	Signal Ground (S3)
5	S5 (PaperEnd)	12	12	S5 (PaperEnd)
	Signal Ground (S4, S5, S6)	24	28	Signal Ground (S5)
6	Data Bit 0 (D0)	2	2	Data Bit 0 (D0)
	Signal Ground (D0, D1)	19	20	Signal Ground (D0)
7	Data Bit 1 (D1)	3	3	Data Bit 1 (D1)
	Signal Ground (D0, D1)	19	21	Signal Ground (D1)
8	Data Bit 2 (D2)	4	4	Data Bit 2 (D2)
	Signal Ground (D2, D3)	20	22	Signal Ground (D2)
9	Data Bit 3 (D3)	5	5	Data Bit 3 (D3)
	Signal Ground (D2, D3)	20	23	Signal Ground (D3)
10	Data Bit 4 (D4)	6	6	Data Bit 4 (D4)
	Signal Ground (D4, D5)	21	24	Signal Ground (D4)
11	Data Bit 5 (D5)	7	7	Data Bit 5 (D5)
	Signal Ground (D4, D5)	21	25	Signal Ground (D5)
12	Data Bit 6 (D6)	8	8	Data Bit 6 (D6)
	Signal Ground (D6, D7)	22	26	Signal Ground (D6)
13	Data Bit 7 (D7)	9	9	Data Bit 7 (D7)
	Signal Ground (D6, D7)	22	27	Signal Ground (D7)
14	C2 (nInit)	16	31	C2 (nInit)
	Signal Ground (C1, $\overline{C2}$, C3)	25	30	Signal Ground (C2)
15	($\overline{C0}$) nStrobe	1	1	($\overline{C0}$) nStrobe
	Signal Ground ($\overline{C0}$)	18	19	Signal Ground ($\overline{C0}$)
16	$\overline{C3}$ (nSelectIn)	17	36	$\overline{C3}$ (nSelectIn)
	Signal Ground ($\overline{C1}$, C2, $\overline{C3}$)	25	30	Signal Ground ($\overline{C3}$)
17	$\overline{C1}$ (nAutoFd)	14	14	$\overline{C1}$ (nAutoFd)
	Signal Ground (C1, $\overline{C2}$, C3)	25	30	Signal Ground ($\overline{C1}$)
18	tied together, no connection at host		18	Host Logic High
			36	Peripheral Logic High
-	Shield			Shield

Reducing Interference

Interference occurs in a cabled link when signals couple from one wire into another, either within a cable or between a cable and a signal outside the cable. The coupling may be capacitive, inductive, or electromagnetic. Capacitive coupling occurs when an electric field, such as that generated by a voltage on a wire, interacts with an adjacent electric field. Inductive, or magnetic, coupling occurs when a magnetic field generated by a voltage on a wire interacts with an adjacent magnetic field. Electromagnetic coupling occurs when a wire acts as a transmitting or receiving antenna for signals that radiate through the air.

You can reduce interference by shielding, or blocking, signals from entering or leaving a wire, or by reducing the amplitude of the interfering signals.

Shielding

Metal shielding is an effective way to block noise due to capacitive, electromagnetic, and high-frequency magnetic coupling. A good parallel-port cable will have a metal shield surrounding the conductors and extending to the metal connectors.

The cable should have no large gaps where the conductors are unshielded. In particular, instead of a single wire, or "pigtail" connecting the shield to the connector, the full 360 degrees of the shield should contact the connector shell. The connectors in turn plug into the metal chassis of the PC or peripheral.

Solid shields provide the best protection, but they tend to be rigid and likely to break. Many cables instead use a more flexible braided shield made by interleaving bundles of thin metal strands into a shield that surrounds the wires. Although a braided shield doesn't cover the wires completely, it's durable, flexible, and effective enough, especially at higher frequencies.

IEEE-1284-compliant cables have two shielding layers. A solid aluminum or polyester foil surrounds the wires, and this is in turn surrounded by braided shield with 85% optical covering. The shield has a 360-degree connection to the connector's shell, which connects to the grounded chassis of both devices. The standard also recommends wire size of AWG 28 or lower. (Lower AWG numbers indicate larger wire diameters.)

Twisted Pairs

Using twisted pairs is another way to reduce interference in a cabled link. A twisted pair has two insulated wires that spiral around each other with a twist every inch or so. IEEE 1284 specifies a minimum of 36 twists per meter. The simple act of twisting results in benefits.

Twisting reduces magnetically coupled interference, especially from low-frequency signals such as 60-Hz power-line noise. Changing voltages on a wire cause the wire to emanate a magnetic field. The magnetic field in turn induces voltages on wires within the field.

The fields that emanate from a signal wire and its ground return have opposite polarities. Each twist causes the wires to physically swap positions, causing the pair's magnetic field to reverse polarity. The result is that the fields emanating from the wires tend to cancel each other out. In a similar way, the twisting reduces electro-magnetic radiation emitted by the pair.

Cable-buying Tips

Buying a cable labeled *IEEE-1284 compliant* is a simple way to guarantee good cable design. Other than this, there often is no easy way to tell how many wires are in a cable, or what type of shielding it has, if any, or whether the wires are in twisted pairs. The connectors are normally molded to the cable, so there's no way to peek inside without cutting the cable apart. Some catalogs do include specifications for the cables they offer. Whatever you do, don't mistakenly buy a 3-wire or 9-wire serial cable for parallel-port use. These cables may have 25-pin D-subs, but because serial links rarely use all 25 lines, they often have just three or nine wires.

Line Terminations

Another factor that affects signal quality in a link is the circuits that terminate the wires at the connector. To understand cable termination, you have to think of the cable as more than a simple series of connections between logic inputs and outputs.

Transmission Lines

When a long wire carries high-frequency signals, it has characteristics of a *transmission line,* defined as a circuit that transfers energy from a source to a load. Because the fast transitions of digital signals contain high-frequency components, most digital circuits are considered high frequency, even if the transmission rate (bits per second) is slow. To ensure reliable performance, transmission lines use line terminations, which are circuits at one or both ends that help ensure that the signals arrive in good shape at the receiver.

In many cases, especially when the cable is short and transmission speed is slow, an interface will work without any special attention to terminations. However, there are basic facts about transmission lines that are helpful when you're dealing with a cabled interface, especially if you need to stretch the limits.

At low speeds and over short distances, you can consider a short wire or PC-board trace to be a perfect connection: a logic high or low at one end of the wire or trace instantly results in a matching high or low at the opposite end. Most of the time, you don't have to concern yourself with delays, signal loss, noise, or other problems in getting a signal from an output to an input.

But when the connection is over a 10-foot or longer cable, and the signals are short pulses with fast rise and fall times, these factors can become important. Specifically, when a cable is physically long in relation to the highest wavelength it carries, it's considered to be a transmission line, which behaves differently than a cable that carries only low frequencies relative to its physical length. Transmission-line effects are significant when the wire length is greater than 1/10 to 1/20 of the wavelength of the highest frequency signal transmitted on the wire.

A 5-Megahertz sine wave has a wavelength of 60 meters, and 1/20 of that is 3 meters, or about 10 feet, which is the length of a typical parallel cable. From this, you might think that a parallel cable isn't a transmission line because the parallel port's maximum rate of transmitting is much less than 5 Mhz. But what's important isn't how often the voltages switch, but rather how quickly they switch.

This is because the frequencies that make up a digital waveform are much higher than the bits-per-second rate of the signal. Mathematically, a square wave (a waveform with equal, alternating high and low times) is the sum of a series of sine waves, including a fundamental frequency plus odd harmonics of that frequency. A 1000-Hz square wave actually consists of sine waves of 1000 Hz, 3000 Hz, 5000 Hz, and so on up.

A perfect square wave has an infinite number of harmonics and instant rise and fall times. Real-life components can pass limited frequencies, and their outputs require time to switch. A signal with fast rise and fall times will contain higher harmonics than a similar signal with slower rise and fall times. Parallel-port signals usually aren't square waves, but the principles apply generally to digital waveforms.

LSTTL and HCMOS logic are fast enough that transmission-line effects can be a factor on a parallel cable. Whether or not the effects will cause errors in an application depends in part on the bits-per-second rate of the transmitted signal and also on the hardware and software that detects and reads the signals. In a slow, short link that allows time between when an output switches and when the corresponding input is read, the software probably won't see any transmission-line effects, which occur mainly as the outputs switch. If you're pushing a link to its limit with either a long cable or high transmitting frequencies, you may have to consider the effects of the cable.

Characteristic Impedance

One way that a transmission line differs from other connections is that the transmission line has a *characteristic impedance.* Measuring the characteristic impedance of a wire involves more than a simple measurement with an ohmmeter. The characteristic impedance is a function of the wire's diameter, insulation type, and the distance between the wire and other wires in the cable.

It doesn't, however, change with the length of the wire. This seems to violate a fundamental rule of electronics, which says that a longer wire has greater resistance from end-to-end than a shorter one. But in most transmission lines, wire length isn't a major factor.

For the most efficient energy transfer from the source (output) to the load (input), the load's input impedance should match the characteristic impedance of the wire. When the impedances match, all of the energy is transferred from the source to the load and the logic level at the receiver matches the logic level at the driver.

If the impedances don't match, some of the energy reflects back to the source, which sees the reflection as a voltage spike. The reflections may bounce back and forth between the source and load several times before dying out. If the receiver reads the input before the reflections die out, it may not read the correct logic level, and in extreme cases, high-voltage reflections can damage the components.

If you're designing an interface from the ground up, you can specify terminations to match your design. But with the parallel port, things aren't as straightforward, because the driver and receiver components can vary. The wrong termination can cause reflected signals and errors in reading the inputs, or it may just slow the signal transitions and reduce the port's maximum speed.

Cable manufacturers often specify the characteristic impedance of their products. Typical values for twisted-pair and ribbon cable are around 100 to 120 ohms.

Example Terminations

A line termination may be located at the output, or source, or at the input, or receiver. In a bidirectional link, each end may have both a source and receiver termination.

Figure 6-3A shows a termination used on some ports. A series resistor at the driver and a high-impedance receiver cause an impedance mismatch that, amazingly, results in a received voltage that equals the transmitted voltage. The series resistor should equal the cable's characteristic impedance, minus the output impedance of the driver. Many parallel ports use series resistors of 22 to 33 ohms. You can add similar resistors in series with outputs that you use to drive the Status or Control inputs on a PC's port.

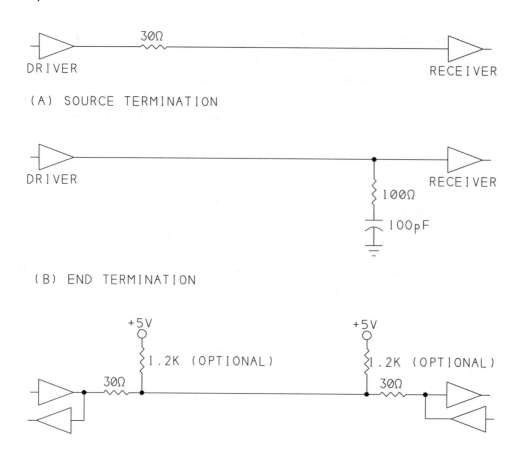

(A) SOURCE TERMINATION

(B) END TERMINATION

(C) TERMINATIONS FOR A BIDIRECTIONAL LINK

Figure 6-3: Line terminations for parallel-port cables.

When the driver switches, half of the output voltage drops across the combination of the series resistor and the driver's output impedance, and the other half reaches the receiver's input. Losing half of the output voltage doesn't sound like a good situation, but in fact, the mismatch has a desirable effect.

On a transmission line, when a signal arrives at a high-impedance input, a voltage equal to the received signal reflects back onto the cable. The reflection plus the original received voltage result in a signal equal to the original voltage, and this combined voltage is what the receiver sees. The reflected voltage travels back to the source and drops across the source impedance, which absorbs the entire reflected signal and prevents further reflections.

The impedance match doesn't have to be perfect, which is a good thing because it's unlikely that it will be. The driver's output impedance varies depending on the output voltage and temperature, so an exact match is impossible. If the impedance at the source doesn't exactly match the cable's impedance, the signal at the receiver won't exactly match the original, and small reflections may continue before dying out. In general, an output impedance slightly smaller than the cable impedance is better than one that is slightly larger.

Figure 6-3B shows another option, an end termination at the receiver, consisting of a resistor and capacitor in series between the signal wire and ground. The resistor equals the characteristic impedance of the wire, and the capacitor presents a low impedance as the output switches. Unlike some other input terminations, this one is usable in both TTL and CMOS circuits. However, this type of termination doesn't work well with a series termination at the driver, because the series termination is designed to work with a high-impedance input. Because many parallel-port outputs have series terminations built-in, it's best not to use this end termination unless you're designing for a specific port that you know can use it effectively.

Figure Figure 6-3C shows IEEE 1284's recommended terminations for a Level-2 bidirectional interface. The standard specifies a characteristic cable impedance of 62 ohms, and assumes that each signal line will be in a twisted pair with its ground return. The outputs have series resistor terminations. If the inputs have pull-ups, they should be on the cable side of the source termination.

Transmitting over Long Distances

If the parallel port's 10 to 15-foot limit isn't long enough for what you want to do, there are options for extending the cable length.

If the interface isn't a critical one, and especially at slower speeds, you can just try a longer cable and see if it works. You may be able to stretch the interface without problems. But this approach is only recommended for casual, personal use, where you can take responsibility for dealing with any problems that occur.

A shielded, 36-wire, twisted-pair cable allows longer links than other cables. If you know that both the port and the device that connects to it have Level 2 interfaces, this type of cable should go 30 feet without problems.

Parallel-port extenders are also available from many sources. One type adds a line booster, or repeater, that regenerates the signals in the middle of the cable, allowing double the cable length. Other extenders work over much longer distances by converting the parallel signals into a serial format, usually RS-232, RS-422, or RS-485.

The serial links use large voltage swings, controlled slew rates, differential signals, and other techniques for reliable transmission over longer distances. You could do the same for each of the lines in a parallel link, but as the distance increases, it makes sense to convert to serial and save money on cabling.

One drawback to the parallel-to-serial converters is that most are one way only, and don't include the parallel port's Status and Control signals. You can use the converters for simple PC-to-peripheral transfers, but not for bidirectional links. Also, serial links can be slow. After adding a stop and start bit for each byte, a 9600-bits-per-second link transmits just 960 data bytes per second.

If you need a long cable, instead of using a serial converter, you might consider designing your circuit to use a serial interface directly.

Port-powered Circuits

Most devices that connect to the parallel port will require their own power supply, either battery cells or a supply that converts line voltage to logic voltages. But some very low-power circuits can draw all the power they need from the port itself.

When to Use Port Power

The parallel-port connector doesn't have a pin that connects to the PC's +5V supply, so you can't tap directly into the supply from the connector. But if your device requires no more than a few milliamperes, and if one or more of the Data outputs is otherwise unused, you may be able to use the port as a power source.

As a rule, CMOS is a good choice for low-power circuits. CMOS components require virtually no power when the outputs aren't switching, and they usually use less power overall than TTL or NMOS.

Powering external circuits is especially easy if the circuits can run on +3V or less. Some components aren't particular about supply voltage. HCMOS logic can use any supply from +2V to +6V, with the logic high and low levels defined in proportion to the supply voltage. (*Minimum logic high input = 0.7(supply voltage); maximum logic low input = 0.3(supply voltage).*) National's LP324 quad op amp draws under 250µa of supply current and can use a single power supply as low as +3V. If you need +5V, there are new, efficient step-up regulator chips that can convert a lower voltage to a regulated +5V.

The parallel port's inputs require TTL logic levels, so any logic-high outputs that connect to the parallel-port inputs should be at least 2.4V. (Status-port inputs may have pullups to +5V, but this isn't guaranteed.)

The source for port power is usually one or more of the Data pins. If you bring a Data output high by writing 1 to it, you can use it as a power source for other circuits. The available current is small, and as the current increases, the voltage drops, but it's enough for some designs.

Of course, if you're using a Data pin as a power supply, you can't use it as a data output, so any design that requires all eight Data lines is out. One type of component that's especially suited to using parallel-port power is anything that uses a synchronous serial interface, such as the DS1620 digital thermometer described in Chapter 9. These require as few as one signal line and a clock line, leaving plenty of bits for other uses.

Abilities and Limits

One problem with using parallel-port power is that the outputs have no specification that every port adheres to. If you're designing something to work on a particular computer, you can experiment to find out if the outputs are strong enough to power your device. If you want the device to work on any (or almost all) computers, you need to make some assumptions. One approach is to assume that the current-sourcing abilities of a port's outputs are equal to those of the original port. Most ports do in fact meet this test, and many newer ports have the more powerful Level 2 outputs. It's a good idea to also include the option to run on an external supply, which may be as simple as a couple of AA cells, in case there is a port that isn't capable of powering your device.

On the original port, the eight Data outputs were driven by the outputs of a 74LS374 octal flip-flop. If you design for the '374's typical or guaranteed source current, your device should work on just about all ports. Typical output current for a 74LS374 is 2.6 milliamperes at 3.1V (2.4V guaranteed). A logic-low output of a '374 can sink much more than this, but a low output doesn't provide the voltage that the external circuits need.

Level 2 outputs can source 12 milliamperes at 2.5V. If you know that your port has Level 2 outputs, you have more options for using parallel-port power.

What about using the Control outputs as a power source? On the original port, these were driven by 7405 inverters with 4.7K pullups. The pull-ups on the outputs make it easy to calculate how much current they can source, because the output is just a 4.7K resistor connected to +5V. These outputs can source a maximum of 0.5 milliampere at 2.5V, so the Data outputs are a much better choice as current sources. On some of the newer ports, in the advanced modes, the Control outputs switch to push-pull type and can source as much current as the Data outputs.

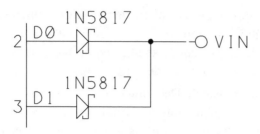

Figure 6-4: You can use spare Data outputs as a power source for very low-power devices. If you use more than one output, add a Schottky diode in series with each line.

Using Control bits as supplies is an option for these ports, but it isn't practical for a general-purpose circuit intended for any port.

I ran some informal tests on a variety of parallel ports, and found widely varying results, as Table 6-5 shows. The port with 74LS374 outputs actually sourced much more current than the specification guarantees, about the same as the Level 2 outputs on an SMC Super I/O controller. A port on an older monochrome video card had the strongest outputs by far, while a port on a multifunction board was the weakest, though its performance still exceeded the '374's specification.

Examples

If the exact supply voltage isn't critical, you can use one or more Data outputs directly as power supplies. If you use two or more outputs, add a Schottky diode in each line to protect the outputs, as Figure 6-4 shows. The diodes prevent current from flowing back into an output if one output is at a higher voltage. Schottky diodes drop just 0.3V, compared to 0.7V for ordinary silicon signal diodes.

How much output current is a safe amount? Again, because the components used in ports vary, there is no single specification. Also, because a power supply isn't the conventional use for a logic output, data sheets often don't include specifications like maximum power dissipation.

The safest approach is to draw no more than 2.6 milliamperes from each output, unless you know the chip is capable of safely sourcing higher amounts. At higher currents, the amount of power that the driver chips have to dissipate increases, and you run the risk of damaging the drivers.

If you need a regulated supply or a higher voltage than the port can provide directly, a switching regulator is a very efficient way to convert a low voltage to a steady, regulated higher (or lower) value. For loads of a few milliamperes,

Table 6-5: Results of informal tests of current-sourcing ability of the Data outputs on assorted parallel ports.

Card	No Load Voltage	Source Current at Data output (milliamperes)		
		4V	3V	2V
Original-type, LS374 outputs	3.5	-	11	25
Monochrome video card, single-chip design	4.9	18	35	35
Older multifunction card, with IDE and floppy controller	4.9	2.7	5	7
SMC Super I/O controller	4.9	0.6	7.5	27

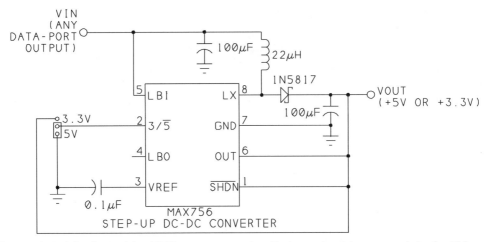

Figure 6-5: Maxim's Max756 can convert a Data output to a regulated +5V or +3.3V supply.

Maxim's MAX756 step-up converter can convert +2.5V to +5V with over 80% efficiency. Figure 6-5 shows a supply based on this chip.

As an example, assume that you want to power a circuit that requires 2 milliamperes at +5V, and assume that the parallel port's Data outputs can provide 2.6 milliamperes at 2.1V (2.4V minus a 0.3V drop for the diodes). This formula calculates how much current each Data pin can provide:

*(load supply (V)) * (output current (A)) =*

*converter efficiency * (source voltage (V)) * (source current (A))*

which translates to:

*5 * (output current) = 0.8 * 2.1 * (0.0026)*

and this shows that each Data pin can provide just under 0.9 milliampere at +5V. Three Data outputs could provide the required total of 2 milliamperes, with some to spare. In fact there is a good margin of error in the calculations, and you could probably get by with two or even one output. If the port has Level 2 outputs, each pin can source 4 milliamperes, so all you need is one pin. You can do similar calculations for other loads.

The '756 has two output options: 5V and 3.3V. The '757 has an adjustable output, from 2.7V to 5.5V.

The selection of the switching capacitor and inductor is critical for the MAX756 and similar devices. The inductor should have low DC resistance, and the capacitor should be a type with low ESR (effective series resistance). Maxim's data sheet lists sources for suitable components, and Digi-Key offers similar components. Because of the '756's high switching speed, Maxim recommends using a PC board with a ground plane and traces as short as possible.

If you just need one supply, Maxim sells an evaluation kit that's a simple, no-hassle way of getting one up and running. The kit consists of data sheets and a printed-circuit board with all of the components installed.

7

Output Applications

One category of use for the parallel port is control applications, where the computer acts as a smart controller that decides when to switch power to external circuits, or decides when and how to switch the paths of low-level analog or digital signals. This chapter shows examples of these, plus a port-expansion circuit that increases the number of outputs that the port controls.

Output Expansion

The parallel port has twelve outputs, including the eight Data bits and four Control bits. If these aren't enough, you can add more by dividing the outputs into groups and using one or more bits to select a group to write to.

Figure 7-1 shows how to control up to 64 TTL- or CMOS-compatible outputs, a byte at a time.

U1 and U4 buffer $D0\text{-}D7$ and $\overline{C0}\text{-}\overline{C3}$ from the parallel port. Four bits on U4 are unused.

U5 is a 74HCT138 3-to-8-line decoder that selects the byte to control. When U5 is enabled by bringing $G1$ high and $\overline{G2A}$ and $\overline{G2B}$ low, one of its Y outputs is low. Inputs A, B, and C determine which output this is. When $CBA = 000$, $Y0$ is low; when $CBA = 001$, $Y1$ is low; and so on, with each value at CBA corresponding to

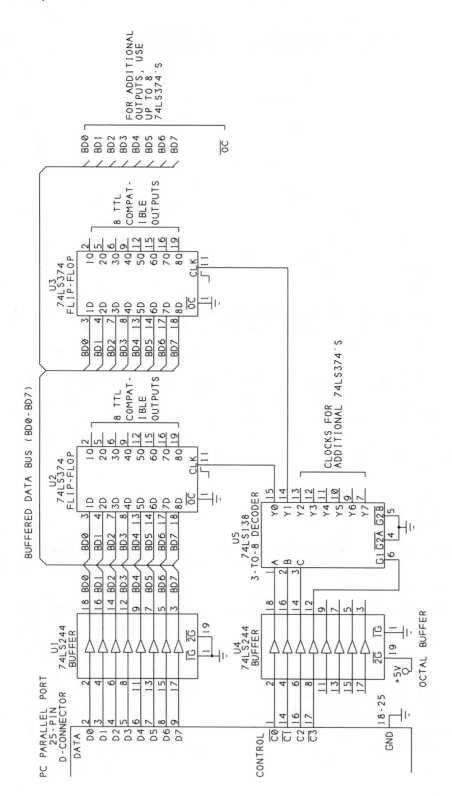

Figure 7-1: The eight data lines on the parallel port can control 64 latched outputs. The four control lines select a byte to write to.

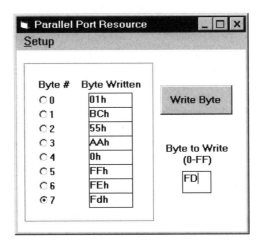

Figure 7-2: User screen for Listing 7-1's program code.

a low *Y* output. At the parallel port, bits $\overline{C0}$-*C2* determine the values at *A, B,* and *C*. If *G1* is low or either $\overline{G2A}$ or $\overline{G2B}$ is high, all of the *Y* outputs are high.

U2 is a 74HCT374 octal flip-flop that latches *D0-D7* to its outputs. The Output Control input ($\overline{OC}$, pin 1) is tied low, so the outputs are always enabled. A rising edge at *Clk* (pin 11) writes the eight *D* inputs to the *Q* outputs.

U3 is a second octal flip-flop, wired like U2, but with a different clock input. You may have up to eight 74HCT374s, each controlled by a different *Y* output of U5.

To write a byte, do the following:

1. Write the data to *D0-D7*.
2. Bring $\overline{C3}$ high and write the address of the desired '374 to $\overline{C0}$, $\overline{C1}$, and *C2* to bring a *Clk* input low.
3. Bring $\overline{C3}$ low, which brings all *Clk* inputs high and latches the data to the selected outputs. You can write just one byte at a time, but the values previously written to other '374's will remain until you reselect the chip and clock new data to it.

Listing 7-1 contains program routines for writing to the outputs. Figure 7-2 shows the form for a test program for the circuit. These demonstrate the circuit's operation by enabling you to select a latch, specify the data to write, and write the data.

You can use HCT-family or LSTTL chips in the circuit. If you can get by with 56 or fewer outputs, you can free up $\overline{C3}$ for another use, and bring *Y0-Y6* high by selecting *Y7*. One possible use for $\overline{C3}$ would be to enable and disable the '374's outputs by tying it to pin 1 of each chip.

```
Sub cmdWriteByte_Click ()
'Write the value in the "Byte to Write" text box
'to the selected output (1-8).
DataPortWrite BaseAddress, CInt ("&h" & txtByteToWrite.Text)
'Select an output by writing its number to
'Control Port, bits 0-2, with bit 3 = 1.
'This brings the output's CLK input low.
'Then set Control bit 3 = 0 to bring all CLK inputs high.
'This latches the value at the data port to the selected output.
ControlPortWrite BaseAddress, ByteNumber + 8
ControlPortWrite BaseAddress, 0
'Display the result.
lblByte(ByteNumber).Caption = ""
lblByte(ByteNumber).Caption = txtByteToWrite.Text & "h"
End Sub
PortType = Left$(ReturnBuffer, NumberOfCharacters)
```

```
Sub optByte_Click (Index As Integer)
ByteNumber = Index
End Sub
```

Listing 7-1: To write to Figure 7-1's bytes, you write a value to the data port, then latch the value to the selected output byte.

Switching Power to a Load

The parallel port's Data and Control outputs can control switches that in turn control power to many types of circuits. The circuits may be powered by a +5V or +12V supply, another DC voltage or voltages, or AC line voltage (115V). In a simple power-control switch, bringing an output high or low switches the power on or off. To decide when to switch a circuit on or off, a program might use sensor readings, time or calendar information, user input, or other information.

Power-switching circuits require an interface between the parallel port's outputs and the switch that you want to control. In an electromagnetic, or mechanical, relay, applying a voltage to a coil causes a pair of contacts to physically separate or touch. Other switches have no moving parts, and operate by opening and closing a current path in a semiconductor.

Choosing a Switch

All switches contain one or more pairs of switch terminals, which may be mechanical contacts or leads on a semiconductor or integrated circuit. In addition, electronically controlled switches have a pair of control terminals that enable opening and closing of the switch, usually by applying and removing a voltage across the terminals.

An ideal switch has three characteristics. When the switch is open, the switch terminals are completely disconnected from each other, with infinite impedance between them. When the switch is closed, the terminals connect perfectly, with zero impedance between them. And in response to a control signal, the switch opens or closes instantly and perfectly, with no delay or contact bounce.

As you might suspect, although there are many types of switches, none meets the ideal, so you need to find a match between the requirements of your circuit and what's available. Switch specifications include these:

Control voltage and current. The switch's control terminals have defined voltages and currents at which the switch opens and closes. Your circuit's control signal must meet the switch's specification.

Load current. The switch should be able to safely carry currents greater than the maximum current your load will require.

Switching voltage. The voltage to be switched must be less than the maximum safe voltage across the switch terminals.

Switching speed. For simple power switches, speed is often not critical, but there are applications where speed matters. For example, a switching power supply may switch current to an inductor at rates of 20 kilohertz or more. You can calculate the maximum switching speed from the switch's turn-on and turn-off times. (*Maximum switching speed = 1/(max. turn-on time + max. turn-off time.*)

Other factors to consider are cost, physical size, and availability.

Figure 7-3 shows some common configurations available in mechanical switches. Electronic switches can emulate these same configurations. You can also build the more complex configurations from combinations of simpler switches.

As the name suggests, a normally open switch is open when there is no control voltage, and closes on applying a control voltage. A normally closed switch is the reverse—it's closed with no control voltage, and opens on applying a voltage.

A single-throw (*ST*) switch connects a switch terminal either to a second terminal or to nothing, while a double-throw (*DT*) switch connects a switch terminal to either of two terminals. In a single-pole (*SP*) switch, the control voltage controls

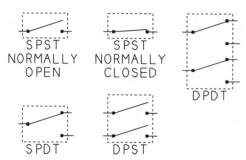

Figure 7-3: Five types of switches.

one set of terminals, while in a double-pole (*DP*) switch, one voltage controls two sets of terminals. A double-pole, double-throw (*DPDT*) switch has two terminals, with each switching between another pair of terminals (so there are six terminals in all).

Logic Outputs

For a low-current, low-voltage load, you may be able to use a logic-gate output or an output port bit as a switch. For higher currents or voltages, you can use a logic output to drive a transistor that will in turn control current to the load. In either case, you need to know the characteristics of the logic output, so you can judge whether it's capable of the job at hand.

Table 7-1 shows maximum output voltages and currents for popular logic gates, drivers, and microcontrollers, any of which might be controlled, directly or indirectly, by a PC's parallel port. The table shows minimum guaranteed output currents at specific voltages, usually the minimum logic-high and the maximum logic-low outputs for the logic family.

To use a logic output to drive a load other than a logic input, you need to know the output's maximum source and sink current and the power-dissipation limits of the chip. Many logic outputs can drive low-voltage loads of 10 to 20 milliamperes. For example, an LED requires just 1.4V. Because you're not driving a logic input, you don't have to worry about valid logic levels. All that matters is being able to provide the voltage and current required by the LED.

Figure 7-4 illustrates source and sink current. You might naturally think of a logic output as something that "outputs," or sends out, current, but in fact, the direction of current flow depends on whether the output is a logic-high or logic-low.

You can think of source current as flowing from a logic-high output, through a load to ground, while sink current flows from the power supply, through a load, into a logic-low output. Data sheets often use negative numbers to indicate source current. In most logic circuits, an output's load is a logic input, but the load can be any circuit that connects to the output.

CMOS logic outputs are symmetrical, with equal current-sourcing and sinking abilities. In contrast, TTL and NMOS outputs can sink much more than they can source. If you want to use a TTL or NMOS output to power a load, design your circuit so that a logic-low output turns on the load.

All circuits should be sure to stay well below the chip's absolute maximum ratings. For example, an ordinary 74HC gate has an absolute maximum output of 25 milliamperes per pin, so you could use an output to drive an LED at 15 milliamperes. (Use a current-limiting resistor of 220 ohms.) If you want 20 milliamperes, a better choice would be a buffer like the 74HC244, with an absolute maximum output of 35 milliamperes per pin. In Figure 7-5, A and B show examples.

Don't try to drive a high-current load directly from a parallel-port output. Use buffers between the cable and your circuits. Because the original parallel port had no published specification, it's hard to make assumptions about the characteristics of a parallel-port output, except that it should be equivalent to the components in the original PC's port. Using a buffer at the far end of the cable gives you known output characteristics. The buffer also provides some isolation from the load-control circuits, so if something goes wrong, you'll destroy a low-cost buffer rather than your parallel port components. A buffer with a Schmitt-trigger input will help to ensure a clean control signal at the switch.

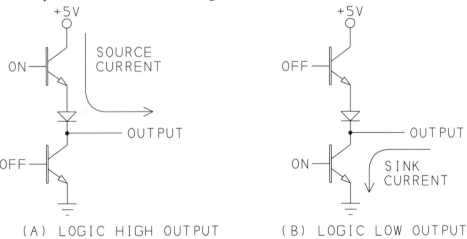

Figure 7-4: A logic-high output sources current; a logic-low output sinks current.

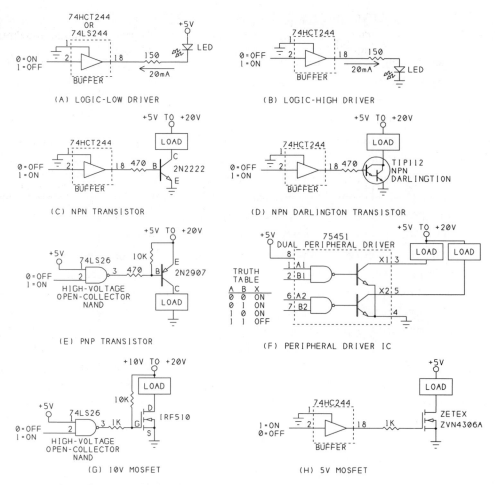

Figure 7-5: Interfaces to high-current and high-voltage circuits.

Bipolar Transistors

If your load needs more current or voltage than a logic output can provide, you can use an output to drive a simple transistor switch.

A bipolar transistor is an inexpensive, easy-to-use current amplifier. Although the variety of transistors can be bewildering, for many applications you can use any

Table 7-1: Maximum output current for selected chips.

Chip	Output high voltage (VOH min)	Output low voltage (VOL max)	Supply Voltage	Absolute maximums
74LS374 flip-flop, 74LS244 buffer	2.4V@-2.6mA	0.5V@24mA	4.5 to 5.5	-
74HC(T)374 flip-flop, 74HC(T)244 buffer	Vcc-0.1@-20μA 3.84V@-6mA	0.1V@20 μA 0.33V@6mA	4.5	35mA/pin, 500mW/package
74LS14 inverter	2.7V@-0.4mA	0.5V@8mA	4.5 to 5.5	-
74HC(T)14 inverter	4.4V@-20μA 4.2V@-4mA	0.1V@20μA 0.33V@4mA	4.5	25mA/pin, 500mW/package
8255 NMOS PPI (programmable peripheral interface)	2.4V@-200μA	0.45V@1.7mA (on any 8 Port B or C pins)	4.5 to 5.5	4mA/pin
82C55 CMOS PPI (programmable peripheral interface)	3V@-2.5mA	0.4V@2.5mA	4.5 to 5.5	4.0mA/pin
8051 NMOS microcontroller	2.4V@-80μA	0.45V@1.6μA	4.5 to 5.5	-
80C51 CMOS microcontroller	Vcc-0.3@-10μA Vcc-0.7@-30μA Vcc-1.5@-60μA	0.3@100μA 0.45@1.5mA 1.0@3.5mA	4 to 5	10mA/pin, 15mA/port, 71mA/all ports
68HC11 CMOS microcontroller	Vdd-0.8@-0.8mA	0.4@1.6mA	4.5 to 5.5	25mA/pin; also observe power dissipation limit for the chip
PIC16C5x CMOS microcontroller	Vdd-0.7@-5.4mA	0.6@8.7mA	4.5	+25/-20mA/pin, +50/-40mA/port, 800mW/package

general-purpose or saturated-switch transistor that meets your voltage and current requirements.

Figure 7-5C uses a 2N2222, a widely available NPN transistor. A logic-high at the control output biases the transistor on and causes a small current to flow from base to emitter. This results in a low collector-to-emitter resistance that allows current to flow from the power supply, through the load and switch, to ground. When the transistor is switched on, there is a small voltage drop, about 0.3V, from collector to emitter, so the entire power-supply voltage isn't applied across the load.

The exact value of the transistor's base resistor isn't critical. Values from a few hundred to 1000 ohms are typical. The resistor needs to be small enough so that the transistor can provide the current to power the load, yet large enough to limit the current to safe levels.

The load current must be less than the transistor's maximum collector current (I_C). Look for a current gain (h_{FE}) of at least 50. Many parts catalogs include these specifications.

The load's power supply can be greater than +5V, but if it's more than +12V, check the transistor's collector-emitter breakdown voltage (V_{CEO}), to be sure it's greater than the voltage that will be across these terminals when the switch is off.

For large load currents, you can use a Darlington pair, as Figure 7-5D shows. One transistor provides the base current to drive a second transistor. Because the total current gain equals the gain of the first times the gain of the second, gains of 1000 are typical. The TIP112 is an example of a Darlington pair in a single TO-220 package. It's rated for collector current of 2 amperes and collector-to-emitter voltage of 100V. A drawback is that the collector-to-emitter voltage of a Darlington is about a volt, much higher than for a single transistor.

The above circuits all use NPN transistors and require current from a logic-high output to switch on. If you want to turn on a load with a logic-low output, you can use a PNP transistor, as Figure 7-5E shows. In this circuit, a logic-low output biases the transistor on, and a voltage equal to the power supply switches it off. If the load's power supply is greater than +5V, use a high-voltage open-collector or open-drain output for the control signal, so that the pullup resistor can safely pull logic-high outputs to the supply voltage.

Another handy way to control a load with logic is to use a peripheral-driver chip like those in the 7545X series (Figure 7-5F). Each chip in the series contains two independent logic gates, with the output of each gate controlling a transistor switch.

There are four members of the series:

75451 dual AND drivers
75452 dual NAND drivers
75453 dual OR drivers
75454 dual NOR drivers

Each output can sink a minimum of 300 milliamperes at 0.7V (collector-to-emitter voltage).

MOSFETs

An alternative to the bipolar transistor is the MOSFET. The most popular type is an enhancement-mode, N-channel type, where applying a positive voltage to the gate switches the MOSFET on, creating a low-resistance channel from drain to source.

P-channel MOSFETs are the complement of N-channel MOSFETs, much as PNP transistors complement NPNs. An enhancement-mode, P-channel MOSFET switches on when the gate is more negative than the source. In depletion-mode MOSFETs (which may be N-channel or P-channel), applying a gate voltage opens the switch, rather than closing it.

Unlike a bipolar-transistor switch, which can draw several milliamperes of base current, a MOSFET gate has very high input resistance and draws virtually no current. But unlike a bipolar transistor, which needs just 0.7V from base to emitter, a MOSFET may require as much as 10V from gate to source to switch on fully.

One way to provide the gate voltage from 5V logic is to use a device with an open-collector or open-drain output and a pull-up resistor to at least 10V, as Figure 7-5G shows. Some newer MOSFETs have lower minimum *on voltages*. Zetex's ZVN4603A can switch 1.5 amperes with just +5V applied to the gate (Figure 7-5H).

MOSFETs do have a small on resistance, so there is a voltage drop from drain to source when the device is switched on. The on resistance of the ZVN4603A is 0.45 ohms at 1.5 amperes, which would result in a voltage drop of about 0.7V. At lower currents, the resistance and voltage drop are less.

Include a gate resistor of around 1K (as shown) to protect the driver's output if you're switching a relay, motor, or other inductive load.

High-side Switches

Another way of controlling a load with a logic voltage is to use a high-side switch like the LTC1156, a quad high-side MOSFET driver chip from Linear Technology, shown in Figure 7-6. The chip allows you to use the cheaper, more widely available N-channel MOSFETs in your designs and adds other useful features. Single and dual versions are also available, and other manufacturers have similar chips.

Most of the previous circuits have used a low-side switch, where one switch terminal connects to ground and the other connects to the load's ground terminal. In a high-side switch, the load's ground terminal connects directly to ground and the switch is between the power supply and load's power-supply terminal.

A high-side switch has a couple of advantages. For safety reasons, some circuits are designed to be off if the switch terminals happen to short to ground. With a low-side switch, shorting the switch to ground would apply power to the load. With a high-side switch, although shorting the switch to ground may destroy the

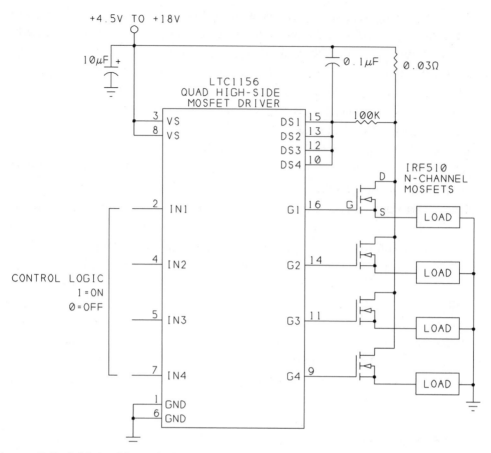

+4.5V TO +18V

Figure 7-6: A high-side switch connects between the load and the power supply. Linear Technology's LTC1156 control high-side MOSFET switches with logic signals.

switch, it removes power from the load. (Most switches fail by opening permanently.)

Connecting the load directly to ground can also help to reduce electrical noise in the circuit. With a low-side switch, the load always floats a few tenths of a volt above ground.

The LTC1156 can control up to four MOSFETs. You can use any 5V TTL or CMOS outputs as control signals, because the switches turn on at just 2V.

Providing a high-enough gate voltage can be a problem when using an N-channel MOSFET in a high-side switch. When the MOSFET switches on, its low drain-to-source resistance causes the source to rise nearly to the supply voltage. For the MOSFET to remain on, the gate must be more positive than the source.

The LTC1156 takes care of this with charge-pump circuits that bring the gate voltages as much as 20V above the supply voltage.

By adding a small current-sensing resistor, you can cause the outputs to switch off if the MOSFETs' drain current rises above a selected value (3.3A with 30 milliohms in the circuit shown). The outputs switch off when the voltage drop across the current-sensing resistor is 100 millivolts.

Solid-state Relays

Another way to switch power to a load is to use a solid-state relay, which offers an easy-to-use, optoisolated switch in a single package. Figure 7-7A shows an example.

In a typical solid-state DC relay, applying a voltage across the control inputs causes current to flow in an LED enclosed in the package. The LED switches on a photodiode, which applies a control voltage to a MOSFET's gate, switching the MOSFET on. The result is a low resistance across the switch terminals, which effectively closes the switch and allows current to flow. Removing the control voltage turns off the LED and opens the switch.

Solid-state relays are rated for use with a variety of load voltages and currents. Because the switch is optoisolated, there need be no electrical connection at all between the control signal and the circuits being switched.

Solid-state relays have an on resistance of anywhere from a few ohms to several hundred ohms. Types rated for higher voltages tend to have higher on resistances. Solid-state relays also have small leakage currents, typically a microampere or so, that flow through the switch even when off. This leakage current isn't a problem in most applications.

There are solid-state relays for switching AC loads as well. These provide a simple and safe way to use a logic signal to switch line voltage to a load. Inside the relay, the switch itself is usually an SCR or TRIAC. Zero-voltage switches minimize noise by switching only when the AC voltage is near zero.

Electromagnetic Relays

Electromagnetic relays have been around longer than transistors and still have their uses. An electromagnetic relay contains a coil and one or more sets of contacts attached to an armature (Figure 7-7B). Applying a voltage to the coil causes current to flow in it. The current generates magnetic fields that move the armature, opening or closing the relay contacts. Removing the coil voltage collapses the magnetic fields and returns the armature and contacts to their original positions.

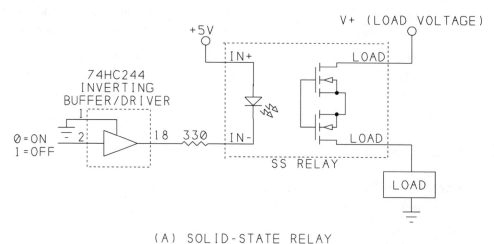

(A) SOLID-STATE RELAY

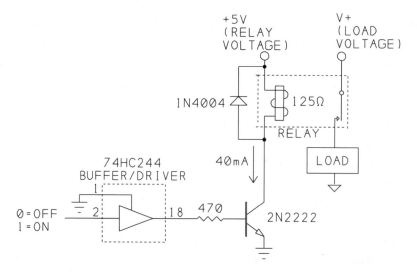

(B) MECHANICAL RELAY

Figure 7-7: Solid-state and electromagnetic, or mechanical, relays are another option for switching power to a circuit. An advantage to relays is that the load is electrically isolated from the switch's control signal.

A diode across the relay coil protects the components from damaging voltages that might otherwise occur when the contacts open and the current in the coil has nowhere to go. In fact, you should place a diode in this way across any switched inductive DC load, including DC motor windings. For AC loads, use a varistor in place of the diode. The varistor behaves much like two Zener diodes connected anode-to-cathode on both ends.

Two attractions of electromagnetic relays are very low on resistance and complete physical isolation from the control signal. Because the contacts physically touch, the on resistance is typically just a few tenths of an ohm. And because the contacts open or close in response to magnetic fields, there need be no electrical connection between the coil and the contacts.

Drawbacks include large size, large current requirements (50-200 milliamperes is typical for coil current), slow switching speed, and the need for maintenance or replacement as the contacts wear. One solution to the need for high current is to use a latching relay, which requires a current pulse to switch, but then remains switched with greatly reduced power consumption.

Controlling the Bits

For simple switches, a single output bit can control power to a load. The bit routines introduced in Chapter 4 make it easy to read and change individual bits in a byte. If you store the last value written to the port in a variable, there's no need to read the port before each write.

X-10 Switches

A different way to control power to devices powered at 115V AC is to use the X-10 protocol, which can send *on, off,* and *dim* commands to a device, using a low-voltage signal carried on 115V, 60-Hz power lines. An X-10 interface is a simple way to control lights and plug-in appliances using only the existing wiring in the building.

Besides the popular manually programmed X-10 controllers and appliance modules, there are devices that enable you to program an X-10 controller from a PC, usually using a serial or parallel link to communicate with the controller.

Signal Switches

One more type of switch worth mentioning is the CMOS switch for low-power analog or digital signals. A logic signal controls the switch's operation.

Simple CMOS Switch

The 4066B quad bilateral switch is a simple and inexpensive way to switch low-power, low-frequency signals. As Figure 7-8 shows, the chip has four control

```
                        4066B
              QUAD BILATERAL SWITCH
    13 CONTROL  A
     1 IN/OUT   A   SWA      OUT/IN A 2
     5 CONTROL  B
     4 IN/OUT   B   SWB      OUT/IN B 3
     6 CONTROL  C
     8 IN/OUT   C   SWC      OUT/IN C 9
    12 CONTROL  D
    11 IN/OUT   D   SWD      OUT/IN D 10
```

Figure 7-8: The 4066B contains four CMOS switches, each controlled by a logic signal.

inputs, each of which controls two I/O pins. A logic-high at a control input closes a switch and results in a low resistance between the corresponding I/O pins. A logic-low opens the switch, and opens the connection between the I/O pins.

The 4066B's power supply can range from 3 to 15V. With a 5V power supply, the on resistance of each switch is about 270 ohms, with the resistance dropping at higher supply voltages. The on resistance has no significant effect on standard LSTTL or CMOS logic or other signals that terminate at high-impedance inputs. An HCMOS version, the 74HC4066, has lower on resistance and, unlike other HCMOS chips, can use a supply voltage of up to 12V.

Controlling a Switch Matrix

A more elaborate switching device is the crosspoint switch, which allows complete control over the routing of two sets of lines. Examples are Harris' 74HCT22106 *Crosspoint Switch with Memory Control* and Maxim's MAX456 *8 x 8 Video Crosspoint Switch*.

Figure 7-9 shows how you can use the parallel port to control an 8 x 8 array of signals with the '22106. You can connect any of eight *X* pins to any of eight *Y* pins, in any combination. Possible applications include switching audio signals to different monitors or recording instruments, selecting inputs for test equipment, or any situation that requires flexible, changeable routing of analog or digital signals.

The '22106 simplifies circuit design and programming. It contains an array of switches, a decoder that translates a 6-bit address into a switch selection, and latches that control the opening and closing of the switches.

To connect an *X* pin to a *Y* pin, set $\overline{MR}$=1 and $\overline{CE}$=0. Then do the following:

1. Write the address of the desired *X* pin to *A0-A2* and write the address of the desired *Y* pin to *A3-A5*. Set $\overline{Strobe}$=1. Set *Data*=1.

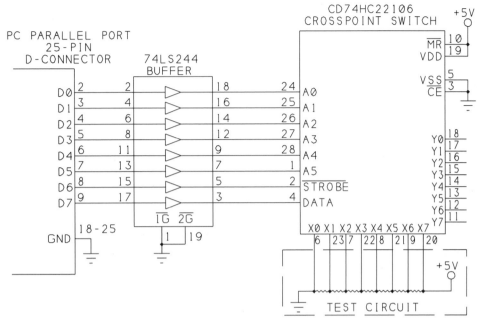

Figure 7-9: The parallel port's data lines can control an 8 x 8 crosspoint switch.

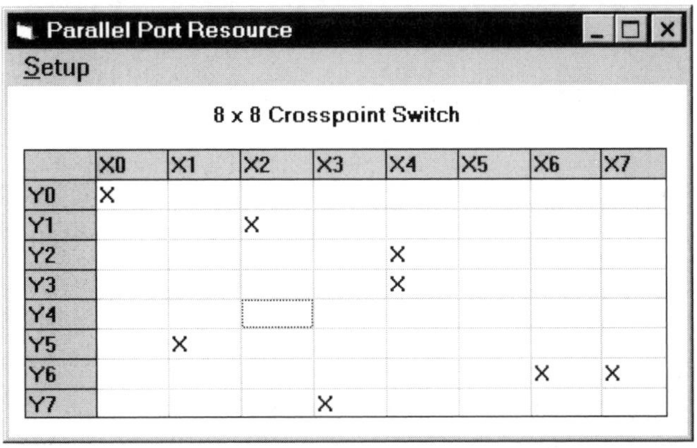

Figure 7-10: Clicking on a grid cell opens or closes the matching switch.

3. Set $\overline{Strobe}$=0 to close the requested switch, connecting the selected X and Y pins.

3. Set $\overline{Strobe}$=1.

To break a connection, do the same thing, except bring the *Data* input low to open the switch.

Figure 7-10 shows the screen for Listing 7-2's program, which demonstrates the operation of the switch matrix. The program uses Visual Basic's Grid control to

```
Const OPENSWITCH% = 0
Const CLOSESWITCH% = 1
```

```
Sub ActivateSwitch (OpenOrClose%)
Dim Strobe%
Dim XY%
'Data port bit 7 = OpenOrClose (0=open, 1=close)
OpenOrClose = OpenOrClose * &H80
'Data port bit 6 = Strobe.
Strobe = &H40
'Data port bits 0-2 hold the X value, bits 3-5 hold the Y value.
XY = grdXY.Col - 1 + (grdXY.Row - 1) * 8
'Write the address, select open or close, Strobe = 1
DataPortWrite BaseAddress, XY + Strobe + OpenOrClose
'Pulse the Strobe input.
DataPortWrite BaseAddress, XY + OpenOrClose
DataPortWrite BaseAddress, XY + Strobe + OpenOrClose
End Sub
```

```
Sub DisplayResults ()
Select Case SwitchState
    Case "Closed"
        grdXY.Text = "X"
    Case "Open"
        grdXY.Text = ""
End Select
End Sub
```

```
Sub Form_Load ()
StartUp
LabelTheGrid
End Sub
```

```
Sub grdXY_Click ()
Select Case grdXY.Text
    Case "X"
        ActivateSwitch OPENSWITCH
        SwitchState = "Open"
        DisplayResults
    Case Else
        ActivateSwitch CLOSESWITCH
        SwitchState = "Closed"
        DisplayResults
End Select
End Sub
```

Listing 7-2: Controlling an 8 x 8 crosspoint switch (Sheet 1 of 2)

```
Sub LabelTheGrid ()
Dim Row%
Dim Column%
grdXY.Col = 0
For Row = 1 To 8
    grdXY.Row = Row
    grdXY.Text = "Y" & Row - 1
Next Row
grdXY.Row = 0
For Column = 1 To 8
    grdXY.Col = Column
    grdXY.Text = "X" & Column - 1
Next Column
lblXY.Caption = "8 x 8 Crosspoint Switch"
End Sub
```

Listing 7-2: Controlling an 8 x 8 crosspoint switch (Sheet 2 of 2)

display the switch matrix. When you click on a cell, the associated switch opens or closes. An *X* indicates a closed switch, an empty cell indicates an open switch.

You can make and break as many connections as you want by writing appropriate values to the chip. All previous switch settings remain until you change them by writing to the specific switch. The switches can connect in any combination. For example, you can connect each *X* pin to a different *Y* pin to create eight distinct signal paths. Or, you can connect all eight *Y* pins to a single *X* pin, to route one signal to eight different paths. The *X* and *Y* pins may connect to external inputs or outputs in any combination.

Figure 7-9 shows the '22106 powered at +5V, but the supply voltage may range from 2 to 10V, and *Vss* (and *Vdd*) may be negative. (The HCT version (74HCT22106) requires a +5V supply.) The chip can switch any voltages within the supply range. However, the maximum and minimum values for the address and control signals vary with the supply voltage. For example, if *Vdd* is +5V and *Vss* is -5V, the address and control signals can no longer use 5V CMOS logic levels, because the logic levels are in proportion to the supply voltage. The maximum logic low for these signals drops from +1.5V to -2V ($Vss + 0.3(|Vdd-Vss|)$), and the minimum logic high drops from +3.5V to +2V ($Vss + 0.7(|Vdd-Vss|)$).

At 5V, the switches' typical on resistance is 64 ohms, dropping to 45 ohms at 9V. The chip can pass frequencies up to 6 Megahertz with ±4.5V supplies.

In Figure 7-9, the parallel port's *D0-D7* control the switch array. The 74HCT244 buffer has TTL-compatible inputs and CMOS-compatible outputs. If you use a 74LS244, add a 10K pull-up resistor from each output to +5V, to ensure that logic highs meet the '22106's 3.3V minimum. If you use a 74HC244, add pullups at the inputs to bring the parallel port's high outputs to valid CMOS logic levels.

For a simple test of the switches, you can connect a series of equal resistors as shown to the X inputs. Each X input will then be at a different voltage. To verify a switch closure, measure the voltages at the selected X and Y inputs; they should match.

Pin 3 ($\overline{CE}$) is tied low. To control multiple switches from a single parallel port, connect each switch's $\overline{CE}$ to one of the Control outputs, and wire $D0$-$D7$ to all of the switches. You then can use the Control lines to select a switch to write to. The Reset input ($\overline{MR}$) is tied high. If you want the ability to reset all of the switches, tie this pin to one of the Control outputs.

Maxim's '456 is similar, but can pass frequencies up to 25 Megahertz, separate analog and digital ground pins, and $V+$ and $V-$ inputs. The address and control signals use 5V logic levels even if the chip uses another supply voltage.

Displays

Because the parallel port resides on a personal computer that has its own full-screen display, there's usually little need to use the port's outputs to control LEDs, LCDs (liquid crystal displays), or other display types. You might want to use LEDs as simple indicators to show troubleshooting or status information. And of course, you can use the port's Data and Control outputs to control other types of displays if the need arises.

8

Input Applications

Because the parallel port's most common use is to send data to a printer, you might think that the port is useful only for sending information from a PC to a peripheral. But you can also use the parallel port as an input port that reads information from external devices. SPPs have five Status inputs and four bidirectional Control lines, and on many newer ports, you can use the eight Data lines as inputs as well.

This chapter shows a variety of ways to use the parallel port for input. The examples include latched digital inputs, an expanded input port of 40 bits, and an interface to an analog-to-digital converter.

Reading a Byte

On the original parallel port, there is no way to read eight bits from a single port register. But there are several ways to use the available input bits to put together a byte of information.

Chapter 2 showed how to perform simple reads of the Status, Control, and bidirectional Data bits, and later chapters show how to use IEEE 1284's Nibble, Byte, EPP, and ECP modes to read bytes and handshake with the peripheral sending the information. The following examples show other options, including a simple way

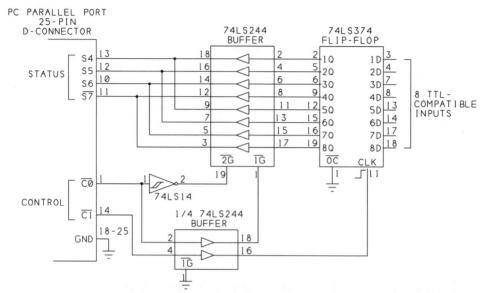

Figure 8-1: A '374 flip-flop latches a byte of data, and a Control bit selects each of two nibbles to be read at the Status port.

to read a byte in two nibbles at the Status port and how to add a latch to store the data to be read.

Latching the Status Inputs

Figure 8-1 and Listing 8-1 show a way to read bytes at the Status port. The circuit stores two nibbles (1 nibble = 4 bits), which the program reads in sequence at the Status port. One Control bit latches the data, and another selects the nibble to read.

The latch is a 74LS374 octal flip-flop. The rising edge of the *Clk* input latches the eight *D* inputs to the corresponding *Q* outputs. Even if the inputs change, the outputs will remain at their latched values until $\overline{C1}$ goes low, then high again. This ensures that the PC's software will read the state of all of the bits at one moment in time. Otherwise, the PC may read invalid data. For example, if the byte is an output from an analog-to-digital converter, the output's value may change by one bit, from *1Fh* when the PC reads the lower four bits, to *20h* when the PC reads the upper four bits. If the data isn't latched, the PC will read *2Fh*, which is very different from the actual values of *1Fh* and *20h*.

A 74LS244 buffer presents the bits to the Status port, four at a time. When $\overline{1G}$ is low, outputs *1Q-4Q* are enabled, and the PC can read inputs *1D-4D*. When $\overline{2G}$ is low, outputs *5Q-8Q* are enabled and the PC can read inputs *5D-8D*. A second '244 buffers the two Control signals. You can substitute HCT versions of the chips.

Parallel Port Complete

```
Option Explicit
Const SelectHighNibble% = 1
Const Clock% = 2
```

```
Sub cmdReadByte_Click ()
Dim LowNibble%
Dim HighNibble%
Dim ByteIn%
'Latch the data
ControlPortWrite BaseAddress, Clock
ControlPortWrite BaseAddress, 0
'Read the nibbles at bits 4-7.
LowNibble = StatusPortRead(BaseAddress) \ &H10
ControlPortWrite BaseAddress, SelectHighNibble
HighNibble = StatusPortRead(BaseAddress) And &HF0
ByteIn = LowNibble + HighNibble
lblByteIn.Caption = Hex$(ByteIn) + "h"
End Sub
```

Listing 8-1: Reading a byte in two nibbles at the Status port.

Listing 8-1 latches a byte of data, then reads it in two nibbles, recombines the nibbles into a byte, and displays the result. The data bits are the upper four Status bits, which makes it easy to recombine the nibbles into a byte. In the upper nibble, the bits are in the same positions as in the original byte, so there's no need to divide or multiply to shift the bits. For the lower nibble, just divide the value read by *&h10.*

Latched Input Using Status and Control Bits

Figure 8-2 is similar to the previous example, but it uses both Status and Control bits for data. Control bits 0-2 are the lower three bits, and Status bits 3-7 are the upper five bits, so each bit has the same position as in the original byte. Control bit 3 latches the data.

For this circuit, multi-mode ports must be in SPP mode to ensure that the Control bits can be used for input. Some multi-mode ports can't use the Control bits as inputs at all.

The three Control lines are driven by 7407 open-collector buffers. The remaining Control input uses another buffer in the package.

You must write *1* to Control bits 0-2's corresponding outputs in order to use them as inputs. (Because bits *0, 1,* and *3* are inverted between the port register and the connector, you actually write *4* to bits *0–3* to bring all outputs high.)

Listing 8-2 latches 8 bits, reads the Status and Control ports, recreates the original byte, and displays the result.

5 Bytes of Input

If you have a lot of inputs to monitor, Figure 8-3 shows how to read up 5 bytes at the Status port. Five outputs of a 74LS244 octal buffer drive the Status inputs, and the other 3 bits buffer the bit-select signals from $\overline{C0}$-C2.

Outputs $\overline{C0}$, $\overline{C1}$, and C2 select one of eight inputs at each of five 74LS151 data selectors. At each '151, the selected input appears at output Y, and also in inverted form at $\overline{W}$. An output of each '151 connects through a buffer to one of the Status inputs. To read a bit from each '151, you write to $\overline{C0}$-C2 to select the bit, then read S3-$\overline{S7}$.

Listing 8-3 reads all 40 bits, 5 bits at a time, combines the bits into bytes, and displays the results. Figure 8-4 is the program screen. Since the '151 has both normal and inverted outputs, you could use the $\overline{W}$ output at $\overline{S7}$ to eliminate having to reinvert the bit in software. Listing 8-3 uses the *StatusPortRead* routine that automatically reinverts bit 7, so Figure 8-3 uses the Y output.

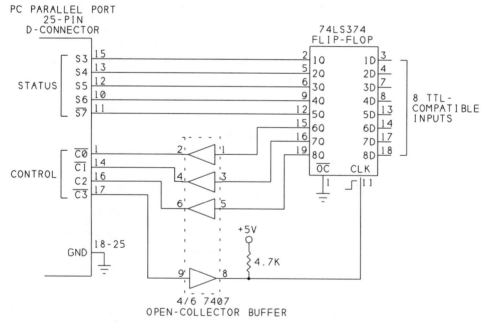

Figure 8-2: Eight latched input bits, using the Status and Control ports.

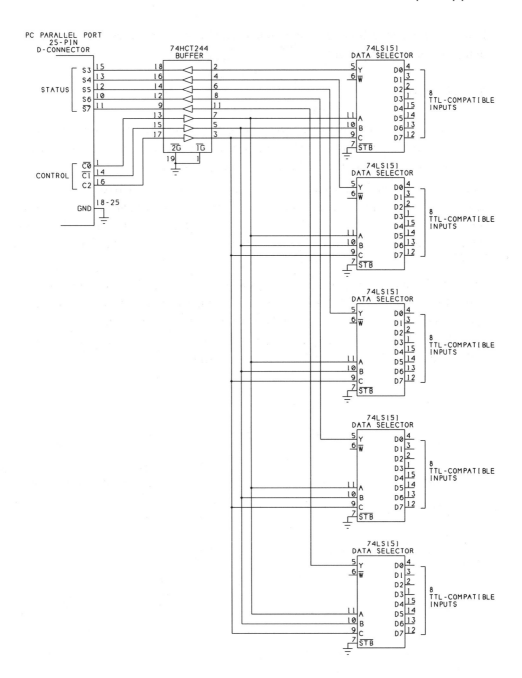

Figure 8-3: Forty input bits, read in groups of five.

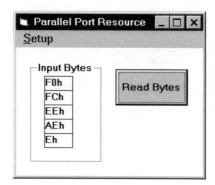

Figure 8-4: Screen for Listing 8-3's program.

Using the Data Port for Input

If you have a bidirectional data port, you can use the eight data lines as inputs. You can also use the port as an I/O port, both reading and writing to it, as long as you're careful to configure the port as input whenever outputs are connected and enabled at the data pins. In other words, when the data lines are configured as outputs, be sure to tristate, or disable, any external outputs they connect to. You can use a '374 to latch input at the Data port, as in the previous examples.

Reading Analog Signals

The parallel port is a digital interface, but you can use it to read analog signals, such as sensor outputs.

Sensor Basics

A sensor is a device that reacts to changes in a physical property or condition such as light, temperature, or pressure. Many sensors react by changing in resistance. If a voltage is applied across the sensor, the changing resistance will cause a change in the voltage across the sensor. An analog-to-digital converter (ADC) can convert the voltage to a digital value that a computer can store, display, and perform calculations on.

Simple On/Off Measurements

Sometimes all you need to detect is the presence or absence of the sensed property. Some simple sensors act like switches, with a low resistance in the presence

```
'Clock is Control bit 3.
Const Clock% = 8
'Write 1 to bits C0-C2 to allow their use as inputs.
Const SetControlBitsAsInputs% = 7
```

```
Sub cmdReadByte_Click ()
Dim LowBits%
Dim HighBits%
Dim ByteIn%
'Latch the data.
ControlPortWrite BaseAddress, SetControlBitsAsInputs + Clock
ControlPortWrite BaseAddress, SetControlBitsAsInputs
'Read the bits at C0-C2, S3-S7.
LowBits = ControlPortRead(BaseAddress) And 7
HighBits = StatusPortRead(BaseAddress) And &HF8
ByteIn = LowBits + HighBits
lblByteIn.Caption = Hex$(ByteIn) + "h"
End Sub
```

```
Sub Form_Load ()
'(partial listing)
'Initialize the Control port.
ControlPortWrite BaseAddress, SetControlBitsAsInputs
End Sub
```

Listing 8-2: Reading 8 bits using the Status and Control ports.

of the sensed property, and a high resistance in its absence. In this case, you can connect the sensor much like a manual switch, and read its state at an input bit. Sensors that you can use this way include magnetic proximity sensors, vibration sensors, and tilt switches.

Level Detecting

Another common use for sensors is to detect a specific level, or intensity, of a property. For this, you can use a comparator, a type of operational amplifier (op amp) that brings its output high or low depending on which of two inputs is greater.

Figure 8-5 shows how to use a comparator to detect a specific light level on a photocell. The circuit uses an LM339, a general-purpose quad comparator. The resistance of a Cadmium-sulfide (CdS) photocell varies with the intensity of light on it. Pin 4 is a reference voltage, and pin 5 is the input being sensed. When the sensed input is lower than the reference, the comparator's output is low. When the sensed input is higher than the reference, the comparator's output is high.

As the light intensity on the photocell increases, the photocell's resistance decreases and pin 5's voltage rises. To detect a specific light level, adjust *R2* so that *Vout* switches from low to high when the light reaches the desired intensity. You can read the logic state of *Vout* at any input bit on the parallel port.

R4 is a pull-up resistor for the LM339's open-collector output. *R3* adds a small amount of hysteresis, which keeps the output from oscillating when the input is near the switching voltage.

You can use the same basic circuit with other sensors that vary in resistance. Replace the photocell with your sensor, and adjust *R2* for the switching level you want.

Reading an Analog-to-digital Converter

When you need to know the precise value of a sensor's output, an analog-to-digital converter (ADC) will do the job. Figure 8-6 is a circuit that enables you to read eight analog voltages. The ADC0809 converter is inexpensive, widely available, and easy to interface to the parallel port. The ADC0808 is the same chip with higher accuracy, and you may use it instead.

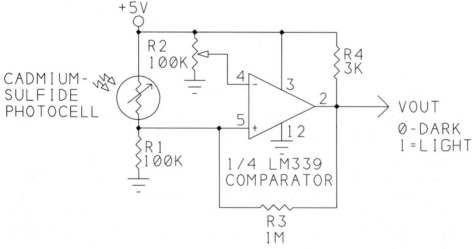

ADJUST R2 SO VOUT SWITCHES AT DESIRED LIGHT LEVEL.

Figure 8-5: A comparator can detect a specific voltage.

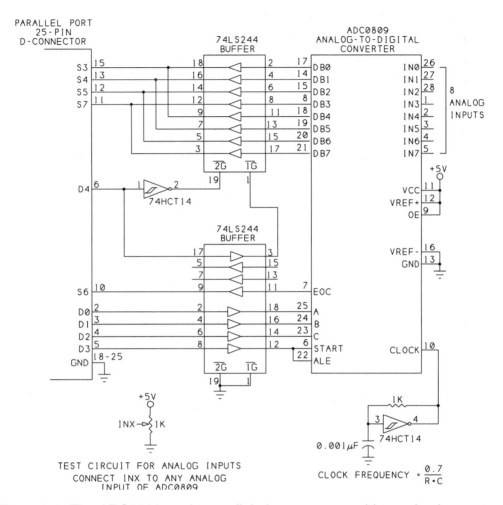

Figure 8-6: The ADC0809 analog-to-digital converter provides a simple way to read 8 analog channels at the parallel port.

The ADC0809 has eight analog inputs (*IN0-IN7*), which may range from 0 to +5V. To read the value of an analog input, you select a channel by writing a value from 0 to 7 to inputs *A-C*, then bringing *Start* and *Ale* high, then low, to begin the conversion. When the conversion is complete, *Eoc* goes high and the digital outputs hold a value that represents the analog voltage read.

The chip requires a clock signal to control the conversion. A 74HCT14 Schmitt-trigger inverter offers a simple way to create the clock. The frequency can range from 10 kilohertz to 1280 kilohertz. If you prefer, you can use a 555 timer for the clock, although the maximum frequency of the 555 is 500 kilohertz. Conversion time for the ADC is 100 microseconds with a 640-kilohertz clock.

```
Dim DataIn%(0 To 7)
Dim DataByte%(0 To 4)
```

```
Sub cmdReadBytes_Click ()
Dim BitNumber%
'The Control port selects a bit number to read.
'The Status port holds the data to be read.
For BitNumber = 0 To 7
    ControlPortWrite BaseAddress, BitNumber
    DataIn(BitNumber) = StatusPortRead(BaseAddress)
Next BitNumber
GetBytesFromDataIn
DisplayResults
End Sub
```

```
Sub DisplayResults ()
Dim ByteNumber%
For ByteNumber = 0 To 4
lblByteIn(ByteNumber).Caption = Hex$(DataByte(ByteNumber)) & "h"
Next ByteNumber
End Sub
```

Listing 8-3: Reading 40 inputs. (Sheet 1 of 2)

```
Sub GetBytesFromDataIn ()
'Bits 3-7 of the 8 bytes contain data.
'To make 5 data bytes from these bits,
'each data byte contains one bit from each byte read.
'For example, data byte 0 contains 8 "bit 3s,"
'one from each byte read.
Dim ByteNumber%
Dim BitNumber%
Dim BitToAdd%
For ByteNumber = 0 To 4
    DataByte(ByteNumber) = 0
    'BitRead gets the selected bit value (ByteNumber + 3)
    'from the selected byte read (DataIn(BitNumber)).
    'To get the bit value for the created data byte,
    'multiply times 2^BitNumber.
    'Add each bit value to the created byte.
    For BitNumber = 0 To 7
        BitToAdd = (BitRead(DataIn(BitNumber), ByteNumber + 3)) _
          * 2 ^ BitNumber
        DataByte(ByteNumber) = DataByte(ByteNumber) + BitToAdd
    Next BitNumber
Next ByteNumber
End Sub
```

Listing 8-3: Reading 40 inputs. (Sheet 2 of 2)

Inputs *Vref+* and *Vref-* are references for the analog inputs. When an analog input equals *Vref-*, the digital output is zero. When the input equals *Vref+*, the digital output is 255. You can connect the reference inputs to the +5V supply and ground, or if you need a more stable reference or a narrower range, you can connect other voltage sources to the references.

Listing 8-4 reads all eight channels and displays the results. It reads the data in two nibbles at *S3–S5* and $\overline{S7}$. Outputs *D0–D2* select the channel to convert, *D3* starts the conversion, and *D4* selects the nibble to read. Optional input *S6* allows you to monitor the state of the ADC's end-of-conversion (*Eoc*) output.

A 74LS244 drives the Status bits. When *D4* is low, you can read the ADC's *DB0–DB3* outputs at the Status port. When *D4* is high, you can read *DB4–DB7*.

A second 74LS244 interfaces the other signals to the ADC. Bringing *D3* high latches the channel address from *D0–D2*, and bringing *D3* low starts a conversion.

Bit *S6* goes high when the ADC has completed its conversion. You can monitor *S6* for a logic high that signals that the conversion is complete, or you can use the

```
Const Start% = 8
Const HighNibbleSelect% = &H10
Dim DataIn%(0 To 7)
Dim ChannelNumber%
Dim LowNibble%
Dim HighNibble%
```

```
Sub cmdReadPorts_Click ()
Dim EOC%
For ChannelNumber = 0 To 7
    'Select the channel.
    DataPortWrite BaseAddress, ChannelNumber
    'Pulse Start to begin a conversion.
    DataPortWrite BaseAddress, ChannelNumber + Start
    DataPortWrite BaseAddress, ChannelNumber
    'Wait for EOC
    Do
        DoEvents
        LowNibble = StatusPortRead(BaseAddress)
        EOC = BitRead(LowNibble, 6)
    Loop Until EOC = 1
    'Read the byte in 2 nibbles.
    DataPortWrite BaseAddress, ChannelNumber + HighNibbleSelect
    HighNibble = StatusPortRead(BaseAddress)
    DataIn(ChannelNumber) = MakeByteFromNibbles()
Next ChannelNumber
DisplayResult
End Sub
```

```
Sub DisplayResult ()
For ChannelNumber = 0 To 7
    lblADC(ChannelNumber).Caption = _
    Hex$(DataIn(ChannelNumber)) & "h"
Next ChannelNumber
End Sub
```

Listing 8-4: Reading 8 channels from an ADC. (Sheet 1 of 2)

```
Function MakeByteFromNibbles% ()
Dim S0%, S1%, S2%, S3%, S4%, S5%, S6%, S7%
S0 = (LowNibble And 8) \ 8
S1 = (LowNibble And &H10) \ 8
S2 = (LowNibble And &H20) \ 8
S3 = (LowNibble And &H80) \ &H10
S4 = (HighNibble And 8) * 2
S5 = (HighNibble And &H10) * 2
S6 = (HighNibble And &H20) * 2
S7 = HighNibble And &H80
MakeByteFromNibbles = S0 + S1 + S2 + S3 + S4 + S5 + S6+ S7
End Function
```

Listing 8-4: Reading 8 channels from an ADC. (Sheet 2 of 2)

rising edge at *S6* to trigger an interrupt, or you can ignore *S6* and just be sure to wait long enough for the conversion to complete before reading the result.

The circuit uses *S6* as end-of-convert because it's the parallel port's interrupt pin. If you don't use interrupts, you can wire the ADC's data outputs to S4–$\overline{S7}$ for an easier (and faster) conversion from nibbles to byte.

At each analog input, you can connect any component whose outputs ranges from 0 to +5V.

Sensor Interfaces

If the output range of your sensor voltages is much less than 5V, you can increase the resolution of the conversions by adjusting the reference voltages to a range that is slightly wider than the range you want to measure.

To illustrate, consider a sensor whose output ranges from 0 to 0.5V. The 8-bit output of the converter represents a number from 0 to 255. If *Vref+* is 5V and *Vref-* is 0V, each count equals 5/255, or 19.6 millivolts. A 0.2V analog input results in a count of 10, while a 0.5V input results in a count of 26. If your input goes no higher than 0.5V, your count will never go higher than 26, and the measured values will be accurate only to within 20 millivolts, or 1/255 of full-scale.

If you lower *Vref+* to 0.5V, each count now equals 0.5/255, or 0.002V. A 0.2-volt input gives a count of 102, a 0.5-volt input gives a count of 255, and the measured values can be accurate to within 2 millivolts.

If you decrease the range, you also increase the converter's sensitivity to noise. With a 5V range, a 20-millivolt noise spike will cause at most a 1-bit error in the

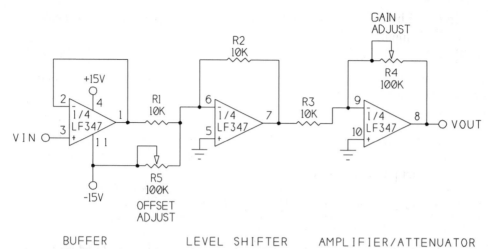

BUFFER   LEVEL SHIFTER   AMPLIFIER/ATTENUATOR

Figure 8-7: With this circuit you can adjust the offset and amplitude of an analog signal.

output. With a 0.5V range, the same spike can cause an error of 10 bits, since each bit now represents just 2 millivolts, rather than 20.

The lower reference doesn't have to be 0V. For example, the output of an LM34 temperature sensor is 10 millivolts per degree Fahrenheit. If you want to measure temperatures from 50 to 100 degrees, you can set *Vref-* to 0.5V and *Vref+* to 1V, for a 50-degree range, or 0.2 degree per bit.

Signal Conditioning

Not every sensor has an output that can connect directly to the ADC0809's inputs. A sensor's output may range from -2 to 0V, from -0.5 to +0.5V, or from -12 to +12V. In all of these cases, you need to shift the signal levels and/or range to be compatible with a converter that requires inputs between 0 and 5 volts.

Figure 8-7 shows a handy circuit that can amplify or reduce input levels, and can also raise or lower the output by adding or subtracting a voltage. Separate, independent adjustments control the gain and offset. The circuit is a series of three op amps: a buffer, a level shifter, and an amplifier. The circuit uses three of the devices in an LF347 quad JFET-input op amp, which has fast response and high input impedance. You can use another op amp if you prefer.

The first op amp is a noninverting amplifier whose output at pin 1 equals *Vin*. The op amp presents a high-impedance input to VIN. The second op amp is an inverting summing amplifier that raises and lowers pin 1's voltage as *R5* is adjusted. Varying *R5* changes the voltage at pin 7, but the signal's shape and peak-to-peak amplitude remain constant. The third op amp is an inverting amplifier whose gain is adjusted by *R4*. This amplifier increases or decreases the peak-to-peak amplitude of its input.

As an example of how to use the circuit, if *Vin* will vary from +0.2V to -0.2V, set *Vin* to +0.2V and adjust *R4* until Vout is +2.5V. Then set *Vin* to -0.2V and adjust *R5* until *Vout* is 0V.

If the range of *Vin* is too large, use R4 to decrease the gain instead of increasing it. If you need to shift the signal level down (to a lower range) instead of up, connect *R5* to +15V instead of -15V. If you don't need level shifting, you can remove *R5* and connect pin 6 only to *R1* and *R2*.

Minimizing Noise

Rapid switching of digital circuits can cause voltage spikes in the ground lines. Even small voltage spikes can cause errors in analog measurements. Good routing of ground wires or printed-circuit-board traces can minimize noise in circuits that mix analog and digital circuits.

To reduce noise, provide separate ground paths for analog and digital signals. Wire or route all ground connections related to the analog inputs or reference voltages together, but keep them separate from the ground connections for the digital circuits, including the clock and buffer/driver chips. Tie the two grounds together at one place only, as near to the power supply as possible. Also be sure to include decoupling capacitors, as described in Chapter 6.

Using a Sample and Hold

An additional component that you may need for rapidly changing analog inputs is a sample-and-hold circuit. To ensure correct conversions, the analog input has to remain stable while the conversion is taking place.

A sample-and-hold circuit ensures that the analog signal is stable by sampling the signal at the desired measurement time and storing it, usually as a charge on a capacitor. The converter uses this stored signal as the input to be converted.

When do you need a sample-and-hold? Clocked at 640 kHz, the ADC0809 requires 100 microseconds to convert, and you'll get good results with inputs that vary less than 1 bit in this amount of time. For rapidly changing inputs, sample-and-hold chips like the LF398 are available, or you can use a converter with a sample-and-hold on-chip.

9

Synchronous Serial Links

The parallel-port interface can transfer eight bits at a time, with each data bit on its own wire. In contrast, in a serial interface, the bits arrive one by one. Although the two interfaces seem very different, there are times when it makes sense to use the parallel port to send and receive certain types of serial data.

This chapter shows how to use the parallel port in a synchronous serial interface, with an example of a link to a digital-thermometer chip.

About Serial Interfaces

One advantage to serial links is that they require fewer wires. If you use a parallel port to transfer serial data, many bits remain available for other uses. Disadvantages to using the parallel port for serial transfers are that the programming is more difficult, because you have to separate each byte into bits, and the transfers are slower, because they're one bit at a time.

A serial link may be synchronous or asynchronous. In an asynchronous link, both ends agree on a clock rate, but each provides its own clock. The receiving end watches for a start bit that indicates the beginning of a transmission, then uses its own clock to determine when to read each of the bits that follow. Because the clock rates may vary slightly, each byte begins with a start bit to resynchronize the receiver to the transmitted data, and ends with a stop bit to indicate end of transmission. The PC uses its serial (RS-232) port for asynchronous communications with modems, serial printers, and other devices. A UART chip in the PC adds and removes start and stop bits and translates between serial and parallel data.

In contrast, synchronous links use a single, common clock. One wire carries the clock signal used by both ends. The transmitting end sends each bit at a defined time in the clock cycle (after a falling edge, for example), and the receiving end uses the clock transitions to determine when to read the incoming bits (on the next rising edge of the clock, for example). Other than the requirement for a common clock, the specific protocols of synchronous serial interfaces can vary. A synchronous link doesn't require start and stop bits, so it doesn't need a UART. Some chips have a built-in synchronous serial interface.

Disadvantages to synchronous links include the need for an extra wire for the clock signal and sensitivity to noise, especially with longer cables. Because the receiver uses clock transitions to determine when to read each bit, a single glitch on the clock line can cause the receiver to misread an instruction or data.

One popular synchronous interface is National Semiconductor's Microwire, which is compatible with many of National's analog-to-digital converters and other components. Chips from other manufacturers, including Dallas Semiconductor and Maxim, use an interface similar to Microwire.

A Digital Thermometer

Dallas Semiconductor's DS1620 D*igital Thermometer and Thermostat* is an 8-pin programmable chip that can measure temperature and detect and respond to alarm temperatures. It uses a 3-wire synchronous serial interface.

The chip measures temperatures from -55 to +125 degrees Celsius (-67 to +257 degrees Fahrenheit), with no calibration required. From 0 to +70°C, thermometer error is ±0.5°, increasing gradually to ±2° at the measuring limits. This makes the chip convenient for many applications, including heating and cooling controls, temperature alarms, or basic temperature logging.

The chip has two modes of operation: 3-wire and standalone. In 3-wire mode, a computer sends commands to start a conversion (to measure and store the current temperature), to read the stored temperature from the chip, to read and write high and low setpoints for the alarm outputs, to set the mode of operation, and to read conversion and alarm status. Three-wire mode requires two output bits to connect to *Clk/$\overline{Conv}$* and *$\overline{Rst}$* on the DS1620, and one bidirectional bit to connect to *DQ*. The recommended power supply is +5V, ±10%.

The chip has three alarm outputs. T_{HIGH} goes high when the measured temperature is greater than the value stored in the *TH* register. T_{LOW} goes high when the temperature is less than the value in *TL*. And T_{COM} (combination) goes high when the temperature is greater than *TH*, and stays high until the temperature falls below *TL*. This output is handy if you want to prevent the output from cycling on and off too often when the temperature is near the setpoint.

You can connect the alarm outputs to input bits on a PC or you can interface alarm or control circuits to them. For example, you could use the T_{COM} output to cause a heater to turn on at 68 degrees and off at 70 degrees.

Using 3-wire mode, you can configure the chip for standalone operation. This mode is more limited but requires no computer interface. If *$\overline{Rst}$* is low and you bring *Clk/$\overline{Conv}$* low, the chip will continuously measure the temperature and indicate alarm conditions as they occur. Or, you can trigger individual temperature measurements at specific times by pulsing *Clk/$\overline{Conv}$* low briefly. Either way, you can use the alarm outputs for monitoring or control functions.

To read or write data to the chip in 3-wire mode, you first send an 8-bit instruction that tells the chip what type of data you're going to read or write. Table 9-1 summarizes the chip's nine instructions.

The temperature registers in the DS1620 are nine bits each, and store positive and negative values with resolution of 0.5 degree. For positive temperatures, bit 8 is 0, bits 1–7 hold the integer value of the temperature, and bit 0, if set, adds 0.5 degree. Negative temperatures are similar, except that bit 8 is 1 and the temperature is stored in two's complement format. (To find the two's complement of a value, complement each bit, then add 1 to the result.) Table 9-2 shows examples of temperatures and their translations into DS1620 format.

To read or write a value to the DS1620, you first must do the following:

1. To begin, *$\overline{Rst}$* is low, *Clk/$\overline{Conv}$* is high. Configure the port bit that connects to *DQ* as an output.
2. Bring *$\overline{Rst}$* high.
3. Bring *Clk/$\overline{Conv}$* low.
4. Set *DQ* equal to bit 0 of the desired instruction.
5. Bring *Clk/$\overline{Conv}$* high.
6. Repeat steps 3-5 for bits 1-7 of the instruction.

Then, to write a value to the chip:

7. Repeat steps 3-5 for bits 0-7 or 0-8 of the data to be written (if any).
8. Bring *$\overline{Rst}$* low for at least 5 milliseconds.

Table 9-1: Command set for the DS1620. Most commands are followed by 8 or 9 data bits read from or written to the chip.

Command (hex)	Name	Description	Number & Type of Bits That Follow
AA	Read Temperature	Read the last conversion result.	9 (output)
01	Write *TH*	Write the high-temperature alarm value.	9 (input)
02	Write *TL*	Write the low-temperature alarm value.	9 (input)
A1	Read *TH*	Read the high-temperature alarm value.	9 (output)
A2	Read *TL*	Read the low-temperature alarm value.	9 (output)
EE	Start Convert	Begin a temperature conversion (1-shot or continuous).	0
22	Stop Convert	Stop temperature conversions after the current conversion completes (continuous mode).	0
0C	Write Config	Write to the configuration register.	8 (input)
AC	Read Config	Read the configuration register.	8 (output)

To read a value from the chip:

7. Do steps 1-6 above, then:

8. Configure the port bit that connects to *DQ* as an input, to prepare to read from *DQ*.

9. Bring *Clk/$\overline{Conv}$* low. *DQ* is now an output that holds the data to be read.

10. Read and store *DQ* (bit 0).

11. Bring *Clk/$\overline{Conv}$* high.

12. Repeat steps 8-10 for bits 1-7 or 1-8 of the data to be read.

13. Bring $\overline{Rst}$ low.

14. Reconfigure the bit that connects to *DQ* as an input.

The data sheet specifies minimum delays between each of the above steps, but most are short enough (125 nanoseconds or less) that you won't have to worry about meeting the requirement in most cases. There are two exceptions. $\overline{Rst}$ must remain low for at least 5 milliseconds after you write to data to the DS1620 (step 8 in the write operation above). The delay gives the chip's internal EEPROM enough time to store the data. The chip also needs one second to execute a start-convert instruction, so after performing a temperature conversion (instruction *EEh*), you must wait one second before you read the result (instruction *AAh*).

Unlike some serial chips, the DS1620's *Clk* frequency has no minimum, so you can clock it as slowly as you want. The maximum is 4 Megahertz.

Table 9-2: The DS1620 stores temperatures in a 9-bit format, with resolution of 1/2 degree. Negative temperatures are stored as two's complements.

Temperature (degrees Fahrenheit)	Temperature (degrees Celsius)	Digital Output (Binary)	Digital Output (Hex)
257	+125	0 1111 1010	0FA
77	+25	0 0011 0010	032
33	+0.5	0 0000 0001	001
32	0	0 0000 0000	000
-31	-0.5	1 1111 1111	1FF
-13	-25	1 1100 1110	1CE
-67	-55	1 1001 0010	192
Fahrenheit degrees = (9/5 * (Celsius degrees)) + 32			

Using the DS1620

You can use a parallel port to communicate with the DS1620. For example, you might have an application where you measure temperatures or monitor for alarms directly at the parallel port. With a portable computer, you can use the program just about anywhere. A parallel-port connection also provides a convenient way to program the chip for standalone mode. You can store setpoints, set the mode, and configure the chip for standalone operation. Then you can use the chip to monitor temperatures on its own, with alarm or control circuits added as needed.

The Interface

Figure 9-1 shows a circuit that uses the parallel port's Status and Control lines to read and write to a DS1620. The circuit adds buffers and drivers to help ensure that all signals arrive in good shape. If you're just programming the chip for use in standalone mode, you can use a short cable and connect the chip directly to the cable.

The *DQ* bit connects through a 74LS245 transceiver to the parallel port's Control bit 0 ($\overline{C0}$). The parallel port must be in SPP mode to ensure that the Control bit is bidirectional (open-collector).

Bit $\overline{C3}$ on the control port is a direction control for the transceiver. When *DQ* is an input (its usual state), $\overline{C3}$ should be low. This enables the DS1620 to read $\overline{C0}$. In other words, signal flow is from pin 18 to pin 2. When *DQ* is an output (when you are reading data from the chip), $\overline{C3}$ should be high. This enables the PC to read *DQ*, and signal flow is from pin 2 to pin 18.

The *Clk/$\overline{Conv}$* and *$\overline{Rst}$* inputs connect to two of the buffers in a 74LS244 octal buffer, which are driven by the two remaining bits of the control port.

The three alarm outputs each connect to a 74LS244 driver that controls a status input (*S3, S4, S5*) on the parallel port. Connecting these is optional.

There are a couple of variations on this circuit that you might use, depending on your port's hardware. If you have a bidirectional Data port, you can use a Data bit instead of a Control bit for reading and writing to DQ. If you do so, be sure to configure the port as input before bringing *$\overline{C3}$* high.

Another option is to use separate input and output bits for reading and writing to DQ. For example, you could connect a Data or Control output through a 3-state buffer/driver to DQ, and also connect DQ through a buffer/driver to a Status input. Use the 3-state driver's control signal to disable the Data bit's buffer/driver except when DQ is an input. To read DQ's state, read its Status bit. To write to DQ, write to the Data bit and enable its buffer/driver. This arrangement will work on any port, and doesn't require any bidirectional bits on the Status port.

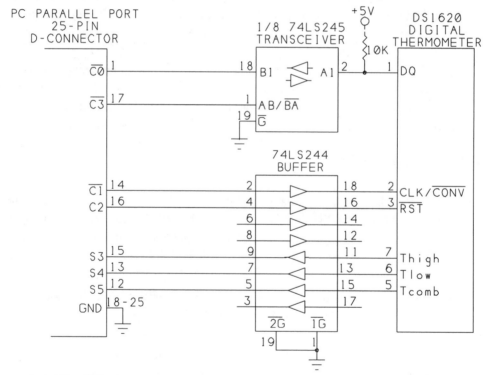

Figure 9-1: The DS1620 stores alarm temperatures and temperature information.

An Application

Figure 9-2 is the screen for a program that enables reading and writing to the chip. The alarm indicators are very simple: grayed text for no alarm, and normal text for alarms. If you wish, you can replace these with more colorful and prominent indicators.

Listing 9-1 is the program code. The code follows the procedures described above for reading and writing to the port. The listing includes routines for setting all of the chip's options and reading the temperatures and configuration information.

Debugging

Debugging serial interfaces can be difficult. If the DS1620 doesn't respond to an instruction, it can be hard to figure out why. Unlike other interfaces where the receiving device acknowledges each transmission, with the DS1620 and similar interfaces, the transmitting end assumes that the receiving end is always ready to accept whatever is sent. The only acknowledgment you get after sending an instruction to the DS1620 is the data returned, if any.

If you have problems getting the circuit up and running, try single-stepping through the program and monitoring the signals at each step to verify that everything is as it should be. A logic probe with a memory LED is useful for detecting

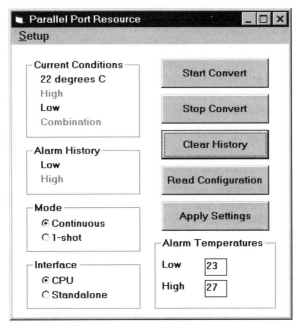

Figure 9-2: Screen for testing and configuring the DS1620.

```
'DS1620 signals:
'Inputs connect to Control port outputs:
Const DataIO = 1: 'bit 0 (this bit is I/O)
Const Clock = 2: 'bit 1
Const ResetOff = 4: 'bit 2
Const ReadDirection = 8: 'bit 3
'Outputs connect to Status port inputs:
Const HighTrigger = 8:  'bit 3
Const LowTrigger = &H10: 'bit 4
Const CombinationTrigger = &H20: 'bit 5
Dim ModeSelect%
Dim InterfaceSelect%
Dim ConfigurationData%
Dim StopConvert%
```

Listing 9-1: Communicating with the DS1620 digital thermostat over a synchronous serial link. (Sheet 1 of 8)

```
Sub cmdApplySettings_Click ()
'Write user changes to the DS1620.
Dim Temperature%
If txtHighAlarmTemperature.Text <> "" Then
    Temperature =
 ConvertToChipFormat(CInt(txtHighAlarmTemperature.Text))
    WriteInstruction (1)
    WriteData Temperature
End If
If txtLowAlarmTemperature.Text <> "" Then
    Temperature =
 ConvertToChipFormat(CInt(txtLowAlarmTemperature.Text))
    WriteInstruction (2)
    WriteData Temperature
End If
'Read the configuration register,
'set or clear the interface and mode-select bits,
'and write the values back.
ConfigurationData = ReadConfiguration()
If optMode(0).Value = True Then
    ModeSelect = 0
Else
    ModeSelect = 1
End If
If optInterface(0).Value = True Then
    InterfaceSelect = 0
Else
    InterfaceSelect = 1
End If
WriteConfiguration ((ConfigurationData And &HFC) Or _
(ModeSelect + InterfaceSelect * 2))
End Sub
```

```
Sub cmdClearHistory_Click ()
Dim Configuration%
'To clear the alarm history,
'write 0 to bits 5 & 6 of configuration register.
Configuration = ReadConfiguration() And &H9F
WriteConfiguration (Configuration)
ReadChip
End Sub
```

Listing 9-1: Communicating with the DS1620 digital thermostat over a synchronous serial link. (Sheet 2 of 8)

```
Sub cmdReadConfiguration_Click ()
ReadChip
UpdateUserControls
End Sub
```

```
Sub cmdStartConvert_Click ()
Dim Temperature%
WriteInstruction (&HEE)
WaitForConversion
WriteInstruction (&HAA)
Temperature = ReadData ()
lblCurrentTemperature.Caption =
  CSng(ConvertFromChipFormat(Temperature)) & " degrees C"
StopConvert = False
End Sub
```

```
Sub cmdStopConvert_Click ()
WriteInstruction (&H22)
StopConvert = True
End Sub
```

```
Function ConvertFromChipFormat! (ValueToConvert%)
'Temperature values read from the chip use 2's complement
'for negative numbers. LSB (bit 0) = 2^-1, or 0.5.
'Bits 0-7 indicate temperature, bit 8 = 1 for negative values.
'This function converts the integer read from the chip
'to a positive or negative floating-point value.
'For negative values, get the temperature value from the _
'2's complement & clear bit 8.
If (ValueToConvert And &H100) = &H100 Then
    ValueToConvert = (ValueToConvert - 1) Xor &H1FF
    ValueToConvert = -(ValueToConvert And &HFF)
End If
'Divide by 2
ConvertFromChipFormat = CSng(ValueToConvert) / 2
End Function
```

Listing 9-1: Communicating with the DS1620 digital thermostat over a synchronous serial link. (Sheet 3 of 8)

```
Function ConvertToChipFormat% (ValueToConvert!)
'Converts a floating-point temperature to the format
'required by the DS1620.
ValueToConvert = ValueToConvert * 2
'If negative, put in 2's complement format.
If ValueToConvert < 0 Then
    ValueToConvert = (Abs(ValueToConvert) Xor &H1FF) + 1
End If
ConvertToChipFormat = CSng(ValueToConvert)
End Function
```

```
Sub Form_Load ()
'(partial listing)
tmrReset.Enabled = False
tmrReset.Interval = 5
tmrWatchForAlarms.Enabled = True
tmrWatchForAlarms.Interval = 1000
lblHigh.Enabled = False
lblLow.Enabled = False
lblCombination.Enabled = False
lblHighFlag.Enabled = False
lblLowFlag.Enabled = False
StopConvert = False
'Initialize control bits.
ControlPortWrite BaseAddress, &HE
ResetChip
ReadChip
UpdateUserControls
End Sub
```

```
Sub optInterface_Click (index As Integer)
InterfaceSelect = index
End Sub
```

```
Sub optMode_Click (index As Integer)
ModeSelect = index
End Sub
```

Listing 9-1: Communicating with the DS1620 digital thermostat over a synchronous serial link. (Sheet 4 of 8)

```
Sub ReadChip ()
'Reads the configuration register & alarms
'& displays the results.
Dim Flag%
Dim Temperature%
Dim Alarms%
Dim Alarm%
ConfigurationData = ReadConfiguration()
'Alarm flags (past alarms)
Flag = BitRead(ConfigurationData, 5)
If Flag = 1 Then
    lblLowFlag.Enabled = True
Else
    lblLowFlag.Enabled = False
End If
Flag = BitRead(ConfigurationData, 6)
If Flag = 1 Then
    lblHighFlag.Enabled = True
Else
    lblHighFlag.Enabled = False
End If
'Alarm inputs (current alarms)
Alarms = StatusPortRead(BaseAddress)
Alarm = BitRead(Alarms, 3)
If Alarm = 1 Then
    lblHigh.Enabled = True
Else
    lblHigh.Enabled = False
End If
Alarm = BitRead(Alarms, 4)
If Alarm = 1 Then
    lblLow.Enabled = True
Else
    lblLow.Enabled = False
End If
Alarm = BitRead(Alarms, 5)
If Alarm = 1 Then
    lblCombination.Enabled = True
Else
    lblCombination.Enabled = False
End If
'Read these, but update only when UpdateUserControls is called.
ModeSelect = BitRead(ConfigurationData, 0)
InterfaceSelect = BitRead(ConfigurationData, 1)
End Sub
```

Listing 9-1: Communicating with the DS1620 digital thermostat over a synchronous serial link. (Sheet 5 of 8)

```
Function ReadConfiguration ()
WriteInstruction (&HAC)
ReadConfiguration = ReadData()
End Function
```

```
Function ReadData% ()
Dim BitValue%
Dim DataIn%
Dim BitIn%
DataIn = 0
'Set the transceiver direction to allow reading DataIO.
'Write 1 to Control bit 0 to allow its use as an input.
ControlPortWrite _
  BaseAddress, Clock + DataIO + ResetOff + ReadDirection
For BitValue = 0 To 8
    'When Clock=0, DS1620 outputs data on DataIO.
    ControlPortWrite _
      BaseAddress, ReadDirection + DataIO + ResetOff
    'Read DataIO and add its value to ReadData
    BitIn = BitRead(ControlPortRead(BaseAddress), 0)
    DataIn = DataIn + BitIn * 2 ^ BitValue
    'Clock=1
    ControlPortWrite _
      BaseAddress, Clock + ReadDirection + DataIO + ResetOff
Next BitValue
'Set ReadDirection=0 to switch transceiver back.
ControlPortWrite BaseAddress, Clock + DataIO + ResetOff
DataIn = DataIn And &H1FF
ReadData = DataIn
End Function
```

```
Sub ResetChip ()
'toggle Reset before each write
ControlPortWrite BaseAddress, Clock + DataIO
'wait at least 5 milliseconds
tmrReset.Enabled = True
Do
    DoEvents
Loop Until tmrReset.Enabled = False
ControlPortWrite BaseAddress, Clock + ResetOff + DataIO
End Sub
```

Listing 9-1: Communicating with the DS1620 digital thermostat over a synchronous serial link. (Sheet 6 of 8)

```
Sub tmrReset_Timer ()
'Ensures a reset pulse of at least 5 milliseconds.
tmrReset.Enabled = False
End Sub
```

```
Sub tmrWaitForConversion_Timer ()
tmrWaitForConversion.Enabled = False
End Sub
```

```
Sub tmrWatchForAlarms_Timer ()
'Read the alarms.
'If continuous mode is selected, read a conversion.
If (optMode(0).Value = True) And (StopConvert = False) Then
    cmdStartConvert.Value = True
End If
ReadChip
End Sub
```

```
Sub UpdateUserControls ()
'Updates the option buttons and alarm settings
'with the values read from the configuration register.
'(Verifies that the values were stored correctly.)
Dim Temperature%
'Read TH
WriteInstruction (&HA1)
Temperature = ReadData()
txtHighAlarmTemperature.Text =
  CSng(ConvertFromChipFormat(Temperature))
'Read TL
WriteInstruction (&HA2)
Temperature = ReadData()
txtLowAlarmTemperature.Text =
  CSng(ConvertFromChipFormat(Temperature))
optMode(ModeSelect).Value = True
optInterface(InterfaceSelect).Value = True
End Sub
```

```
Sub WaitForConversion ()
tmrWaitForConversion.Enabled = True
Do
    DoEvents
Loop Until tmrWaitForConversion.Enabled = False
End Sub
```

Listing 9-1: Communicating with the DS1620 digital thermostat over a synchronous serial link. (Sheet 7 of 8)

```
Sub WriteConfiguration (ConfigurationData%)
WriteInstruction (&HC)
WriteData (ConfigurationData)
End Sub
```

```
Sub WriteData (DataToWrite%)
'Writes data to the DS1620 after a write instruction
'Chip ignores bit 8 if unneeded
Dim BitNumber%
Dim BitValue%
For BitNumber = 0 To 8
    BitValue = BitRead(DataToWrite, BitNumber)
    'Clock=0
    ControlPortWrite BaseAddress, ResetOff
    'Set or clear DataIO to match the bit value.
    ControlPortWrite BaseAddress, BitValue + ResetOff
    'Clock=1
    ControlPortWrite BaseAddress, BitValue + Clock + ResetOff
Next BitNumber
End Sub
```

```
Sub WriteInstruction (Instruction%)
Dim BitNumber%
Dim BitValue%
'Toggle Reset before each write.
ResetChip
ControlPortWrite BaseAddress, Clock + ResetOff
For BitNumber = 0 To 7
    BitValue = BitRead(Instruction, BitNumber)
    'Clock=0
    ControlPortWrite BaseAddress, ResetOff
    'Set or clear DataIO to match the bit value
    ControlPortWrite BaseAddress, ResetOff + BitValue
    'Clock=1
    ControlPortWrite BaseAddress, Clock + ResetOff + BitValue
Next BitNumber
End Sub
```

Listing 9-1: Communicating with the DS1620 digital thermostat over a synchronous serial link. (Sheet 8 of 8)

glitches on the *Clk* or $\overline{Rst}$ lines. (A single glitch on either of these can cause an instruction to be misread.)

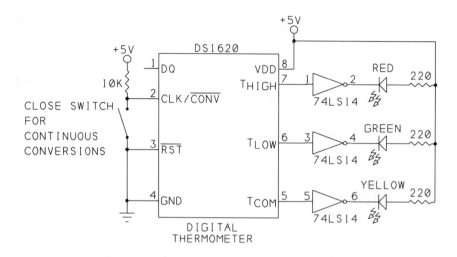

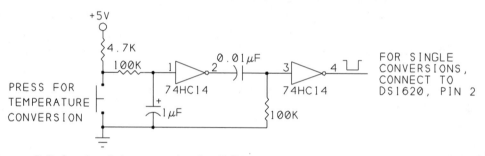

Figure 9-3: In standalone mode, the DS1620 monitors temperature and outputs alarm signals.

Standalone Mode

Figure 9-3 shows the DS1620 in standalone mode. It also shows circuits you can connect to the alarm outputs in standalone or 3-wire mode. Before you can use this circuit, you have to use 3-wire mode to program the chip by setting bit 1 in the configuration register to 0 and writing the desired values to the alarm setpoints.

For continuous temperature conversions, close the switch at pin 2. ($Clk/\overline{Conv}$ must be high on power-up.) To start a single conversion, use the alternate circuit shown instead of the switch and resistor at pin 2. Press the switch to cause a single pulse of about 1 millisecond at $Clk/\overline{Conv}$.

The DS1620's alarm outputs can source just 1 milliampere at 2.4V, and sink 4 milliamperes at 0.4V, so most alarm interfaces will require some buffering.

In the example, LEDs connect to the alarm outputs. The red one lights when the temperature exceeds *TH*, the green one lights when the temperature is less than

TL, and the yellow one turns on at the same time as the red and stays on until the green turns on.

Chapter 7 showed how to use a logic signal to control power to a circuit. For the DS1620, possible uses might be to control a fan that runs when T_{COM} is high, or a heater that runs when T_{COM} is low.

Table 9-3 shows the functions for each of the bits in the DS1620's configuration byte.

Other Serial Chips

Many other chips use serial interfaces similar to the DS1620's. Maxim's Max186 and '188 are low-power, 8-channel analog-to-digital converters, and National Semiconductor's DAC0854 is a quad digital-to-analog converter.

If you're considering using a device, examine its data sheet carefully, because the specifics of the interfaces do vary. On National's ADC0838 analog-to-digital converter, the maximum time that the serial clock can remain high is 60 microseconds, although the clock can remain low indefinitely as long as the analog input is stable. Other chips are more flexible, and can be clocked as slowly as you wish.

Table 9-3: Bit functions in the DS1620's configuration register.

Bit	Name	Value	Function
0	1-shot mode	0	Start Convert causes continuous conversions
	Start Convert	1	causes one conversion
1	CPU use	0	$Clk/\overline{Conv}$ begins a conversion when $\overline{Rst}$ is low
		1	3-wire mode, $Clk/\overline{Conv}$ acts as clock
2	-	don't care	unused
3	-	don't care	unused
4	-	don't care	unused
5	TLF	0	temperature > value in TL
		1	temperature <= value in TL
6	THF	0	temperature < value in TH
		1	temperature >= value in TH
7	DONE	0	conversion in progress
		1	conversion complete

10

Real-time Control

Programs that access the parallel port may use any of a number of ways to decide when to read or write to a port. User actions are one obvious way. In many of the examples in this book, the user triggers a port read or write by clicking a command button. Other examples of user actions are a request to print a file or read a file from a parallel-port-based drive.

Other types of triggers include events that occur at a periodic rate (every five seconds; every hour), at a specific time of day (2:10 pm; every hour on the hour), or in response to an external event (a switch's closing; an analog-to-digital converter's end-of-conversion pulse). This chapter shows how to do all of these in Visual-Basic programs.

Periodic Triggers

Some applications need to read or write to the parallel port at a periodic rate. For example, to control a (very slow) stepping motor, you might write to the port once per second. A monitoring system might read a sensor once a day.

Visual Basic's Timer control makes it easy to do these. You set the Timer control to trigger a Timer event at regular intervals that you define. When the Timer event occurs, the program run a subroutine that performs the desired actions.

The Timer control is best suited for measuring intervals of a few hundred milliseconds to 1 minute, and when absolute accuracy isn't essential. The longest interval a Timer control can detect is 64.676 seconds, or a little over a minute. However, using the Time function along with the Timer control enables measuring longer periods. An 18-Hz clock updates the Timer's contents, so the minimum interval that the Timer control can measure is 1/18 second, or 56 milliseconds. The 18-Hz clock is the same signal the computer uses to update its real-time-clock.

Visual Basic allows you to set the timer interval as short as 1 millisecond, but the timer event won't execute until the next clock tick, which may occur after 1 or 56 milliseconds. This also means that all timer events are no more precise than within 56 milliseconds.

In addition to the Timer control's limited resolution, other system events can reduce the Timer control's accuracy. If other things keep the CPU busy for more than 1/18 second, the Timer Control will miss one or more clock ticks and the length between Timer events will increase. For example, if a Timer event is supposed to occur after 1 second, but the Timer misses two clock ticks, the event will occur 2/18 second late, or after 1.11 seconds. If your program is the only application running, and if the program does little more than wait for Timer Events, missing Timer ticks won't be a problem.

Tasks that can block timer updates include long loops or calculations, and lengthy disk, network, or port accesses. In Visual-Basic programs, adding a DoEvents statement in a long loop enables the Timer to update, although other applications may still block additional Timer updates during DoEvents.

Simple Timer Control

Listing 10-1 is a program that demonstrates the use of the Timer Control, and Figure 10-1 is the program's screen. Users can select the period between Timer events. The Timer-event subroutine just sounds a beep. You can replace the beep with whatever code you want to execute periodically.

The program allows intervals of hours, minutes, hours and minutes, or seconds. For intervals of less than 1 minute, the Timer's interval property equals the interval time in milliseconds, and the Timer event calls an Alarm subroutine that contains the code the program wants to execute periodically. If the interval is longer than a minute, the time is too long to set directly in the Interval property, so the program uses a different approach. The Timer event occurs once per minute, and the Timer subroutine has an internal counter that keeps track of the remaining minutes. Every minute, the Timer subroutine decrements the counter. When the count equals zero, the Alarm subroutine executes.

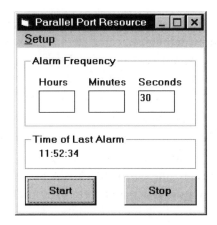

Figure 10-1: This program allows you to set an alarm interval in hours, minutes, and seconds. When the selected time has elapsed, an Alarm subroutine runs.

Although the subroutine is called Alarm, you can use similar Timer routines for any type of application with periodic events, not just security or alarm indicators.

Time-of-day Triggers

Another way of triggering an event by time is to trigger at a specific time of day. With the Timer control described above, you can cause an event to occur once an hour, but there's no way of ensuring that the events occur on the hour, at 1:00, 2:00, 3:00, and so on. The Timer control begins timing when it's enabled, and that may be on the hour or any time between.

The solution is in Visual Basic's Time function, which can trigger an event when the system time matches the time specified in the application. The Time function is as accurate as the computer's system clock. It's also a convenient way of timing longer intervals of minutes and hours, whether or not they have to occur on the minute or hour. The Time function requires more programming effort than using the Timer control alone, because the program has to check periodically to see if the current time matches the event time.

Listing 10-2 is a program that enables the user to select an alarm time in hours, minutes, and/or seconds, and then set, or turn on, the alarm. Figure 10-2 is the program's user screen. When the alarm is set and the system time matches the selected values, the Alarm subroutine executes.

The program uses the Timer control to read the system time once per second. A shorter interval gives greater precision in the alarm time, with the tradeoff that the system spends more time checking the time. A longer interval is less precise, but the Timer events take up less of the system's time.

The program uses Visual Basic's type 7 variant variable `Date`, which can store time as well as date information. The time can use a variety of formats. Listing 10-2 uses the format "`hh:nn:ss`", with 2-digit numbers for hours (0-23), minutes (0-59), and seconds (0-59). (The interval name for minutes is `n` because months uses `m`.)

Visual Basic's `DateAdd` and `DateDiff` functions make it easy to execute Timer events that occur more than once per hour or minute. For example, you might want a Timer event to occur on the hour and at 15, 30, and 45 minutes after the hour. The `DateAdd` function enables you to add 15 minutes to a date variable. The function automatically increments the hours and other fields when appropriate. If each Timer event adds 15 minutes to the alarm time, the event will execute every 15 minutes.

This statement adds one 15-minute interval to the variable AlarmTime:

```
DateAdd("n",15,AlarmTime)
```

Use of `DateAdd` and `DateDiff` requires the financial function *msafinx.dll*, provided with Visual Basic.

If you want to trigger actions on a specific date, use the `Date` function, which works similar to `Time`.

Loop Timers

Another way to cause periodic events is to use a `For` loop to cause delays between events:

```
For I = 1 to 10: Next I
```

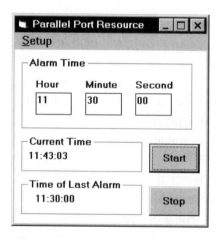

Figure 10-2: This program allows you to set an alarm time for a specific time of day.

```
Dim IntervalSeconds&
Dim IntervalMinutes%
Dim IntervalHours%
Dim LongDelay%
Dim Alarm%
Dim SecondsCounter%
Dim MinutesCounter%
```

```
Sub AlarmEvents ()
Beep
'Place code to execute periodically here.
End Sub
```

```
Sub cmdStart_Click ()
SetTimerInterval
tmrAlarm.Enabled = True
End Sub
```

```
Sub cmdStop_Click ()
tmrAlarm.Enabled = False
End Sub
```

Listing 10-1: Triggering periodic events. (Sheet 1 of 3)

```
Sub SetTimerInterval ()
Dim Hours$
Dim Minutes$
Dim Seconds$
LongDelay = False
Alarm = False
Hours = txtHours.Text
Minutes = txtMinutes.Text
Seconds = txtSeconds.Text
If Hours = "" Then Hours = "0"
If Minutes = "" Then Minutes = "0"
If Seconds = "" Then Seconds = "0"
IntervalSeconds = _
 Val(Hours) * 3600 + Val(Minutes) * 60 + Val(Seconds)
If IntervalSeconds < 60 Then
    tmrAlarm.Interval = IntervalSeconds * 1000
Else
    'For long delay, check the time once/minute
    tmrAlarm.Interval = 60000
    LongDelay = True
    'Get the number of minutes.
    IntervalMinutes = IntervalSeconds \ 60
End If
End Sub
```

```
Sub tmrAlarm_Timer ()
If LongDelay Then
    'Decrement the minutes remaining; see if count is finished.
    IntervalMinutes = IntervalMinutes - 1
    If IntervalMinutes <= 0 Then
        Alarm = True
    End If
Else
    Alarm = True
End If
If Alarm = True Then
    'Reset time variables
    SetTimerInterval
    lblTimeOfLastAlarm.Caption = Time$
    AlarmEvents
End If
text1.Text = _
  Time$ & " " & ";" & IntervalMinutes & ";" & IntervalSeconds
End Sub
```

Listing 10-1: Triggering periodic events. (Sheet 2 of 3)

```
Sub txtHours_Change ()
If txtHours.Text <> "" Then
    txtSeconds.Text = ""
    txtSeconds.Enabled = False
    lblSeconds.Enabled = False
    End If
End Sub
```

```
Sub txtMinutes_Change ()
If txtMinutes.Text <> "" Then
    txtSeconds.Text = ""
    txtSeconds.Enabled = False
    lblSeconds.Enabled = False
End If
End Sub
```

Listing 10-1: Triggering periodic events. (Sheet 3 of 3)

This method can create very short delays, but the time will vary depending on the system. For this reason, creating timing loops like the one above isn't a good idea unless you need a simple, short, and very non-critical delay time.

Triggering on External Signals

Some applications, especially those that access circuits outside of the computer, need to respond to external events. The event might be a user's pressing a switch, an alarm signal generated by an external condition, an analog-to-digital converter's signaling that it has a value waiting to be read, or any condition that toggles one of the port inputs.

Two methods for detecting external signals are by polling and by hardware interrupts. In polling, the software must read, or poll, a signal periodically to find out if an event has occurred. With interrupts, the computer's hardware is programmed to detect a change at an external signal automatically.

The main advantage of polling is that the programming involved is relatively simple. The disadvantage is that the computer can waste a lot of time checking for events. Interrupts eliminate the wasted time, but programming an interrupt routine is more difficult. This is especially true under Windows, where multiple programs may be running and the interrupt routine has to be able to execute without disrupting any of them.

```
Dim Alarm%
Dim AlarmTime$
Dim AlarmSounded%
Dim SkipHours%
Dim SkipMinutes%
Dim SkipSeconds%
```

```
Sub AlarmEvents ()
Beep
'Place code to execute on alarm here.
End Sub
```

```
Sub cmdStart_Click ()
Dim AlarmHour$
Dim AlarmMinute$
Dim AlarmSecond$
AlarmHour = txtHour.Text
AlarmMinute = txtMinute.Text
AlarmSecond = txtSecond.Text
If AlarmHour = "" Then
    SkipHours = True
    AlarmHour = "00"
Else
    SkipHours = False
End If
If AlarmMinute = "" Then
    SkipMinutes = True
    AlarmMinute = "00"
Else
    SkipMinutes = False
End If
If AlarmSecond = "" Then
    SkipSeconds = True
    AlarmSecond = "00"
Else
    SkipSeconds = False
End If
AlarmTime = Format$(AlarmHour & ":" & _
 AlarmMinute & ":" & AlarmSecond, "hh:mm:ss")
AlarmSounded = True
tmrAlarm.Enabled = True
End Sub
```

Listing 10-2: Triggering events according to time of day. (Sheet 1 of 3)

```
Sub cmdStop_Click ()
tmrAlarm.Enabled = False
End Sub
```

```
Sub Form_Load ()
'(partial listing)
'This determines how often the program checks for alarm
'conditions:
tmrAlarm.Interval = 500
End Sub
```

Listing 10-2: Triggering events according to time of day. (Sheet 2 of 3)

```
Sub tmrAlarm_Timer ()
Dim CurrentTime$
Dim CurrentHour%
Dim CurrentMinute%
Dim CurrentSecond%
Dim HourMatch%
Dim MinuteMatch%
Dim SecondMatch%
'Save the current time.
CurrentTime = Time$
lblCurrentTime.Caption = CurrentTime
CurrentHour = DatePart("h", CurrentTime)
CurrentMinute = DatePart("n", CurrentTime)
CurrentSecond = DatePart("s", CurrentTime)
'See if the current hours, minutes, and seconds match the
'alarm conditions.
'If a field in AlarmTime is blank (unused), use the value
'from CurrentTime.
If SkipHours Then
    AlarmTime = Format$((DatePart("h", CurrentTime) & ":" _
        & DatePart("n", AlarmTime) & ":" & _
        DatePart("s", AlarmTime)), "hh:nn:ss")
End If
If SkipMinutes Then
    AlarmTime = Format$((DatePart("h", AlarmTime) & ":" & _
        DatePart("n", CurrentTime) & ":" & _
        DatePart("s", AlarmTime)), "hh:nn:ss")
End If
If SkipSeconds Then
    AlarmTime = Format$((DatePart("h", AlarmTime) & ":" & _
        DatePart("n", CurrentTime) & ":" & _
        DatePart("s", CurrentTime)), "hh:nn:ss")
End If
If (CurrentTime >= AlarmTime) And Not AlarmSounded Then
    AlarmSounded = True
    Beep
    lblTimeOfLastAlarm.Caption = CurrentTime
    AlarmEvents
End If
If (CurrentTime < AlarmTime) And AlarmSounded Then
    'If the alarm field(s) have cycled back to 0,
    'set AlarmSounded to false to allow the next alarm.
    AlarmSounded = False
End If
End Sub
```

Listing 10-2: Triggering events according to time of day. (Sheet 3 of 3)

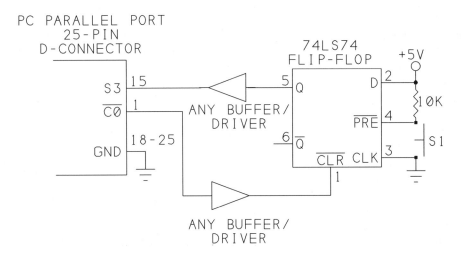

Figure 10-3: A flip-flop can store a logic level that indicates a switch press. When the PC reads the signal, it clears the flip-flop.

Polling

Polling means checking periodically to see if an event has occurred. For parallel-port applications, the event may be a transition at an input. The conventional signal that indicates that the peripheral has received a byte and is ready for another is *nAck*, but you can use any Status bit, or even a Control or Data bit configured as input. In Visual Basic, you can use the Timer control or Time function to poll an input at a rate you select.

If the signal you're watching for is a brief pulse, you need to be sure that the program doesn't miss it. For example, to detect when a user presses a pushbutton, you might connect the pushbutton to an input that goes low while the switch is pressed. But if the software polls the input every 200 milliseconds, and the user presses the switch for just 100 milliseconds, the software may not see the switch press at all. Decreasing the time between polls will solve the problem, but the increased time spent polling will degrade system performance in other areas.

Another problem with detecting manual switch presses is key bounce. When a user presses a mechanical switch, the switch contacts usually bounce open and closed a few times before making positive contact, and bounce again when the switch is released. With a short time between polls, a program watching for a switch closure may detect two or more switch presses when the user pressed the switch just once.

One way to solve both of these problems is to latch the signal that indicates a key press until the program detects and clears it. Figure 10-3 shows a circuit that does just this. The Q output of a 74LS74 flip-flop connects to a Status input, and a Control output drives the flip-flop's $\overline{Clr}$ (Clear) input. A switch controls the $\overline{Pre}$ (Preset) input. Bringing $\overline{Clr}$ low causes Q to go low. When the user presses the switch, $\overline{Pre}$ goes low, setting the flip-flop and bringing Q high. When the software detects the change at its Status input, it pulses $\overline{Clr}$ low briefly to clear the flip-flop and bring Q low again.

This circuit will reliably detect brief switch presses. For manual switches like the one shown, if the flip-flop has already been cleared when the switch re-opens, switch bounce may retrigger the flip-flop. The solution is to delay a bit before clearing the flip-flop, or use a hardware debouncing circuit, such as a 1-shot multivibrator, to ensure that the flip-flop doesn't see the switch bounce. You can use any parallel-port input and output bits with this circuit.

Listing 10-3 is a program that polls the Status port. When bit 3 is high, the program runs an `Alarm` subroutine that displays a message and pulses Control bit 0 to clear the flip-flop.

Polling Frequency

The program uses the Timer control to determine when to read the status port. The ideal frequency of polling, or period between polls, depends on how fast the program needs to respond to the events.

If you poll often, you'll know very quickly if the event occurred, but you'll probably waste a lot of time checking when nothing has happened. If you poll less often, you won't waste as much time looking, but you also won't be able to guarantee a fast response. In an alarm circuit where the program needs to take action within 1 second, the program should poll the alarm input more often than once per second, even if the chance that an alarm has occurred at any single poll is slim. If the computer has nothing else to do, there's no harm in polling frequently. If the computer has a lot of other things to do while it waits, it makes sense to set the time between polls to the longest time that the application can tolerate.

Hardware Interrupts

A hardware interrupt is another way to cause a computer to respond to an external event. When an interrupt occurs, the CPU stops what it's doing and executes an interrupt-service routine (ISR) that performs the desired actions. When the ISR is finished executing, the CPU returns to what it was doing before the interrupt occurred.

At the parallel port, a transition at *nAck* (Status bit 6) can cause a hardware interrupt.

```
Dim PollBit%
Dim FlipFlopClearBit%
Dim ControlPortData%

Sub Alarm ()
lblAlarm.Caption = "Switch pressed at " + Time$
End Sub

Sub ClearFlipFlop ()
'Pulse the Clear input of the flip-flop
'so new switch presses can be detected.
ControlPortData = ControlPortRead(BaseAddress)
BitReset ControlPortData, FlipFlopClearBit
ControlPortWrite BaseAddress, ControlPortData
BitSet ControlPortData, FlipFlopClearBit
ControlPortWrite BaseAddress, ControlPortData
End Sub

Sub Form_Load ()
StartUp
'The Status-port bit that the program polls:
PollBit = 3
'The Control-port bit that clears the flip-flop:
FlipFlopClearBit = 0
ClearFlipFlop
tmrPoll.Interval = 1000
tmrPoll.Enabled = True
lblAlarm.Caption = "Waiting for alarms..."
End Sub

Sub tmrPoll_Timer ()
Dim SwitchPress%
'Read the bit being polled.
'If the bit = 1, call the Alarm subroutine.
SwitchPress = BitRead(StatusPortRead(BaseAddress), PollBit)
If SwitchPress = 1 Then
    ClearFlipFlop
    Alarm
End If
End Sub
```

Listing 10-3: Program code for Figure 10-3's circuit.

Interrupts are fast and efficient. They can give the quickest response possible to a hardware event. They're efficient because the software doesn't have to waste time polling just in case an event has occurred. Instead, the hardware detects events automatically.

But although they have advantages, hardware interrupts aren't always a practical solution. There are several reasons why programming with hardware interrupts is challenging.

First, to use the interrupt, the system must know where the ISR resides in memory. Many programming languages, including Visual Basic, have no way of setting or finding the memory location of a program, so you're out of luck entirely unless you can use another programming language or a control with this ability.

Also, bugs in an interrupt-driven program are very likely to crash the computer or cause other problems that require rebooting. Getting an interrupt-driven program up and running takes more time and effort than other types of programs.

And finally, when you're using the parallel-port interrupt, although the interrupt works in a similar way on most systems, there are exceptions to be aware of if you want your application to work on all PCs.

Programming Options

Under Windows 3.x, a DLL may handle hardware interrupts. Windows 95 requires a VxD. Although you can't write an ISR in Visual Basic, you can use hardware interrupts in Visual-Basic programs. The quick and simple way to add parallel-port interrupts is to use a commercial Ocx designed for this purpose.

Using an Ocx

An example of an Ocx for port access is BlueWater Systems' WinRT Ocx, for use in 32-bit programs. Figure 10-4 shows its properties screens, which enable you to select a range of port addresses and select and enable a hardware interrupt. You can also use WinRT for port accesses under Windows NT, which doesn't allow direct port I/O.

Port reads and writes using WinRT use this syntax:

```
Value = Inp(PortOffset)
Outp PortOffset, Value
```

where `PortOffset` is the relative address of the port (for example, 0 for the Data port, 1 for the Status port, 2 for the Control port), and `Value` is the byte to write to the port (with `Outp`) or the byte read from the port (with `Inp`).

To use WinRT with hardware interrupts, you do the following:

1. In WinRT's *Resources* property sheet, enter a port address and IRQ level and click *Apply,* then *Restart Driver.* You need to set and apply the properties only once, but you must start the driver each time the system boots. If you want to start

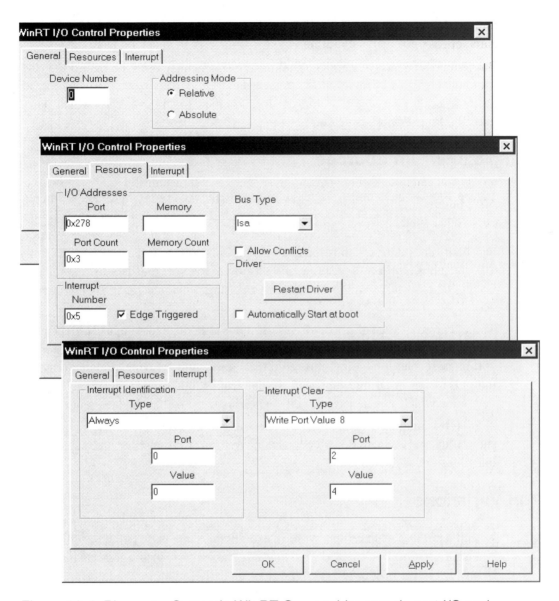

Figure 10-4: Bluewater System's WinRT Ocx enables you do port I/O and hardware interrupts under Windows 95. The properties screens enable you to configure the Ocx.

the driver automatically on bootup, check *Automatically Start at Boot* on the Resources property sheet.

2. Place the code you want to execute on interrupts in the *OcxName*_interrupt subroutine, where *OcxName* is the Ocx's *Name* property.

3. Run the program. Whenever the Ocx's assigned interrupt occurs, the program runs the `Interrupt` subroutine.

When WinRT loads, it checks Windows 95's system registry to ensure that the port addresses and other resources it needs aren't reserved by other drivers. It also stores WinRT's resources in the registry, so other drivers can learn which ports and IRQ level WinRT is using.

Multiple Interrupt Sources

Figure 10-5 is an example of interrupt use that allows a program to detect when a user presses any of four switches. Each switch sets one of four flip-flops, whose outputs you can read at *S3-S5* and *$\overline{S7}$*. Listing 10-4 is a program that uses WinRT and hardware interrupts to respond to the switch presses in Figure 10-5. Listing 10-5 includes routines for reading and writing to the port registers using WinRT, because the syntax is different than when using `Inp` and `Out` for direct port access.

The *$\overline{Q}$* output of each flip-flop drives an input to a 74LS20 4-input NAND gate. When any *$\overline{Q}$* output goes low, the NAND's output goes high and triggers a 200-microsecond low-going pulse at *nAck* (Status port bit 6). The rising edge of the pulse triggers an interrupt, and the interrupt routine reads the Status port to determine which switch was pressed, and clears the flip-flops by bringing *$\overline{C0}$* low.

A 74HC14 Schmitt-trigger inverter generates the interrupt pulse. To lengthen or shorten the pulse, increase or decrease the values of the resistor and capactor at pin 1.

Port Variations

Not all parallel-port interrupts work in exactly the same way. On the original PC, when the interrupt is enabled, a rising edge at *nAck* (*S6*) triggers an interrupt. However, on the original PC and many of its early imitators, the interrupt signal isn't latched internally, and these computers may not respond properly to a very brief pulse at *nAck*. On these systems, the interrupt signal must remain high until the CPU acknowledges it, and this may take anywhere from 10 to 100 microseconds or more, depending on your computer's speed and whatever else the computer has to do before it can service the interrupt. A 100-microsecond pulse is long enough for most systems to detect.

Another difference is that a few ports trigger interrupts on the falling edge of *nAck*. However, in conventional use, where the interrupt signal is a brief pulse to acknowledge receiving a byte, it usually doesn't matter which edge triggers the

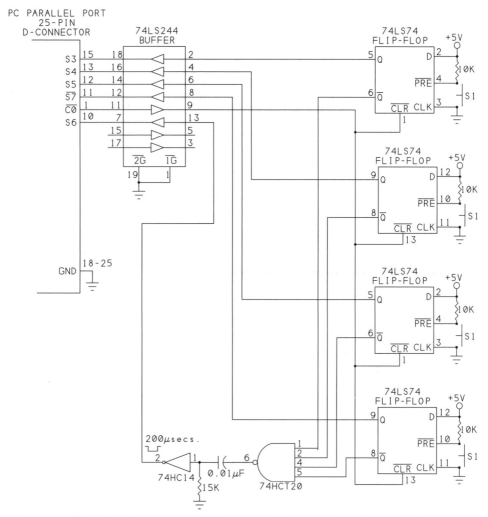

Figure 10-5: This circuit causes an interrupt when any of 4 switches is pressed. Reading the Status port tells you which switch was pressed

interrupt. Newer port designs will almost certainly have latched interrupts and trigger on the rising edge.

```
Dim FlipFlopClearBit%
Dim ControlPortData%
```

```
Sub DisableInterrupt()
'Disable the parallel-port interrupt.
'(Set Control port bit 4 = 0.)
ControlPortData = ControlPortRead()
BitReset ControlPortData, 4
ControlPortWrite ControlPortData
End Sub
```

```
Sub EnableInterrupt()
'Enable the parallel-port interrupt.
'(Set Control port bit 4 = 1.)
ControlPortData = ControlPortRead()
BitSet ControlPortData, 4
ControlPortWrite ControlPortData
End Sub
```

```
Sub Form_Load()
'The WinRt driver must be loaded!
'In the WinRT property sheets,
'click "Restart Driver" for manual loading
'or select "Automatically start at boot" for autoloading
'on bootup.
'The Control-port bit that clears the flip-flops:
FlipFlopClearBit = 0
DisableInterrupt
ClearFlipFlops
'Rearm automatically after an interrupt:
ocxParallelPort.ArmInterrupt True
EnableInterrupt
End Sub
```

```
Private Sub Form_Unload(Cancel%)
DisableInterrupt
End
End Sub
```

Listing 10-4: Using WinRT's Ocx to detect hardware interrupts. (Sheet 1 of 2)

Parallel Port Complete

```
Sub ClearFlipFlops()
'Pulse the flip-flops' clear input (Control port bit 0).
ControlPortData = ControlPortRead()
BitReset ControlPortData, FlipFlopClearBit
ControlPortWrite ControlPortData
BitSet ControlPortData, FlipFlopClearBit
ControlPortWrite ControlPortData
End Sub
```

```
Sub ocxParallelPort_Interrupt(ByVal Status As Long)
'Read the status port.
'Determine which switch was pressed.
'Clear the flip-flops.
Dim StatusPortData%
Dim S3%
Dim S4%
Dim S5%
Dim S7%
Dim ResultCaption$
ResultCaption = "Switch pressed = "
StatusPortData = StatusPortRead()
S3 = BitRead(StatusPortData, 3)
If S3 = 1 Then ResultCaption = ResultCaption + " S3"
S4 = BitRead(StatusPortData, 4)
If S4 = 1 Then ResultCaption = ResultCaption + " S4"
S5 = BitRead(StatusPortData, 5)
If S5 = 1 Then ResultCaption = ResultCaption + " S5"
S7 = BitRead(StatusPortData, 7)
If S7 = 1 Then ResultCaption = ResultCaption + " S7"
lblSwitchPressed.Caption = ResultCaption + " at " + Time$
ClearFlipFlops
End Sub
```

Listing 10-4: Using WinRT's Ocx to detect hardware interrupts. (Sheet 2 of 2)

```
Function DataPortRead%()
'Reads a parallel port's data port.
DataPortRead = frmMain.ocxParallelPort.Inp(0)
End Function
```

```
Sub DataPortWrite(Value%)
'Writes a byte to a parallel port's data port.
frmMain.ocxParallelPort.Outp BaseAddress, Value
End Sub
```

```
Function StatusPortRead%()
'Reads a parallel port's status port.
'Calculates the status-port address from the port's
'base address, and inverts bit 7 of the byte read.
'The status-port hardware reinverts these bits,
'so the value read matches the value at the connector.
StatusPortRead = frmMain.ocxParallelPort.Inp(1) Xor &H80
End Function
```

```
Function ControlPortRead%()
'Reads a parallel port's control port.
'Calculates the control-port address from the port's
'base address, and inverts bits 0, 1, & 3 of the byte read.
'The control-port hardware reinverts these bits,
'so the value read matches the value at the connector.
Dim ControlPortData%
ControlPortData = frmMain.ocxParallelPort.Inp(2)
ControlPortRead = ControlPortData Xor &HB
End Function
```

```
Sub ControlPortWrite(Value%)
'Writes a Value to a parallel port's control port.
'Calculates the control-port address from the port's
'base address, and inverts bits 0, 1, & 3.
'The control-port hardware reinverts these bits,
'so Value is written to the port connector.
frmMain.ocxParallelPort.Outp 2, (Value Xor &HB)
End Sub
```

Listing 10-5: Routines for reading and writing to the parallel-port registers using WinRT.

Parallel Port Complete

11

Modes for Data Transfer

The IEEE-1284 standard documents five types of data transfers: Compatibility, Nibble, Byte, EPP and ECP. All of these were in use before the standard's publication, but the standard provides a reference that circuit designers and programmers can use when designing products.

The standard also describes a software negotiation that enables a PC and a peripheral to decide on a protocol for transferring data. Other documents fill in topics that IEEE 1284 doesn't cover, such as information that is specific to the PC's architecture. Unfortunately a few aspects, such as the basic setup and configuration procedures for a port, aren't standardized, and vary with the controller chip.

This chapter introduces the new modes, describes IEEE-1284's negotiation protocol, and shows ways of determining which modes a port supports and how to select a mode from those available.

The IEEE 1284 Standard

The IEEE 1284 standard is a document that defines and describes all of the popular conventions and protocols for parallel-port communications. A committee of the The Institute of Electrical and Electronic Engineers (IEEE) developed the standard, which was released in 1994.

The IEEE is an organization of engineers and engineering companies. One of its activities is to develop and publish standards, or documents that recommend specifications for engineering practices, including computer interfacing. The idea behind developing the standards is to reduce the extra work, confusion, and incompatibilities that result when every manufacturer develops products independently and customers have to choose from among variations on a single idea, such as the parallel port.

The parallel-port standard has the designation *IEEE Std 1284-1994* and the lengthy full title of *Standard Signaling Method for a Bi-directional Parallel Peripheral Interface for Personal Computers.* This book refers to it as IEEE 1284. The complete document is available from the IEEE.

The standard describes Compatibility, Nibble, Byte, EPP, and ECP transfers. It defines the parallel-port signals and their uses in the different modes, including timing specifications. It also describes connectors and cables, including the original ones and new, high-performance types (described in Chapter 6.)

IEEE 1284 doesn't cover everything, however. Most notably, it doesn't say anything about how to program or access the interface in a PC or peripheral. There's no mention of the PC's parallel-port registers and how to use them to configure, read, and write to the port.

However, other sources have documented conventions for these. A document published by Microsoft (see Appendix A) describes register use and protocol for ECPs. Data sheets for parallel-port controller chips also describe the use of the parallel-port registers. Another IEEE committee is developing a standard BIOS, or API, for using the new modes.

Definitions

The purpose of IEEE 1284 is to describe methods for asynchronous, fully interlocked, bi-directional communications between a host and a peripheral device. This means, a term at a time:

Asynchronous. As explained in Chapter 9, in synchronous communications, the devices share a common clock signal, and events occur at defined times in relation to the clock. The clock often runs at a fixed frequency, which causes each data transfer to take the same amount of time.

Parallel-port data transfers are normally asynchronous, where the devices don't share a common clock, and the timing of events is defined in relation of one event to another. For example, when the PC brings *nStrobe* low, the peripheral brings *Busy* high in response. The delay before *Busy* goes high can vary from 0 to 10 microseconds, and the width of the *nStrobe* pulse can vary from 0.75 to 500 microseconds. The peripheral is responsible for detecting *nStrobe*, reading the data, then bringing *Busy* high, rather than depending on a clock signal to tell it when to do each of these. The peripheral may bring *Busy* low again whenever it's ready to receive another byte. (It is possible to use the parallel port as a synchronous interface, as Chapter 9 showed with the DS1620 thermometer chip.)

Fully interlocked. Every control signal is acknowledged with an answering control signal. This ensures that the transmitting device sends data only when the receiving device is ready, and that the receiving devices acknowledges receiving all data.

Bi-directional. Data may travel in both directions.

Host. This is usually a PC, though it can be any device that controls the interface.

Peripheral device. This may be a printer, scanner, A/D or D/A converter, a micro-controller, another PC, or any device that connects to the host's parallel port.

Communication modes

IEEE 1284 defines five communication modes. It uses the term *forward channel* to refer to transfers from the host to the peripheral, and *reverse channel* to refer to transfers from the peripheral to the host. Below is a summary of each mode:

Register Use

Table 11-1 summarizes the registers used by each of the modes. The functions of some of the registers vary depending on the mode.

Compatibility mode

Compatibility mode is similar to the data-transfer protocol used by the BIOS in the original PC. The host sends a byte at a time to the peripheral, and *Busy* and *nAck* provide handshaking. This is the default mode that all PCs and PC-compatible devices can use.

Nibble mode

Nibble mode defines a way that all ports can use to transfer data in the reverse direction, from the peripheral to the host. Each byte of data arrives four bits (a nibble) at a time, at four of the Status inputs. The remaining Status bit and a Data bit provide handshaking.

Table 11-1: Registers used by different port types.

Address	Port Type	Function
base address	SPP, PS/2, EPP, ECP modes 000, 001	Data port
	ECP mode 011	ECP FIFO (address)
base address + 1	all	Status port
base address + 2	all	Control port
base address + 3	EPP	EPP address
base address + 4	EPP	EPP data
base address + 5	EPP	varies
base address + 6	EPP	varies
base address + 7	EPP	varies
base address + 400h	ECP mode 010	Parallel Port FIFO (data)
	ECP mode 011	ECP FIFO (data)
	ECP mode 110	Test FIFO
	ECP mode 111	Configuration Register A
base address + 401h	ECP mode 111	Configuration Register B
base address + 402h	ECP all modes	ECR (extended control register)

Byte Mode

Byte mode defines a way to transfer data in the reverse direction, from the peripheral to the host, when the data lines are bidirectional. For faster data transfers, PS/2 ports, ECPs, and some EPPs can use Byte mode instead of Nibble mode.

EPP Mode

Enhanced Parallel Port (EPP) mode allows high-speed transfers of bytes in either direction. Handshaking signals distinguish between data and address transfers.

ECP Mode

Like EPP mode, Extended Capabilities Port (ECP) mode can do high-speed transfers in either direction. Handshaking signals distinguish between data and control bytes. A control byte may contain an address or data-compression information. A FIFO buffer stores bytes received and bytes to be sent.

Compatible and Compliant Devices

The 1284 standard defines the terms *compatible* and *compliant* in relation to the standard. You might think that a device labeled as *1284-compatible* or *1284-compliant* would have to support all of the above modes, but this isn't so.

According to the standard, 1284-compatible devices include any device that can use Compatibility mode. This includes the SPP and all of its imitators and derivatives.

A device that is 1284-compliant must also support the IEEE 1284's protocol for negotiating. However, the only additional mode that a 1284-compliant device must support is Nibble mode. An SPP or other 1284-compatible device can also use Nibble mode, but it doesn't support the negotiation protocol, so the host and peripheral must have another way of selecting the mode.

According to the IEEE 1284's definitions, neither compatible nor compliant devices have to support EPP or ECP modes. So, if you're buying a parallel port labeled as 1284-compatible or compliant, it's a good idea to verify that it also supports EPP and ECP modes.

Signal names

IEEE 1284 assigns new names to the port bits to reflect their new purposes. Some of the bits have as many as five names, depending on the mode. Table 11-2 shows the signal names for the bits in the Data, Status, and Control ports in each mode.

Detecting Port Types

On many of the ports that support the new modes, the new abilities go unused or cause problems when the software expects to communicate with an old-style port and accesses one of the new modes by mistake. Confusion about the new ports includes very basic issues like how to find out what modes are available, how to enable and disable the different modes, and how and when to use each mode.

Just figuring out what type of parallel port is in a system can be a challenge. Many ports, no matter how many modes they support, default to SPP type, which can use only Compatibility and Nibble modes. Before you can use the new modes, you have to configure the port to allow their use.

Using the New Modes

To use Byte, EPP, or ECP mode, both the host and peripheral must have supporting hardware and software. These are the basic requirements:

PC Requirements

To use one of the new modes, the PC must have both hardware and software support for the mode:

Table 11-2: The functions of the parallel-port's bits change depending on the data-transfer mode.

Bit	Function according to Mode				
	Compatibility	Nibble	Byte	EPP	ECP
D0	data bit 0	not used	data bit 0	address/data bit 0	data bit 0
D1	data bit 1	not used	data bit 1	address/data bit 1	data bit 1
D2	data bit 2	not used	data bit 2	address/data bit 2	data bit 2
D3	data bit 3	not used	data bit 3	address/data bit 3	data bit 3
D4	data bit 4	not used	data bit 4	address/data bit 4	data bit 4
D5	data bit 5	not used	data bit 5	address/data bit 5	data bit 5
D6	data bit 6	not used	data bit 6	address/data bit 6	data bit 6
D7	data bit 7	not used	data bit 7	address/data bit 7	data bit 7
S3	nError	nDataAvail, data bits 0, 4	nDataAvail	User defined bit 2	nPeriphReq
S4	Select	XFlag, data bits 1, 5	XFlag	XFlag/User defined bit 3	XFlag
S5	PaperEnd	AckDataReq, data bits 2, 6	AckDataReq	User defined bit 1	nAckReverse
S6	nAck	PtrClk	PtrClk	Intr	PeriphClk
$\overline{S7}$	Busy	PtrBusy, data bits 3, 7	PtrBusy	nWait	PeriphAck
$\overline{C0}$	nStrobe	HostClk	HostClk	nWrite	HostClk
$\overline{C1}$	nAutoLF	HostBusy	HostBusy	nDStrb	HostAck
C2	nInit	nInit	nInit	nInit	nReverseReq
$\overline{C3}$	nSelectIn	1284Active (optional)	1284Active	1284Active nAStrb	1284Active

1. The mode must be enabled at the port.

2. The PC's software has to know how to do the transfers using the new mode. The application software or the operating system may provide a software driver for Nibble, Byte, EPP, or ECP transfers. The following chapters have details about the modes and how to program them.

Peripheral Requirements

The peripheral must also support the mode you want to use. A peripheral with an EPP- or ECP-capable port will almost certainly contain its own computer chip—a microprocessor or microcontroller—to manage the parallel-port communications. Some peripherals have a dedicated controller chip just for the parallel-port communications, and a separate CPU that performs other tasks and accesses the port controller as needed. Other peripherals may use a single computer chip for all device functions.

The control program in a peripheral is normally stored as firmware: the code is in ROM, EPROM, or another nonvolatile memory chip, and the peripheral's CPU reads the program directly from the chip, rather than loading from disk into RAM, as on a PC. If you're designing your own peripheral and you don't use a dedicated parallel-port controller, you'll have to program the hardware to perform the transfers.

Port Detecting in Software

If you're writing a parallel-port application that will run on many different computers, the application may want to detect what modes the PC's and peripheral's ports support, so it can choose the best communication mode available.

Chapter 4 included software routines for detecting port types (and supported modes) in a PC. IEEE 1284 defines a negotiation protocol, a series of signals and responses, for determining which modes a peripheral supports. A PC can request different modes until it finds one that both the PC and peripheral support. A peripheral that is IEEE-1284-compliant will support the protocol.

Disabling the Advanced Modes

Some peripheral devices are designed for use only with SPPs. They may use the Status and Control lines in unconventional ways that will confuse an EPP or ECP. With these devices, you want to be sure to configure the port as an SPP.

One way to do so is to disable the advanced modes entirely, as described in Chapter 1. This method is fine if you use the port only as an SPP. If you sometimes use the port to connect to devices that use the newer modes, they won't be able to use the modes until you re-enable them.

A second option is to get a PS/2, EPP, or ECP to act like an SPP without disabling the new modes entirely. A PS/2-type port or EPP will act like an SPP as long as you don't set bit 5 of the control port to 1, disabling the data outputs. To configure an ECP to emulate an SPP, select mode 000 in the ECR. In mode 011 (ECP), writing to the Data port (the base address) causes the port to try to do an ECP Address-Write cycle, with automatic handshaking, which you don't want.

If you have an unknown port and want it to emulate an SPP, first test for the presence of an ECP and if it exists, select mode 000 in the ECR. Otherwise, just remember to keep control bit $5 = 0$.

One difference on some of the newer ports is that even in SPP mode, the port doesn't have open-collector outputs on the Control bits, so you can't use these bits as inputs. Also, some EPPs don't support Byte mode, so to do Byte-mode transfers, you'll need to configure the port as PS/2-type, or as ECP with the ECP's PS/2 mode selected.

Saving the Original Configuration

A final note for parallel-port experimenting: before you change any of the configurations, save the original values of the configuration registers. In most cases you'll want to restore these values on exiting your program. Rebooting resets the chip's configuration, then applies any settings in the CMOS setup.

Negotiating a Mode

With so many modes to choose from, when a host and peripheral want to communicate, they need a way to decide which mode to use. IEEE 1284's *negotiation phase* enables devices to talk back and forth to decide the best mode to use. This way, users don't have to concern themselves with configuring the software for a particular mode, or even knowing which modes their ports support.

Through negotiating, the host can find out which modes a peripheral supports. When a peripheral supports multiple modes, the negotiation tells the peripheral which mode the host wants to use.

A 1284-compliant device will negotiate according to the standard. Some peripheral controllers have internal state machines that perform the negotiating automatically. Otherwise, the peripheral's firmware does the negotiating. If a host tries to negotiate with a port that doesn't respond to the negotiation, the host should default to Compatibility mode.

Protocol

Figure 11-1 is a timing diagram for the negotiation between a host and peripheral. These are the negotiating steps:

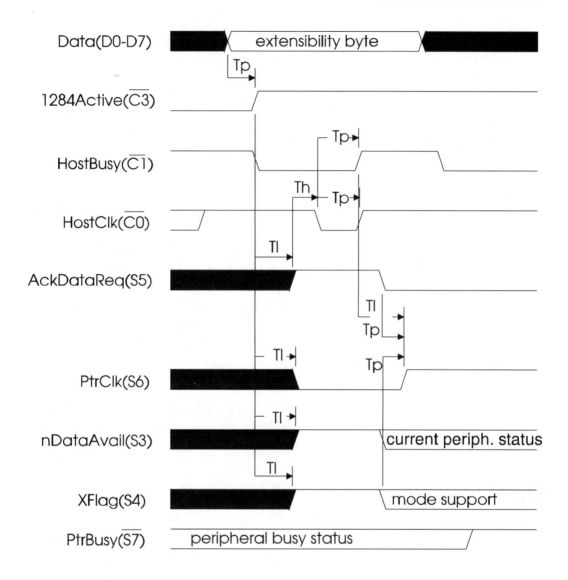

Time	Minimum	Maximum
Tl	0	35 millisecs.
Th	0	1.0 sec.
Tp	0.5 μsec	–

Figure 11-1: The IEEE 1284 standard includes a negotiation protocol that enables a PC and peripheral to decide which communications mode to use.

1. The host requests a mode by writing an extensibility request value to the data lines (*D0-D7*), then bringing *1284Active* ($\overline{C3}$) high, and *HostBusy* ($\overline{C1}$) low. Table 11-3 lists the extensibility bytes.

2. In response, a 1284-compliant peripheral brings *PtrClk* (*S6*) low and *AckDataReq* (*S5*), *XFlag* (*S4*), and *nDataAvail* (*S3*) high. On a peripheral that isn't 1284-compliant and thus doesn't support negotiating, this situation is unlikely to occur because an event that causes *S5* (*PaperEnd*) to go high would cause *S3* (*nError*) to go low. If *PaperEnd* and *nError* are not both high, the peripheral doesn't support IEEE 1284 negotiation and the host brings *1284Active* ($\overline{C3}$) low to end the negotiation attempt. The link may then use compatibility mode to transfer data.

3. If the peripheral supports negotiating, the host brings *HostClk* ($\overline{C0}$) low to latch the extensibility byte into the peripheral. The host then brings *HostClk* and *HostBusy* high.

4. In response, the peripheral brings *AckDataReq* low. If it supports the requested mode, it leaves *XFlag* high. The exception is Nibble mode, which all 1284-compliant devices must support, and for which XFlag goes low. If the peripheral has data to send to the host, it brings *nDataAvail* low.

5. The peripheral brings *PtrClk* (*S6*) high to complete the negotiation.

If the requested mode isn't supported by the peripheral, the host returns to compatibility mode and may try again with a different extensibility request byte. When the host finds a mode that the peripheral supports, data transfer can begin.

Controller Chips

There are many different parallel-port controller chips. Some are designed for use in a PC or other host device, while others are designed for use in peripherals, and a few can be configured for either use.

Host Chips

If you have an ECP or EPP, it's often possible to identify the controller chip. Knowing the manufacturer and part number can be useful if you need to learn more about configuring the chip or want to check compatibility with a peripheral's driver.

On a typical EPP- or ECP-capable chip, performing basic configuration functions such as selecting the port's base address, IRQ level, and port type requires accessing configuration registers in the controller. To protect from accidental writes, the

Table 11-3: The host sends an extensibility byte to the peripheral to request a transmission mode.

Extensibility byte	Function
1000 0000	Request extensibility link
0100 0000	Request EPP mode
0011 0000	Request ECP mode with RLE
0001 0000	Request ECP mode
0000 1000	Reserved
0000 0100	Request Device ID, return data using Nibble mode
0000 0101	Request Device ID, return data using Byte mode
0001 0100	Request Device ID, return data using ECP mode without RLE
0011 0100	Request Device ID, return data using ECP mode with RLE
0000 0010	Reserved
0000 0001	Byte mode transfer
0000 0000	Nibble mode transfer

configuration registers often require a special series of writes before they can be accessed. There is no standard method for accessing the configuration registers, however. The addressing and protection methods vary with the chip.

Table 11-4 lists some parallel-port chips. The part number and manufacturer's name or logo are usually stamped on the chip.

SMC's Super I/O

An example of parallel-port chips that support ECP and EPP modes is SMC (Standard Microsystems Corporation)'s FDC37C665GT and FDC37C666GT. Their full name is *Advanced High-Performance Multi-Mode Parallel Port Super I/O Floppy Disk Controllers*. I'll call them SMC Super I/O for short.

As the name suggests, these chips include both a floppy-disk controller and a parallel port. You can even configure the parallel port as a floppy-disk port for external drives—a useful feature for diskless portable computers. The chip also has two serial-port UARTs and an IDE interface.

The two chips are similar. The -65GT is optimized for use on motherboards and includes software configuration logic for the floppy controller. The -66GT is optimized for use on expansion cards and includes a game-port select. Both support all of the parallel-port modes: Compatibility, Nibble, Byte, EPP, and ECP.

The chips have 16 configuration registers, but you access the registers using just two port addresses. One address holds the index of the register to access (0-Fh), and the other holds the data to be written or read from the register.

Table 11-4: Parallel-port controller chips for PCs.

Manufacturer	Part Number	Part Name	Package
Intel	82091AA	Advanced Integrated Peripheral (AIP)	100-pin QFP
National Semiconductor	PC87332VLJ	Super I/O III Premium Green	100-pin QFP
National Semiconductor	NS486SXF	486-Class Controller with On-chip Peripherals for Embedded Systems	160-pin QFP
SMC (Standard Microsystems Corporation)	FDC37C665, FDC37C666	Advanced High-Performance Multi-Mode Parallel Port Super I/O Floppy Disk Controller	100-pin QFP
SMC (Standard Microsystems Corporation)	FDC37C93X	Plug and Play Compatible Ultra I/O Controller	160-pin QFP
Startech	ST78C34	General-purpose parallel port with 83-byte FIFO	44-pin PLCC, 40-pin DIP
Startech	ST78C36	ECP/EPP parallel printer port with 16-byte FIFO	44-and 68-pin PLCC

To prevent accidental writes to the configuration registers, the software must first enter the chip's Configuration Mode. On the '65 chip, you do so by writing 55h twice to port 3F0h. SMC recommends disabling interrupts during these writes, because any port access that occurs between the two writes will prevent the chip from entering Configuration mode. You can re-enable interrupts after entering Configuration Mode.

In Configuration mode, software may read and write to the configuration registers. To access a register, you write the register number to port 3F0h, then read or write data at port 3F1h. You can verify that you're in Configuration mode by changing a bit in a configuration registers and reading back the result. When you're finished accessing the registers, you exit Configuration Mode by writing *AAh* to port 3F0h.

On the '66 chip, the configuration registers may be at *3F0h-3F1h* or at *370h-371h*, depending on the logic states of two of the chip's pins. An expansion card with a '66 may include jumpers or a utility to select the address range. To enter configuration mode, you write *44h* twice in a row to the lower address, either *3F0h* or *370h*.

A single system may have three SMC Super I/O ports: a '65 on the motherboard, one '66 on an expansion card with configuration registers at 3F0h, and another

'66 expansion card with configuration registers at 370h. The different access codes and configuration register addresses enable all three to co-exist. (Each port must have a different base address as well.)

Only some of the configuration registers are related to parallel-port use. Table 11-5 lists the relevant bits. From the table, you can see that the default configuration for the '66 is SPP, with all of the other modes disabled. In order to use PS/2, EPP, or ECP modes, you have to set Configuration Register 1's bit 3 to 0. You then can select a mode with bits 0 and 1 of Configuration Register 4.

The Configuration Registers also allow you to select a base address, place the port in low-power mode, and select an EPP type, FIFO threshold for ECP transfers, and interrupt-request polarity. Unlike other controller chips, these don't include an IRQ-level select, so external circuits have to perform that function.

On the '66, the port address and mode (SPP, EPP, ECP, or ECP+EPP) are hardware-selected by the logic states of pins on the chip. Expansion cards may include jumpers or software to allow changing these.

Most data-transfer modes are available in more than one of the modes selected in the Configuration Registers or in hardware. For example, on the '65, if CR1, bit 3, is 0, any of the modes in CR4 will allow SPP transfers. For EPP transfers, you can use either mode 01 or 11 in CR4.

With all of these options, it may take two or three steps to select a mode. For example, in order to do ECP transfers on a '65, you would:

1. Enable the extended modes by setting bit 3 of CR1 to 0.
2. Select *ECP* port type by writing 10 or 11 to bits 0 and 1 of CR4.
3. Select the ECP's internal ECP mode by writing 011 to bits 7-5 in the ECP's ECR.

For EPP transfers, you can either select *SPP & EPP* port type in CR4, or:

1. Select *ECP & EPP* port type.
2. Select the ECP's internal EPP mode in the ECR.

FarPoint Communications' F/PortPlus is an example of an expansion card that uses the '66. The chip is hardwired as *ECP+EPP*, and FarPoint provides a utility for selecting the ECP's internal modes. Farpoint also includes a program for accessing the configuration registers, though you'll need the chip's data sheet for documentation on the registers themselves.

SMC's Ultra I/O

An enhancement to the Super I/O is SMC's FDC37C93X *Plug and Play Compatible Ultra I/O Controller*. It has the same abilities as the Super I/O, and also supports Microsoft's Plug and Play standard.

Table 11-5: Parallel-port configuration bits in SMC's Super I/O Chips

Configuration Register	Bit	Name	Description
CR1	1,0	Parallel port address (note 4)'	0 0 disabled
			0 1 3BCh
			1 0 378h
			1 1 278h (default)
	2	Parallel port power	1 power supplied (default)
			0 low power mode
	3	Parallel Port Mode (note 4)	1 SPP (default)
			0 extended modes allowed (see CR4, bits 0, 1)
	4	IRQ polarity (affects IRQ3, IRQ4, FINTR, and LPT IRQ (5 or 7)	1 active high, inactive low (default)
			0 active low, inactive high-Z (always true in ECP, EPP modes)
CR4	0,1	Parallel Port Extended Modes (if CR1 bit 3 = 0) (note 4)	1 0 SPP, PS/2 (default)
			0 1 SPP & EPP (note 1)
			1 0 ECP (note 3)
			1 1 ECP & EPP (notes 2 & 3)
	6	EPP type	0 EPP 1.9 (default)
			1 EPP 1.7
CRA	0-3	ECP FIFO Threshold	threshold for ECP service requests (0-15, default = 0)

Note 1: Read/writes to SPP registers are SPP mode, read/writes to EPP registers are EPP mode.

Note 2: For EPP, set ECR register of ECP to mode 100.

Note 3: For SPP, set ECR register of ECP to mode 000.

Note 4: In the '65GT, this option is set by hardware and can't be changed in the configuration registers.

The port on this card may have any of 480 base addresses, on any byte boundary from 100h to FF8h. Of course, other devices will use many of these locations, and most parallel ports will continue to use the conventional addresses. But it is handy to have the ability to choose a nonstandard address if necessary.

NSC's Super I/O

National Semiconductor's PC87332VLJ Super I/O, or NSC Super I/O for short, is much like SMC's Super I/O, with an EPP/ECP parallel port plus two serial ports, control logic for an IDE interface (for hard drives), and a floppy-disk interface.

This chip has eight configuration registers, and various bits in six of them configure the parallel port. The parallel-port functions in the configuration registers are similar to those in SMC's Super I/O. You can enable the port, select an address, power down, select an IRQ level and polarity, and enable PS/2, ECP, and EPP modes. However, the register assignments are different from those in SMC's chips.

As with SMC's chips, NSC's Super I/O uses two consecutive port addresses for accessing the Configuration Registers. The addresses and method for accessing them differs, however. There are four possible address pairs. The active pair is selected in hardware. The first address in the pair is an index register. The second address is the data register, and holds the data to write or data read. To change the configuration data, you write the index to the index register, then write the data twice to the data register. Writing twice protects against inadvertent writes.

Five pins on the chip allow selecting of different combinations of default port addresses in hardware.

NSC's Embedded 486

National Semiconductor's NS486SXF is nearly a complete computer system on a chip. It contains an 80486 microprocessor and peripheral functions that you would expect to find on a PC's motherboard, including a parallel port that supports ECP. The chip is intended as a controller for devices like fax machines, multi-function peripherals, TV set-top boxes, and computer-based organizers and communicators.

The NS486's ECP can be configured in Host or Slave (peripheral) mode. In Host mode, the signals emulate the signals on a PC's parallel port, while in Slave mode, they emulate the signals on a peripheral's port. For example, in Host mode, the Status lines are inputs; in Slave mode, they're outputs. If the NS486 is functioning as a PC, the port uses Host mode and connects to a peripheral device. If the chip is the controller for a peripheral, the port uses Slave mode and connects to a PC's parallel port.

Peripheral Chips

In addition to chips designed for use in the host PC, there are parallel-port controllers designed for use in peripherals. Like the controller chips in PCs, many of the peripheral chips support Byte, EPP, and ECP modes. But the peripheral chips don't have to interface to a PC's ISA expansion bus, and they may not use the standard PC addresses for the port registers. (Some peripherals do have 80x86 CPUs, however.) Some chips have a pass-through port that allows their use in a daisy chain of devices connected to a single port on the PC. And, as mentioned above, the bits on the peripheral have different functions: the Status bits are output, the Control bits are input, and the Data bits are input, or bidirectional bits that are input on powerup.

The previous section described NSC's Embedded 486, which can be configured for use in peripherals as well as PCs. Table 11-6 lists other peripheral controllers that support EPP and ECP modes.

SMC's 34C60

SMC's 34C60 Parallel Port Interface chip is a companion to SMC's Super I/O. It handles the peripheral side of a parallel-port link. Like SMC's Super I/O, it's a 100-lead surface-mount chip and is a computer in itself. It has inputs and outputs that can buffer and drive a parallel-port cable. It also has an interface to an ISA-type bus. The peripheral doesn't have to include a full ISA bus, of course, but using the familiar ISA interface makes it easy for designers to interface a CPU to the chip.

Other features include the ability to daisy-chain up to eight peripherals on the port, support for interrupt-sharing among multiple devices, a low-battery sensor, and an output for driving a piezo buzzer.

Cirrus Logic's CD1283

Cirrus Logic's CD-1283 is designed for use in printers, scanners, and tape drives. It has a 64-byte FIFO, automatic compressing and decompressing of data, and DMA support. A 16-bit data bus and 7 address lines interface to the peripheral's CPU. The chip's internal state machine automatically responds to IEEE 1284 negotiations from the host. A Negotiation Status register indicates the current mode and the success or failure of the latest negotiation attempt.

Peripheral Daisy Chains

Although you can easily add a second and third port to most desktop systems, and there's always the option of using a switch box to select a device at a single port, it would be more convenient to be able to connect several devices to one port and use each whenever you want. A supplement to the IEEE 1284 standard documents a daisy-chain protocol that allows up to nine devices to connect to a single port. At this writing, the supplement is still under development, but a preliminary version, IEEE P1284.3, is available for review. The following information is based on the preliminary version, which is subject to change.

Table 11-6: Controller chips for peripherals with EPP and ECP support.

Manufacturer	Part Number	Part Name	Package
Cirrus Logic	CL-CD1283	IEEE 1284-Compatible Parallel Interface Controller	100-pin QFP
SMC (Standard Microsystems Corporation)	34C60	Parallel Port Interface Chip - Peripheral Side	100-pin QFP

All of the devices in the chain use the same signal paths for communicating with the host PC. Except for the PC and the last device in the chain, each device connects both to the device ahead of it and to the device behind it in the chain. The PC selects the device it wants to communicate with, and all of the others remain in transparent, or pass-through, mode. In transparent mode, the device ignores all transmissions and allows signals to pass to the next device in the chain. Only the selected device communicates with the host.

Except for the last device in the chain, all devices have to understand the daisy-chain protocol. The last device can be daisy-chain-unaware (in other words, any conventional peripheral). This device can communicate when none of the others is selected.

Protocol

The host communicates with the peripherals by sending commands in packets, using the Command Packets Protocol (CPP). This is the format of the packets:

Escape Sequence	Command	Terminator
AA 55 00 FF 87 78	xx	FF

Table 11-7 shows the commands. The escape sequence is a series of bytes sent without any handshaking. The peripheral has to monitor the Data inputs, watching for the sequence. (An internal state machine may perform this function.) An escape byte is considered valid if it remains for a least one microsecond. The peripheral responds by setting the Status port as follows: After receiving the first FFh, the peripheral sets the Status port to 00x10xxx (x = don't care). After receiving 87h, it sends 11011xxx. After receiving 78h, if the device is selected, it sends 00111xxx, or 01111xxx if it's the last device in the chain. If the device is not selected, bit 4 in the byte sent after 78h is 0. The bytes are those on the daisy chain; in the PC's Status register, bit 7 is inverted from the values shown. After the escape sequence, the PC sends the Command byte and pulses *nStrobe*, then sends the FFh terminator with no handshaking.

Table 11-7: MAP commands for parallel-port daisy chains.

Command (hexadecimal)	Command (binary)	Description
00-07	0000 0aaa	Assign address *aaa* to current device.
08-0F	0000 1aaa	Query interrupt from device *aaa*
10-17	0001 0aaa	Query protocol ID from device *aaa*
20-27	0010 0aaa	Select device *aaa* in EPP mode
30	0011 xxxx	De-select all devices
40	0100 0xxx	Disable daisy-chain interrupts
48	0100 1xxx	Enable daisy-chain interrupts
50-57	0101 0aaa	Clear interrupt latches on device *aaa*
58-5F	0101 1aaa	Set interrupt latch on device *aaa*
D0-D7	1101 0aaa	Select device *aaa* in ECP mode
E0-E7	1110 0aaa	Select Device *aaa* in Compatible mode

All of the daisy-chain-aware devices power up in transparent mode. Before communications can begin, the host assigns each device an address corresponding to its number in the chain. To assign an address to the first device in the chain, the host writes the escape sequence followed by 00 to the data lines. When a daisy-chain-aware peripheral recognizes this as an assign-address command (00 through 07), it blocks all Control signals from passing to the next device, so when the host brings *nStrobe* low, the first device in the chain is the only one to see it. It accepts the address and returns to transparent mode. The host then sends the next address (01) to the next device in the chain, and continues until it reaches the last device.

After each device has an address, the host can use the Select-Device commands to select a device and communications mode.

Programming Options

There are several approaches to writing a program that uses one of the IEEE-1284 modes.

You can write your own software from scratch, using the IEEE 1284 specification and other parallel-port conventions as a guide. Of course, the device that connects to the host computer must also be capable of using the modes you program. With IEEE-1284-compliant peripherals, you can use the standard's negotiation protocol to select a mode. If you're designing your own peripheral, you can implement the new modes by using a dedicated controller chip or by programming the transfers yourself.

To make accessing the new modes easier, the IEEE 1284.3 supplement will define a device driver, or software interface, for parallel-port data transfers, including functions for detecting a port's mode, transferring data, and selecting a device when several are connected to one port.

There are also a few commercial device drivers available for parallel ports, including support for the advanced modes. Peripheral manufacturers can license these drivers for use with their products.

12

Compatibility and Nibble Modes

Every PC's parallel port can use two communications modes: Compatibility mode for eight-bit PC-to-peripheral transfers, and Nibble mode for four-bit peripheral-to-PC transfers. This chapter describes these modes and introduces a circuit that you can use to interface a parallel port to a microcontroller or other peripheral circuit.

Compatibility Mode

Compatibility mode is the default mode for sending data from the host to the peripheral. The host writes bytes to the Data port, and Status and Control bits provide handshaking. The Compatibility mode described in IEEE 1284 uses handshaking that is compatible with the handshaking in the original PC's BIOS routine for parallel-port transfers.

Handshaking

Three of the parallel port's signals are intended as handshaking signals for controlling the flow of data. The handshaking performs several functions. The peripheral's *Busy* output tells the PC when it's ready to receive data. The PC's *nStrobe* output tells the peripheral that a byte is available to be read on the Data lines. When the peripheral reads a byte, it sends a *nAck* pulse to tell the PC that the byte was received.

You don't have to use handshaking with parallel-port operations. For example, if you're using the port outputs to control a set of relays, simple Out statements that write to the data port may be all you need. The handshaking signals are necessary if there's a chance that the receiving device won't be ready when the transmitting device has something to send, or if the PC wants the receiving device to acknowledge receiving each byte.

Figure 12-1 shows the handshaking and data signals for Compatibility mode, which should work with just about all existing parallel-port peripherals. The transfer works like this:

1. The PC brings *SelectIn ($\overline{C3}$)* low to tell the peripheral it wants to communicate. In response, the peripheral brings *Select (S4)* high. The PC reads the Status port and verifies that *Select* is high and that *Busy ($\overline{S7}$)* is low.

If you use one of the MS-DOS functions to write to the port, *PaperEnd (S5)* must also be low and *nError (S3)* must be high.

2. When all looks OK, the PC writes a byte to *D0-D7*.

3. After a delay of at least 0.75 microseconds, the PC pulses *nStrobe ($\overline{C0}$)* low. The pulse is typically 1 to 5 microseconds wide, but may range from 0.75 to 500 microseconds. The PC holds *D0-D7* valid for at least 0.75 microseconds after *nStrobe* returns high.

4. On the falling edge of *nStrobe*, the peripheral reads and latches (stores) *D0-D7* and brings *Busy* high to tell the computer not to send another byte yet. *Busy* should go high within 0.5 microsecond after *nStrobe* goes low.

5. When the peripheral has latched the data, it pulses *nAck (S6)* low to tell the PC that it received the byte. The *nAck* pulse is typically 5 microseconds, but may range from 0.5 to 10 microseconds. The PC may use *nAck* as an interrupt that tells the PC when to write the next byte to the data port. When the peripheral is ready to receive another byte, it brings *Busy* low and a new data transfer may begin.

Variations

Because IBM didn't fully document the timing requirements and other details of the parallel-port interface in the original PC, manufacturers of compatible computers and peripherals had to resort to examining the design of the PC's parallel port and the PC's BIOS functions, and designing products that were compatible

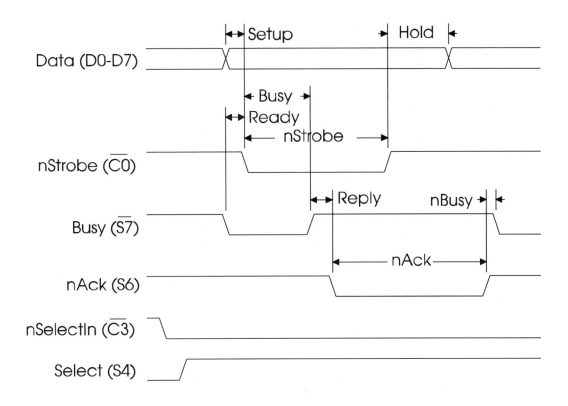

Signal	Minimum (microseconds)	Maximum (microseconds)
Ready	0	-
Setup	0.75	-
Hold	0.75	-
Busy	0	0.5
nStrobe	0.75	500
Reply	0	-
nBusy	0	2.5 (typical)
nAck	0.5	10

Figure 12-1: Compatibility mode handshaking.

with these. With many companies making PCs, printers, and other parallel-port devices, some variations were bound to occur along the way. (Now, of course, designers of parallel-port hardware can use the IEEE-1284 standard as a basis for port designs.)

If you're writing programs that will run on many different computers or with many different printers or other parallel-port devices, you want to be sure that the program will work with all of them. For the most part, this is easy to do, though there are some minor differences to be aware of. Specifically, there are variations in the timing of the *Busy* and *nStrobe* signals, in the timing, definition, and use of *nAck*, and in the triggering and latching of interrupts.

Busy and nStrobe

In the compatibility-mode timing described above, the peripheral must bring *Busy* high within 0.5 microsecond after *nStrobe* goes low. IEEE 1284 calls this *Busy While Strobe* timing. On some peripherals (and in the original Centronics interface), *Busy* doesn't go high until after *nStrobe* goes high (*Busy after Strobe* timing) (Figure 12-2A).

Busy and nAck

In Compatibility mode, the entire *nAck* pulse occurs while *Busy* is high (*Ack in Busy* timing). *Busy* returns low either at the same time as *nAck* returns high, or up to 2.5 microseconds later. There are two variations of this timing. With *Ack while Busy* timing (Figure 12-2B), *nAck* goes low while *Busy* is high, but doesn't go high until after *Busy* has returned low. With *Ack after Busy* timing (Figure 12-2C), *nAck* doesn't go low until after *Busy* has returned low, so the entire *nAck* pulse is outside the *Busy* pulse.

Interrupts

In addition, the interrupt circuits on some PCs varies from the original design.

In the original interface and most of the designs that imitate it, the rising edge of *nAck* triggers interrupts. But a few ports interrupt on *nAck*'s falling edge instead.

Also, the parallel port on the original PC, XT, and some compatibles of the same era didn't latch the interrupt pulses. If the pulse isn't latched, or stored, when it occurs, there's a chance that the PC won't detect the interrupt request (if the entire pulse occurs while interrupt requests are disabled, for example). To ensure compatibility with ports that don't latch the interrupt signal internally, *nAck* should be as long as 200 microseconds.

On some systems, the parallel port's interrupt line is disabled, possibly because all available IRQ levels are in use by other devices. The parallel-port BIOS routines, MS-DOS functions, and Windows printer drivers will all function without using parallel-port interrupts. If you want your software to be compatible with all ports, include the ability to transfer data without using interrupts. (Chapter 10 has more on interrupts.)

Tips for Reliable Data Transfers

For software that works with PCs or peripherals that have any of the above variations, data transfers should meet both of these requirements:

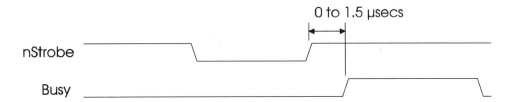

(A) With Busy After Strobe timing, the peripheral doesn't assert Busy until nStrobe has returned high.

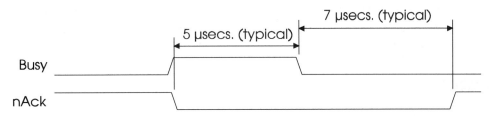

(B) With Ack While Busy timing, nAck goes low while Busy is high, and returns high after Busy has returned low.

(C) With Ack After Busy timing, the entire nAck pulse occurs after Busy has returned low.

Figure 12-2: Three variations on the Compatibility-mode timing.

1. Before sending a byte, verify that *Busy* is low.

2. After sending a byte, wait at least 1.5 microseconds after *nStrobe* goes high before checking *Busy* in preparation for sending the next byte. Otherwise, if the device uses *Busy After Strobe* timing, there's a chance that the PC will send a byte before the device has latched the previous byte. A 1.5 microsecond delay is quite short, however, and most programs will have this much delay built-in.

When *Busy* is low again, the PC can send another byte.

This method ignores *nAck*, so there is no acknowledgment from the peripheral that it received the previous byte. When *Busy* is low, the peripheral must detect *nStrobe*'s going low and bring *Busy* high before the PC tries to send another byte. On most ports, it is possible to use *nAck* to interrupt the PC to let it know that the peripheral received the previous byte and is ready for another.

Another way to guarantee that the peripheral received the byte is to use a hand-shake where each control signal remains asserted until the opposite end acknowledges it. The Byte, EPP, and ECP handshakes use this technique.

Nibble Mode

Nibble mode enables any parallel port interface to receive bytes of data from a peripheral. The peripheral uses four Status outputs to send a byte in two nibbles. Nibble transfers were in use long before IEEE 1284, but the standard formalizes a protocol.

Handshaking

Chapter 2 showed a simple way to read a byte by reading four Status bits twice. IEEE-1284's Nibble mode uses the same idea, though the bit assignments differ and the handshaking is more complex. Figure 12-3 shows a Nibble-mode transfer, and Table 12-1 lists the Nibble-mode signals.

There are two phases, or parts, associated with Nibble mode. The data transfer phase includes the writing of a byte from the peripheral to the host, or PC. Idle phase defines the signal states when a transfer isn't occurring.

Nibble mode works like this:

1. The host brings *HostBusy* ($\overline{C1}$) low to say that it's ready to accept the first nibble from the peripheral.

2. The peripheral writes data bits 0-3 to *S3*, *S4*, *S5*, and $\overline{S7}$ and brings *PtrClk* (*S6*) low to indicate that the nibble is available to be read.

3. The host reads the four data bits and brings *HostBusy* high to indicate that it received the nibble.

4. The peripheral brings *PtrClk* high.

5. When the host is ready for the second nibble, it brings *HostBusy* low.

6. The peripheral places data bits 4-7 on *S3*, *S4*, *S5*, and $\overline{S7}$ and brings *PtrClk* low to indicate that the nibble is available to be read.

7. The host reads the four data bits and brings *HostBusy* high to indicate that it received the nibble.

8. The peripheral sets the status bits as follows:

   PtrBusy ($\overline{S7}$), high if the peripheral is busy, low if not busy
   nDataAvail (*S3*), low if another byte is ready to be sent, high if no byte ready to send

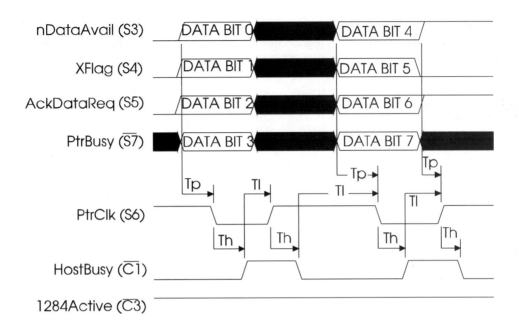

Time	Minimum	Maximum
Tl	0	35 millisecs.
Th	0	1.0 sec.
Tp	0.5 μsec	-

Figure 12-3: Nibble-mode transfer (PC to peripheral).

AckDataReq (S5), same as *S3*
XFlag (S4), same as in previous negotiation

9. The peripheral brings *PtrClk* high.

10. The host may now read *nDataAvail* to find out if another byte is available to read, and *PtrBusy* to find out if the peripheral is busy.

After it receives a byte, the host may do any of the following:

Bring *HostBusy* low and wait for more data.
Leave *HostBusy* high to prevent the peripheral from sending another nibble.
Bring *1284Active* low to return to compatibility mode.

Table 12-1: Nibble mode signals

Port Bit	Signal Name	Source	Function (reverse data transfer)	Function (reverse idle)
S3	nDataAvail	Peripheral	Low if there is a byte to send, then data bit 0, then 4	Low when there is a byte to send
S4	Xflag	Peripheral	Data bit 1, then 5	-
S5	AckDataReq	Peripheral	Data bit 2, then 6	High until host requests a data transfer, then follows S5
S6	PtrClk	Peripheral	High in response to C1's going high	Low to signal host that a byte is available to be read
$\overline{S7}$	PtrBusy	Peripheral	Data bit 3, then 7, then peripheral busy status	-
$\overline{C1}$	HostBusy	Host	High when host receives a byte, low when host is ready to receive another	High in response to S6's going low.

Making a Byte from Two Nibbles

In most applications, after receiving two nibbles, the host will combine them into a byte. The following table shows the bits and their positions in the status register:

Status Bit	Nibble 1	Nibble 2
S3	D0	D4
S4	D1	D5
S5	D2	D6
$\overline{S7}$	D3	D7

The host reads the nibbles from the Status register, in bits 3–5 and 7. One way to create a byte may be to extract the value of each bit in the nibbles and then construct the byte from the individual bits.

These calculations divide a byte into two nibble-mode nibbles:

```
D0 = (ByteToSend And 1)  * 8
D1 = (ByteToSend And 2)  * 8
D2 = (ByteToSend And 4)  * 8
D3 = (ByteToSend And 8)  * &h10
D4 = (ByteToSend And &h10) \ 2
D5 = (ByteToSend And &h20) \ 2
D6 = (ByteToSend And &h40) \ 2
D7 = ByteToSend And &h80
LowNibble = D0 + D1 + D2 + D3
```

```
HighNibble = D4 + D5 + D6 + D7
```

Using the fact that bits 0–2 use same multiplier, as do bits 4–6, another way to divide a byte into nibbles is like this:

```
'Get D3's value and shift it right 4 places
D3 = (ByteToSend And 8) * &h10
'Get the values of D0-D2 and shift left 3 places
'Store all four bits in LowNibble
LowNibble = (ByteToSend And 7) * 8 + D3
'Get D7's value; no shifting necessary
D7 = (ByteToSend And &h80)
'Get the values of D4-D6 and shift left 1 place
'Store all four bits in HighNibble
HighNibble = (ByteToSend And &h70) \ 2 + D7
```

At the receiving end, these calculations recreate the byte from two Nibble-mode nibbles:

```
D0 = (LowNibble And 8) \ 8
D1 = (LowNibble And &h10) \ 8
D2 = (LowNibble And &h20) \ 8
D3 = (LowNibble And &h80) \ &h10
D4 = (HighNibble And 8) * 2
D5 = (HighNibble And &h10) * 2
D6 = (HighNibble And &h20) * 2
D7 = HighNibble And &h80
ByteRead=D0+D1+D2+D3+D4+D5+D6+D7
```

Again, another way to do it is:

```
'Get D3's value from LowNibble and shift left 4 places
D3 = (LowNibble And &h80) \ &h10
'Get the values of D0-D2 from LowNibble
'and shift left 3 places
LowNibble = (LowNibble And &h38) \ 8 + D3
'Get D7's value from HighNibble; no shifting required
D7 = HighNibble And &h80
'Get the values of D4-D6 from HighNibble
'and shift right 1 place
HighNibble = (HighNibble And &h38) * 2 + D7
ByteRead = LowNibble + HighNibble
```

If you're programming your own interface on both ends, you don't have to use IEEE 1284's bit assignments. For example, you could use Status bits 4-7 for the data bits in ascending order, and use Status bit 3 for handshaking. Then all you would need to do is shift the lower nibble left four places (divide by 10h) and add this value to the higher nibble. Status bit 6 is conventionally left for handshaking, however, because it's the PC's interrupt input.

A Compatibility & Nibble-mode Application

In Compatibility and Nibble modes, the peripheral has to provide handshaking to complement the signals from the PC. All but the simplest peripherals will have a microcontroller or other computer chip that controls the interface and reads and writes the handshaking signals at appropriate times. On some general-purpose microcontrollers, such as Microchip's PIC series, the port drivers are strong enough that you can connect them directly to a parallel-port cable without external drivers Otherwise, you need to add buffers and drivers between the cable and microcontroller. Another option is to use a dedicated parallel-port controller chip. Most of these can connect directly to a cable, and have the three port registers built in, along with a CPU interface. A third option is to use a chip that's designed as a general-purpose interface, with I/O ports, a CPU interface, and handshaking support, but that isn't designed specifically as a PC's printer interface.

In the examples that follow, I use the 82C55 Programmable Peripheral Interface chip as an interface between a parallel port and a microcontroller. The 82C55 is a general-purpose interface that offers a fairly simple way to experiment with the different modes without having to use one of the more complex port chips or program all of the handshaking yourself. The chip is widely available, and you can interface it to many different microcontrollers and microprocessors. The hardware interface and programming strategy in the examples are typical of many microcontroller circuits, so you can use similar designs with other chips and any programming language.

About the 82C55 PPI

To understand the circuits that follow, you need to know a little about the architecture and operation of the 82C55.

Chip Options

The 8255 is the original NMOS version of the chip, and the 82C55 is the CMOS version, which is recommended for its lower power consumption. Some compatible chips use different part numbers, such as NEC's µPD71055.

Ports

The 82C55 has three 8-bit I/O ports and an 8-bit data bus for interfacing to a microcontroller or other computer chip. You can configure the ports as inputs or outputs, and one of these ports can function as a bidirectional port.

The 8255 was first designed for use with Intel's 8085 and similar microprocessors. The port pins were intended to connect to peripheral devices controlled by the microprocessor. Over the years, the 8255 has found uses in all kinds of circuits and with many different computer chips. The original IBM PC contained an 8255 that performed a variety of functions, including reading system settings on DIP switches, reading keyboard input, and controlling timer/counter functions.

In modern systems, a peripheral is likely to contain its own microprocessor or microcontroller. This enables the peripheral to do much of its own processing instead of burdening the system CPU with all of the work. In this situation, instead of acting as a simple CPU-to-peripheral interface, the 82C55 can interface a PC's parallel port—which is controlled by the PC's CPU—to a second CPU that controls one or more peripheral devices. The second CPU may even control another 82C55, whose ports in turn control peripheral devices.

The 82C55 has enough port bits to interface to the parallel port's 17 signals, with 7 bits left for other uses. The chip can automatically generate handshaking signals that are compatible with parallel-port handshaking, including Compatibility, Byte, and EPP modes. For the other modes, you can program the handshaking in software or firmware.

One drawback of the 82C55 is that its outputs can't source or sink the amount of current recommended for parallel-port interfaces. Unless your cable is very short, you'll want to add drivers and buffers between the port pins and the cable.

Port Modes

The 82C55's three ports function in two groups: Group 1 consists of Port A and the lower four bits of Port C, and Group 2 consists of Port B and upper four bits of Port C. Writing a value to the Configuration Register selects a mode for each group. Figure 12-4 shows the possibilities.

Mode 0 (*Basic Input/Output*) is simple I/O. A write operation to an output port latches the byte written to the data bus to the port pins. A read of an input port places the byte on the port pins on the data bus, where the CPU can read it.

Mode 1 (*Strobed Input/Output*) adds handshaking to Port A or B. Port C provides the handshaking signals.

In Mode 1, when a port is programmed as input, the 82C55's *STB* (Strobe) input corresponds to the PC's *nStrobe* ($\overline{C0}$) output, and its *IBF* (input buffer full) output corresponds to the PC's *Busy* ($\overline{S7}$) input. When *STB* goes low, *IBF* goes high to tell the PC that the peripheral is busy. *STB* can also cause an *INTR* (interrupt) output to signal the peripheral's CPU that a byte is available to be read. Reading a byte at the 82C55 automatically brings *IBF* low, telling the PC that the peripheral is ready for another byte.

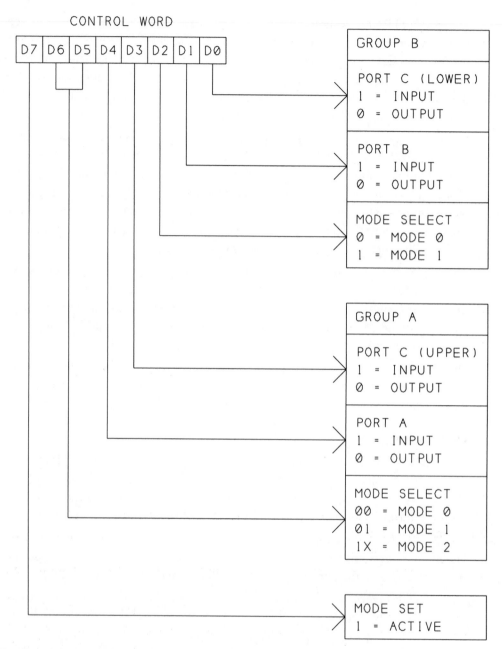

Figure 12-4: The 82C55's control word selects the modes for its three ports.

When a port is programmed as output, the peripheral writes a byte to the port and brings the 82C55's $\overline{OBF}$ low to signal the PC that a byte is available. The PC brings the 82C55's $\overline{ACK}$ input low, then high to tell the peripheral that it has

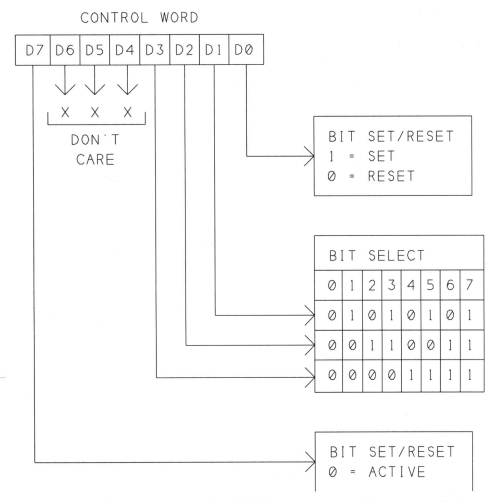

Figure 12-5: Another function of the 82C55's control word is to set and clear individual bits on Port C.

latched the byte. $\overline{ACK}$'s going high can cause the 82C55's *INTR* output to signal the CPU to write another byte to the port.

Mode 2 (Strobed Bidirectional Bus I/O) is the 82C55's third mode of operation. It allows using Port A as a bidirectional port, using an interface similar to Mode 1's input and output interfaces. The port is output when the peripheral's CPU writes to the port, input when the peripheral's CPU reads the port, and high impedance at other times.

Another feature of the Configuration register is the ability to set and reset individual bits on Port C with a single write operation. Figure 12-5 shows the Port-C values to accomplish this.

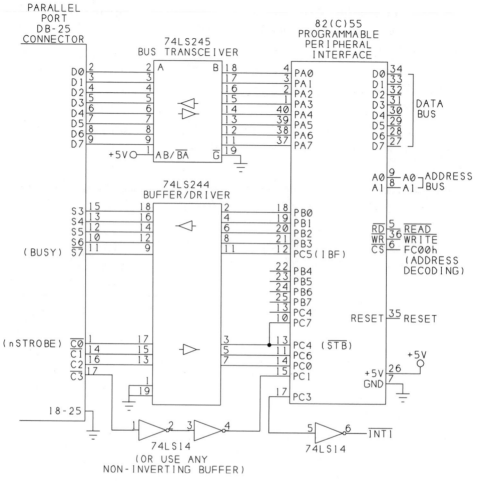

Figure 12-6: This circuit connects to an 8052 microcontroller, and can do Compatibility and Nibble-mode transfers.

Compatibility and Nibble-mode Interface

Figure 12-6 shows an interface that can do Compatibility and Nibble-mode transfers. In this and other example circuits in this book, the 82C55 interfaces to an 8052-Basic microcontroller, which is a variant of an Intel 8052 microcontroller with a Basic interpreter stored in the chip's internal ROM.

The Basic interpreter provides a simple way to program the microcontroller using the familiar Basic language, although the Basic-52 interpreter is by necessity nowhere near as complex or capable as Visual Basic or other Basics used on PCs. You can use an 8052-Basic chip as the brains in a data logger, controller circuit, or other device that doesn't require the computing power of a personal computer.

The chip can access up to 120 kilobytes for storing Basic programs and data. (The Basic interpreter uses the remaining 8 kilobytes.)

Appendix C shows a 8052-Basic circuit that Figure 12-6's circuit can connect to. The companion disk includes the Basic-52 code for the applications in this and the following chapters.

You can also use Figure 12-6's circuit with any microcontroller in Intel's 8051 family, using any programming language for the microcontroller. The 82C55 also interfaces in a similar way to other microcontrollers that can access external memory.

On the 82C55, a chip-select ($\overline{CS}$) input connects to address-decoding circuits that select a range of at least four addresses. In Figure 12-6, $\overline{CS}$ selects a base address of FC00h, but it can be any available series of addresses. Two address inputs (*A0, A1*) select one of the four addresses in the range. Port A is at the base address, Port B is at *baseaddress + 1*, Port C is at *base address + 2*, and the Configuration Port is at *base address + 3*. Other control signals are read ($\overline{RD}$) and write ($\overline{WR}$), which interface to the microcontroller's $\overline{RD}$ and $\overline{WR}$ outputs, and *Reset*, which is brought low on powerup. A data bus (*D0-D7*) transfers bytes between the microcontroller and the 82C55.

In the example, on the 82C55, Port A is input, Mode 1, and Port B is output, Mode 0. Port C, bits 4 and 5 are handshaking signals for Port A. The handshaking bits are defined by the 82C55's architecture, and can't be changed. The remaining bits on Port C are inputs.

The parallel port's Data outputs control Port A. Bits 0–3 of Port B control four of the parallel port's Status inputs, and Port C, bit 5 controls the fifth Status input. The parallel port's four Control-port outputs control bits 0, 1, 4, and 6 of Port C.

A 74LS245 bus transceiver buffers the parallel port's data lines to Port A on the 82C55. Pin 1 is tied high to set the direction so that data passes from the parallel port to the 82C55. A 72LS244 buffer/driver drives the five status outputs and buffers three of the control inputs. The fourth control input may use any buffer.

Instead of the '245 at the data lines, you can use a second 74LS244, with pins 1 and 19 tied low. I used a '245 because, with just a few wiring changes, I was able to use a similar circuit for the other 82C55 interfaces in this book. Control bits 2 and 3 are unused in the example program, but I included them in case a particular application has a use for them. If you have no use for these bits, you don't have to connect them. On the 82C55, four of Port B's outputs and one of Port C's inputs are unused and available for other uses.

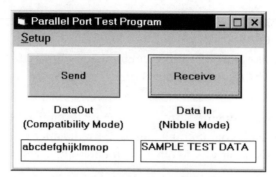

Figure 12-7: The test program allows users to send and receive blocks of 16 bytes. The screen displays the data to send and data received.

Example Program

Figure 12-7 shows the screen for a Visual Basic program that you can use to send and receive data using this circuit. Listing 12-1 shows the program code. The example program illustrates what's involved in transferring blocks of data. You can revise the example to suit a specific application.

The program transfers data in 16-byte blocks. In the example screen, the data displays as text, but it may be control commands, sensor readings, or other information. Arrays store the data to be sent and data received, and command buttons enable you to send or request to receive a block of data.

The PC controls the interface. The default direction for transmissions is from the PC to the peripheral. Clicking the *Send* command button causes 16 bytes to be written to the parallel port. The peripheral reads and stores the bytes. When the link is idle, the peripheral polls Control bit 1. Clicking the *Receive* command button causes the PC to request data from the peripheral by bringing Control bit 1 low. When the peripheral detects the change, it sends a block of data to the PC.

PC-to-Peripheral Transfers

To receive data from the PC, the 82C55 uses its Mode 1, with automatic handshaking. The parallel port's *nStrobe*($\overline{C0}$) output drives the 82C55's Strobe ($\overline{STB}$) input, and the 82C55's Input Buffer Full (*IBF*) output drives the parallel port's *Busy* ($\overline{S7}$) input.

In the example program, the PC reads the characters in the *Send* text box, and writes their ASCII codes in sequence to the port. The program could instead read bytes from an array variable, or from a file. The 8052 stores the received bytes in an array variable.

The PC waits for *Busy* to be low, then writes a byte to *D0-D7* and brings *nStrobe* low, then high. When *nStrobe* goes low, the 82C55 latches the byte at Port A and

```
Dim StatusPortData%
Dim ControlPortData%
Dim TimedOut%
Dim DirectionSet%
Dim DataIn%
Dim LowNibble%
Dim HighNibble%
Dim ReadAnother%
Dim Character$
```

Listing 12-1: Transferring blocks of data using Compatibility and Nibble modes. (Sheet 1 of 7)

```
Sub cmdReadDataFromPort_Click ()
'Read characters from the parallel port.
'Display the received characters on the form.
Dim TextData$
Dim FileLength&
Dim BufferSize%
Dim CharNumber%
CharNumber = 0
TimedOut = False
lblDataInDisplay.Caption = ""
DirectionSet = DirectionRequest("PeripheralToPC")
tmrTimedOut.Enabled = True
If DirectionSet Then
    'Read characters at the port.
    'After each character, read the status port.
    'Stop reading if S3, S5, or S7 =1.
    ReadAnother = True
    Do
     DoEvents
     ReadByteFromPort
     lblDataInDisplay.Caption = lblDataInDisplay.Caption _
       + Chr$(DataIn)
     CharNumber = CharNumber + 1
    Loop Until ReadAnother = False Or TimedOut = True
    'Return to default direction
    DirectionSet = DirectionRequest("PcToPeripheral")
    If Not (TimedOut) Then
     MsgBox "Successful transfer", 0, "Result"
    End If
    CharNumber = 0
    tmrTimedOut.Enabled = False
End If
End Sub
```

Listing 12-1: Transferring blocks of data using Compatibility and Nibble modes. (Sheet 2 of 7)

```
Sub cmdWriteDataToPort_Click ()
Dim CharNumber%
TimedOut = False
tmrTimedOut.Enabled = True
'Write the characters in the text box to the parallel port.
For CharNumber = 1 To 16
    If Not (TimedOut) Then
     'Write each character in sequence
     Character = Mid$(txtDataOut.Text, CharNumber, 1)
     If Character = "" Then Character = " "
     WriteByteToPort
    End If
Next CharNumber
If Not (TimedOut) Then
    MsgBox "Successful transfer", 0, "Result"
End If
tmrTimedOut.Enabled = False
End Sub
```

Listing 12-1: Transferring blocks of data using Compatibility and Nibble modes. (Sheet 3 of 7)

```
Function DirectionRequest% (Direction$)
Dim C1%
Dim S6%
'Control port, bit 1 is the direction control for the data port.
'1=PC-to-peripheral (default), 0=peripheral-to-PC
'The peripheral acknowledges a direction change by setting
'Status bit 6 to match.
Direction = LCase$(Direction)
ControlPortData = ControlPortRead(BaseAddress)
'Set Control port bits to match the selected direction.
Select Case Direction
    Case "pctoperipheral"
     C1 = 1
     BitSet ControlPortData, 1
    Case "peripheraltopc"
     C1 = 0
     BitReset ControlPortData, 1
    Case Else
    End Select
ControlPortWrite BaseAddress, ControlPortData
tmrTimedOut.Enabled = True
'Wait for the peripheral to accept direction change by setting
  S6=C1
Do
    DoEvents
    If TimedOut Then Exit Function
    StatusPortData = StatusPortRead(BaseAddress)
    S6 = BitRead(StatusPortData, 6)
Loop Until S6 = C1 Or TimedOut = True
tmrTimedOut.Enabled = False
If S6 = C1 Then DirectionRequest = True
End Function
```

```
Sub Form_Load ()
'(partial listing)
'Timeout limit for peripheral.
tmrTimedOut.Interval = 5000
tmrTimedOut.Enabled = False
'Set the initial direction.
DirectionSet = DirectionRequest("PcToPeripheral")
End Sub
```

Listing 12-1: Transferring blocks of data using Compatibility and Nibble modes. (Sheet 4 of 7)

```
Sub MakeByteFromNibbles ()
'Get the 8 bits from LowNibble and HighNibble
'and arrange them into a byte.
Dim Bit0%
Dim Bit1%
Dim Bit2%
Dim Bit3%
Dim Bit4%
Dim Bit5%
Dim Bit6%
Dim Bit7%

Bit0 = BitRead(LowNibble, 3)
Bit1 = BitRead(LowNibble, 4) * 2
Bit2 = BitRead(LowNibble, 5) * 4
Bit3 = BitRead(LowNibble, 7) * 8
Bit4 = BitRead(HighNibble, 3) * &H10
Bit5 = BitRead(HighNibble, 4) * &H20
Bit6 = BitRead(HighNibble, 5) * &H40
Bit7 = BitRead(HighNibble, 7) * &H80
DataIn = Bit0 + Bit1 + Bit2 + Bit3 + Bit4 + Bit5 + Bit6 + Bit7
End Sub
```

Listing 12-1: Transferring blocks of data using Compatibility and Nibble modes.
(Sheet 5 of 7)

```
Sub ReadByteFromPort ()
'Read one character from the parallel port
'Uses nibble mode.
Dim S6%
'Read the control port.
ControlPortData = ControlPortRead(BaseAddress)
'When S6=0, read the status port into LowNibble and set C1=1.
Do
    LowNibble = StatusPortRead(BaseAddress)
    S6 = BitRead(LowNibble, 6)
    DoEvents
    If TimedOut Then Exit Sub
Loop Until S6 = 0
BitSet ControlPortData, 1
ControlPortWrite BaseAddress, ControlPortData
'When the peripheral responds by setting S6=1, set C1=0.
Do
    StatusPortData = StatusPortRead(BaseAddress)
    S6 = BitRead(StatusPortData, 6)
    DoEvents
    If TimedOut Then Exit Sub
Loop Until S6 = 1
BitReset ControlPortData, 1
ControlPortWrite BaseAddress, ControlPortData
'When S6=0 again, read the status port into HighNibble
'and set C1=1.
Do
    HighNibble = StatusPortRead(BaseAddress)
    S6 = BitRead(HighNibble, 6)
    DoEvents
    If TimedOut Then Exit Sub
Loop Until S6 = 0
BitSet ControlPortData, 1
ControlPortWrite BaseAddress, ControlPortData
'When the peripheral responds by setting S6=1, set C1=0.
Do
    StatusPortData = StatusPortRead(BaseAddress)
    S6 = BitRead(StatusPortData, 6)
    DoEvents
    If TimedOut Then Exit Sub
Loop Until S6 = 1
BitReset ControlPortData, 1
ControlPortWrite BaseAddress, ControlPortData
```

Listing 12-1: Transferring blocks of data using Compatibility and Nibble modes. (Sheet 6 of 7)

```
MakeByteFromNibbles
'If any of S3 or S5 =1, the transmission is complete.
If (StatusPortData And &H28) > 0 Then ReadAnother = False
End Sub
```

```
Sub tmrTimedOut_Timer ()
TimedOut = True
MsgBox "Peripheral not responding", 0
DirectionSet = DirectionRequest("PcToPeripheral")
tmrTimedOut.Enabled = False
End Sub
```

```
Sub WriteByteToPort ()
'Write one character to the parallel port
'Uses compatibility mode handshaking.
'Wait for S7 (Busy) to be low.
Dim S7%
Do
    StatusPortData = StatusPortRead(BaseAddress)
    S7 = BitRead(StatusPortData, 7)
    DoEvents
    If TimedOut Then Exit Sub
    Loop Until S7 = 0
'Write the character.
If Character = "" Then Character = " "
DataPortWrite BaseAddress, Asc(Character)
'After each write, toggle C0 (nStrobe).
BitReset ControlPortData, 0
ControlPortWrite BaseAddress, ControlPortData
BitSet ControlPortData, 0
ControlPortWrite BaseAddress, ControlPortData
End Sub
```

Listing 12-1: Transferring blocks of data using Compatibility and Nibble modes. (Sheet 7 of 7)

brings Busy high. When *nStrobe* goes high, the 82C55 brings its Port C, bit 3, high to trigger an interrupt (*INT1*) on the 8052. When the 8052 detects *INT1*'s going low, it reads and stores the received byte at Port A on the 82C55. The read operation automatically brings *Busy* low, to signal the PC that the 82C55 is ready for another byte.

Other Programming Considerations

On the 82C55, all of the handshaking is built into the chip, so the only programming required is configuring the chip for the appropriate modes and writing the interrupt-service routine to read the bytes as they arrive. At the PC, the software must do the handshaking (toggling *nStrobe* and checking *Busy*).

If you use a peripheral interface that doesn't have handshaking functions built in, you'll need to program these. If you don't use an interrupt at the microcontroller, you can poll the Control port, watching for a change at $\overline{C0}$, but you must poll it often enough not to miss the brief *nStrobe* pulse.

Compatibility mode requires *Busy* to go high within 10 microseconds after *nStrobe* goes low. If you're programming your own interface on both ends, you don't have to meet this limit, but you do want to be sure that the peripheral reads the byte before the PC has removed it. One way of doing so is to have the PC wait until *Busy* goes high before it brings *nStrobe* high.

The example program doesn't use *nAck* (*S6*), but if you wish, you can program the 82C55's Port B, bit 3, to provide a *nAck* pulse.

Peripheral-to-PC Transfers

The reverse direction is more complicated, because the 82C55 has to break each byte into nibbles and send them to the PC, and the PC has to recombine the received nibbles into bytes on the other end.

Clicking the *Receive* command button causes the PC to request data from the peripheral by bringing $\overline{C1}$ low. When the 82C55 detects the request, it places the lower nibble of the byte to send on *S3-S5* and $\overline{S7}$, then brings *S6* low. The PC reads the nibble and brings $\overline{C1}$ high. To complete the handshake, the 82C55 brings *S6* high, and the PC brings $\overline{C1}$ low. The 82C55 then places the higher nibble on the status lines and the handshake repeats: *S6* goes low, $\overline{C1}$ goes high, *S6* goes high, and $\overline{C1}$ goes low. The 82C55 then sends the next byte.

The 8052 stores the bytes to send in an array variable. The PC displays the values received in the *Receive* text box. The program could also store the data in a file or array variable.

After sending the last byte, the 82C55 brings *S3* and *S5* high to signal the PC that the transmission is complete. Both devices then switch to the default PC-to-peripheral direction, and the 82C55 waits for a strobe pulse that signals received data or a low at $\overline{C1}$ that signals a request to send data.

At the peripheral, the 82C55 doesn't have a Nibble-mode handshake, so the program must provide the handshake signals The 82C55's Port C, bit 5 bit controls $\overline{S7}$ at the parallel port. In Mode 1, this bit indicates input-buffer full. In Nibble mode, *nStrobe* ($\overline{C0}$) must remain high to keep $\overline{S7}$ from falsely detecting a PC-to-peripheral transfer.

When Port A is in Mode 1, there is no way to read Port C, bit 4 ($\overline{STB}$). (Reading this bit instead returns the state of the interrupt-enable flag for the port.) Control bit 0 is unused during Nibble transfers, but in the circuit shown, the bit is routed to Port C, bit 7, where the 8052 can read it if desired.

The example program uses IEEE 1284's Nibble-mode bit assignments, which require some bit-shuffling to rearrange into a byte. If you prefer, you can use bit assignments that are more convenient, and change the software to match.

Detecting Timeouts

One consideration with data transfers like these is providing a way out when the interface hangs—when for some reason, one end of the link stops responding. The programs on both ends should be able to detect when this has occurred, and exit the transfer gracefully.

In the example program, on both ends, if a transfer takes longer than 5 seconds, the program stops trying and returns to the idle, PC-to-peripheral state.

In the Visual Basic program, a `Timer` control watches for timeouts. If the peripheral doesn't respond in 5 seconds, the `Timer` event displays a message and sets the `TimedOut` variable to `True`. The data-transfer routines monitor the `TimedOut` variable, and quit the transfer when `TimedOut` is `True`.

In order for the routines to detect the `TimedOut` condition, every `Do` loop that waits for a response from the peripheral contains one of these:

```
DoEvents
If TimedOut then Exit Sub
```

or

```
DoEvents
Until (condition) or TimedOut
```

The `DoEvents` statement enables Visual Basic to update the `Timer` and perform other system functions while the program is waiting for a response. The `Exit Sub` statement quits the subroutine when the `TimedOut` variable is `True`. If the subroutine needs to continue after the timeout, the `Until` statement in the loop checks the timeout condition and ends the loop if there's no response.

In a similar way, at the peripheral, Basic-52's `Timer` detects timeouts, and an `On Time` routine restarts the program if there is no response from the PC.

Having to test for `Timeout` conditions slows the transfers, but it ensures that the programs will recover if something goes awry. You can adjust the `TimedOut` value to suit your application. You could also add a command button in the `TimedOut` Message Box to allow users to retry the transfer instead of quitting.

13

Byte Mode

Many parallel ports, including PS/2-type, EPPs, and ECPs, have bidirectional data ports. PS/2-type ports, ECP, and many EPPs can use Byte mode for software-controlled, 8-bit peripheral-to-PC transfers, where the peripheral writes a byte at a time to the data port, rather than having to chop every byte into nibbles and write them in sequence to the status port. This chapter describes Byte mode and presents two applications that build on the example in the previous chapter. The first application allows a PC to communicate with a peripheral in Compatibility and Byte modes. The second allows a PC to communicate in Compatibility, Nibble, and Byte modes, and uses IEEE 1284 negotiation to tell the peripheral which mode to use for peripheral-to-PC transfers.

Handshaking

To use Byte Mode, the host must have a bidirectional data port, and the peripheral must be able to write a byte to the data lines. IEEE 1284's Byte mode describes a handshaking protocol for Byte-mode transfers.

Like the Compatibility-mode handshake, the Byte-mode handshake includes a Busy signal to tell the sending device when it's OK to send a byte, and a Strobe signal to tell the receiving device that data is available. The Busy signal is *Host-Busy* ($\overline{C1}$), and the Strobe is *PtrClk* (*S6*).

In Byte mode, after asserting a control signal, the asserting device waits for an acknowledgment from the other device before de-asserting the signal. As a result, the timing requirements aren't stringent, and the transfers can allow generous delays.

If the peripheral isn't IEEE-1284 compliant, the host can't use IEEE-1284 negotiation to select Byte mode, but any device with the required number of signals can use Byte mode to exchange data, as long as both the host and peripheral agree on the mode.

Figure 13-1 shows a timing diagram for Byte transfers. The transfers work like this:

1. The host disables outputs *D0-D7*. On most bidirectional ports, bringing bit *C5* high accomplishes this.

2. The host brings *HostBusy* ($\overline{C1}$) low to indicate that it's ready to receive data.

3. The peripheral places data on *D0-D7* and brings *PtrClk* (*S6*) low.

4. In response to *PtrClk*'s going low, the host reads *D0-D7* and brings *HostBusy* high. The host brings *HostClk* ($\overline{C0}$) low, either at the same time as or after bringing *HostBusy* high.

5. The peripheral sets the status bits as follows:

PtrBusy ($\overline{S7}$), high if the peripheral is busy, low if not busy
nDataAvail (*S3*) low if another byte is ready to be sent, high if no byte ready to send
AckDataReq (*S5*), same as *nDataAvail*
XFlag (*S4*), same as in previous negotiation

6. The peripheral brings *PtrClk* high.

7. The host brings *HostClk* high to indicate that it received the byte. This can occur before or at the same time that *HostBusy* goes low in step 2 of the next transfer. (Toggling both in one port write is quicker.)

After it receives a byte, the host may:

Bring *HostBusy* low and wait for more data.
Leave *HostBusy* high to prevent the peripheral from sending another byte.
Bring *1284Active* low to return to compatibility mode.

Applications

The following two application examples show how to do Byte-mode transfers. As in Chapter 12, the peripheral uses an 82C55 PPI for its parallel-port interface. Both examples do Compatibility and Byte-mode transfers. In the second example,

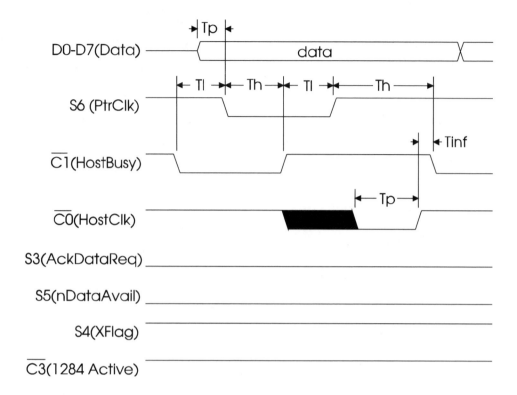

Parameter	minimum	maximum
Td	0	-
Th	0	1 sec.
Tl	0	35 msec.
Tp	0	-
Tinf	0	infinite

Figure 13-1: Timing diagram for a Byte-mode transfer.

the PC negotiates with the peripheral to select Byte or Nibble mode for reverse transfers.

Compatibility & Byte Mode

Figure 13-2 shows a circuit that you can use to transfer bytes in both directions over the data lines.

The PC-to-peripheral transfers use Compatibility-mode handshaking. The peripheral-to-PC transfers use handshaking that is similar to IEEE 1284's Byte mode, with minor differences because the 82C55's built-in handshaking doesn't exactly match the Byte-mode handshake. The next example in this chapter follows the IEEE-1284 Byte-mode interface more closely.

All in all, the exact details of the handshake don't matter, as long as the receiving end can identify when a byte is available and the transmitting end can identify when the peripheral has read a byte sent to it and is ready for another.

Figure 13-2's circuit is very similar to the example in Chapter 12. The differences are:

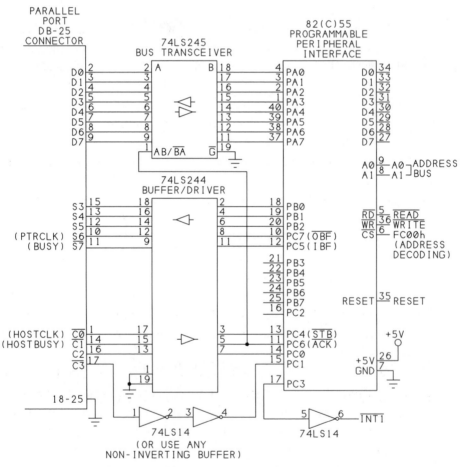

Figure 13-2: This circuit can communicate with a PC in Compatibility or Byte mode.

The 82C55's Port A uses bidirectional mode (Mode 2) instead of input only (Mode 1). As before, two Port C bits provide handshaking for PC-to-peripheral transfers. Two other Port C bits provide handshaking for peripheral-to-PC transfers. *PtrClk* (*S6*) connects to Port C, bit 7. (In the previous circuit, Port C, bit 7 was input, so *S6* connected to Port B, bit 3.)

The 82C55's Port C, bit 6, output controls the direction of the '245 transceiver. In the previous circuit, this bit was tied high, because the PC's data port was output-only.

The PC-to-peripheral transfers are exactly like those in Chapter 12's circuit. The PC writes bytes to its data port, and the 82C55 detects their arrival and stores the received bytes.

An application similar to Chapter 12's transfers blocks of data. Listing 13-1 shows the subroutines and functions that differ. On both ends, the programming for peripheral-to-PC transfers changes from Nibble to Byte mode. When switching between Byte and Compatibility modes, the program code has to switch the direction of the '245 transceiver and the direction of the Data port on both ends at the appropriate times. When using Nibble and Compatibility modes, you don't have to worry about this because the Data lines don't change direction.

The Byte transfers are much simpler than Nibble transfers. Using Figure 13-2's circuit, the 82C55 places a byte on *D0-D7* and brings *PtrClk* (*S6*) low. When the PC detects that *PtrClk* is low, it brings *HostBusy* ($\overline{C1}$) low and reads the byte. The 82C55 responds by bringing *PtrClk* high, and the PC then brings *HostBusy* high to complete the transfer.

As with Compatibility mode, the handshake is automatic at the 82C55. When *HostBusy* goes low, the 82C55 automatically brings *PtrClk* high. When *HostBusy* goes high in response, the 82C55 automatically brings Port C, bit 3 high, which generates an interrupt on the 8052. The 8052's interrupt-service routine writes another byte to Port A, and this automatically brings *PtrClk* low to begin the next transfer.

HostBusy ($\overline{C1}$) also provides the direction-control for the '245. It goes low only during a peripheral-to-PC transfer. To ensure that two drivers aren't enabled at the same time on the same line, the PC's Control port, bit 5, should be set to 0 only after *HostBusy* goes high, returning the '245 to the PC-to-peripheral direction.

The circuit uses $\overline{C3}$ as a direction-control request line. For PC-to-peripheral transfers, $\overline{C3}$ is high. When the PC wants to receive data, it brings $\overline{C3}$ low. The peripheral detects this, and sends a series of bytes to the PC. When the transfer is complete, the peripheral brings *S3* high to indicate the end of the transfer and switches to the PC-to-peripheral direction. The PC detects the direction change, sets $\overline{C3}$ high, and re-enables its data outputs in preparation for a PC-to-peripheral

```
Sub cmdReadDataFromPort_Click ()
'Read characters from the parallel port.
'Display the received characters on the form.
Dim TextData$
Dim FileLength&
Dim BufferSize%
Dim CharNumber%
CharNumber = 0
TimedOut = False
lblDataInDisplay.Caption = ""
tmrTimedOut.Enabled = True
DirectionSet = DirectionRequest("PeripheralToPc")
'Read bytes at the port.
'After each byte, read the status port.
'Stop reading if S3 =1 (indicates end of transmission).
ReadAnother = True
Do Until ReadAnother = False Or TimedOut = True
    DoEvents
    ReadByteFromPort
    lblDataInDisplay.Caption = _
     lblDataInDisplay.Caption + Chr$(DataIn)
    CharNumber = CharNumber + 1
Loop
    If Not (TimedOut) Then
     MsgBox "Successful transfer", 0, "Result"
    End If
CharNumber = 0
tmrTimedOut.Enabled = False
'Re-enable the data outputs.
DirectionSet = DirectionRequest("PcToPeripheral")
End Sub
```

Listing 13-1: Byte-mode transfers data from a peripheral to a PC. (Sheet 1 of 3)

```
Function DirectionRequest% (Direction$)
Dim S3%
Dim C3%
Direction = LCase$(Direction)
ControlPortData = ControlPortRead(BaseAddress)
BitSet ControlPortData, 1
'Set Control port bits to match the selected direction.
'For control bit 5,
'0 enables the data outputs, 1 tristates the outputs.
Select Case Direction
    Case "pctoperipheral"
     BitSet ControlPortData, 0
     BitSet ControlPortData, 3
     BitReset ControlPortData, 5
     C3 = 1
    Case "peripheraltopc"
     BitReset ControlPortData, 0
     BitReset ControlPortData, 3
     BitSet ControlPortData, 5
     C3 = 0
    Case Else
    End Select
ControlPortWrite BaseAddress, ControlPortData
tmrTimedOut.Enabled = True
Do
    StatusPortData = StatusPortRead(BaseAddress)
    S3 = BitRead(StatusPortData, 3)
    DoEvents
    If TimedOut Then Exit Function
Loop Until C3 = S3
If C3 = S3 Then tmrTimedOut.Enabled = False
End Function
```

Listing 13-1: Byte-mode transfers data from a peripheral to a PC. (Sheet 2 of 3)

```
Sub ReadByteFromPort ()
'Read one character from the parallel port
'Similar to byte mode, but slightly different
'handshake to accommodate the 82C55's Mode 2.
Dim S6%
Dim S3%
Dim DataPortData%
'Read the control port.
ControlPortData = ControlPortRead(BaseAddress)
'Wait for S6=0.
Do
    StatusPortData = StatusPortRead(BaseAddress)
    S6 = BitRead(StatusPortData, 6)
    DoEvents
    If TimedOut Then Exit Sub
Loop Until S6 = 0
'C1=0 enables data outputs
BitReset ControlPortData, 1
ControlPortWrite BaseAddress, ControlPortData
'Read the byte
DataIn = DataPortRead(BaseAddress)
'When the peripheral responds with S6=1, set C1=1.
Do
    StatusPortData = StatusPortRead(BaseAddress)
    S6 = BitRead(StatusPortData, 6)
    DoEvents
    If TimedOut Then Exit Sub
Loop Until S6 = 1
BitSet ControlPortData, 1
ControlPortWrite BaseAddress, ControlPortData
'If S3 =1, the transmission is complete.
StatusPortData = StatusPortRead(BaseAddress)
If (StatusPortData And 8) > 0 Then
    ReadAnother = False
End If
End Sub
```

Listing 13-1: Byte-mode transfers data from a peripheral to a PC. (Sheet 3 of 3)

transfer. The direction line also tells the 8052 which interrupt-service routine to use. When $\overline{C3}$ is high, an interrupt causes the 8052 to read a byte at Port A, and when $\overline{C3}$ is low, an interrupt causes the 8052 to write a byte to Port A.

The IEEE 1284's Byte mode differs from the above interface in a couple of respects. In an IEEE 1284 Byte-mode transfer:

HostBusy's polarity is the reverse. *HostBusy* is low to begin a transfer, and high after reading the data.

An additional control signal, *HostClk* ($\overline{C0}$), is an *Ack* signal. It goes high, then low, after *PtrClk* returns high, to indicate that the byte was received. In the 82C55's handshake, instead of using *HostClk*, *HostBusy*'s going high after *Ptr-Clk* goes high tells the 82C55 that the PC has received the byte.

Compatibility, Nibble & Byte Mode with Negotiating

A final example enables an 82C55 to do Compatibility, Nibble, and Byte-mode transfers. For reverse (peripheral-to-PC) transfers, the PC determines whether or not its port can do Byte-mode transfers, and uses IEEE 1284 negotiating to request the appropriate mode from the peripheral.

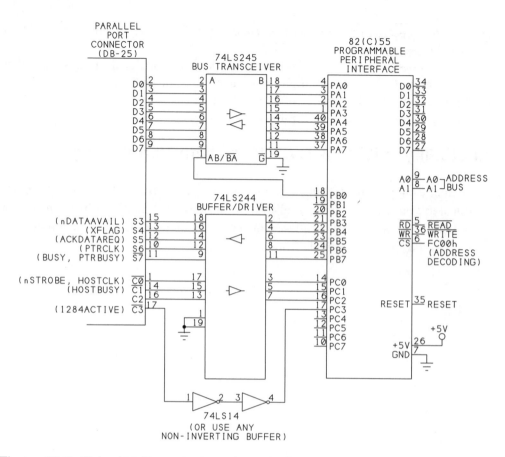

Figure 13-3: This circuit can communicate in Compatibility, Nibble, and Byte modes.

Figure 13-3 shows the circuit. All of the 82C55's ports use Mode 0 (simple I/O), with no built-in handshaking, so program code must control and read all of the handshaking signals at the peripheral. Port A switches from input to output as needed. Port B's bits 3-7 correspond to the Status Ports bits 3-7, and Port C's bits 0-3 correspond to the Control Port's bits 0-3. Port B, bit 0, controls the direction of the '245 transceiver. Two of Port B's outputs and the upper nibble of Port C are free for other uses.

The program for the circuit uses IEEE 1284's protocols for Compatibility, Nibble, and Byte modes, and negotiating a mode. The only difference is that due to the slowness of the Basic-52 program controlling the 82C55, Busy ($\overline{S7}$) may not go high within 10 microseconds after *nStrobe* ($\overline{C0}$) goes low. To ensure that each byte is transferred, the PC holds *nStrobe* low until *Busy* goes high. Listing 13-2 shows the PC's program code, where it differs from Listing 13-1's code.

```
Sub cmdReadDataFromPort_Click ()
'Read characters from the parallel port.
'Display the received characters on the form.
Dim CharNumber%
Dim RequestedMode$
Dim SuccessfulNegotiation%
CharNumber = 0
Timedout = False
lblDataInDisplay.Caption = ""
'Tell the peripheral which mode to use.
Select Case Port(IndexOfSelectedPort).PortType
    Case "SPP"
     RequestedMode = "NibbleMode"
     lblReceiveMode.Caption = "(Nibble Mode)"
    Case Else
     RequestedMode = "ByteMode"
     lblReceiveMode.Caption = "(Byte Mode)"
End Select
SuccessfulNegotiation = Negotiate(RequestedMode)
If SuccessfulNegotiation Then
    tmrTimedOut.Enabled = True
    'Read characters at the port.
    ReadAnother = True
    Do
     DoEvents
     ReadByteFromPort (RequestedMode)
     lblDataInDisplay.Caption = lblDataInDisplay.Caption _
      + Chr$(DataIn)
     CharNumber = CharNumber + 1
    Loop Until ReadAnother = False Or Timedout = True
    If Not (Timedout) Then
     MsgBox "Successful transfer", 0
    End If
    CharNumber = 0
    tmrTimedOut.Enabled = False
Else
    MsgBox "Failed negotiation", 0
End If
ReturnToCompatibilityMode
End Sub
```

Listing 13-2: Program code for the PC in Compatibility, Nibble, and Byte modes, with negotiating. (Sheet 1 of 7)

```
Sub cmdWriteDataToPort_Click ()
Dim CharNumber%
Timedout = False
tmrTimedOut.Enabled = True
'Write the characters in the text box to the parallel port.
For CharNumber = 1 To 16
    If Not (Timedout) Then
     'Write each character in sequence
     Character = Mid$(txtDataOut.Text, CharNumber, 1)
     If Character = "" Then Character = " "
     WriteByteToPort
    End If
Next CharNumber
If Not (Timedout) Then
    MsgBox "Successful transfer", 0
End If
tmrTimedOut.Enabled = False
End Sub
```

Listing 13-2: Program code for the PC in Compatibility, Nibble, and Byte modes, with negotiating. (Sheet 2 of 7)

```
Function Negotiate (RequestedMode$)
Dim ExtensibilityByte%, S4%
Select Case RequestedMode
    Case "NibbleMode"
     ExtensibilityByte = 0
    Case "ByteMode"
     ExtensibilityByte = 1
    End Select
ControlPortData = ControlPortRead(BaseAddress)
DataPortWrite BaseAddress, ExtensibilityByte
BitSet ControlPortData, 3
BitSet ControlPortData, 0
BitReset ControlPortData, 1
ControlPortWrite BaseAddress, ControlPortData
tmrTimedOut.Enabled = True
'Wait for S3=1, S4=1, S5=1, S6=0.
Do
    DoEvents
    StatusPortData = StatusPortRead(BaseAddress)
Loop Until ((StatusPortData And &H78) = &H38) Or Timedout
S4 = BitRead(StatusPortData, 4)
If S4 = 1 Then
    Negotiate = True
Else
    Negotiate = False
End If
'Peripheral latches the byte.
BitReset ControlPortData, 0
ControlPortWrite BaseAddress, ControlPortData
BitSet ControlPortData, 0
BitSet ControlPortData, 1
ControlPortWrite BaseAddress, ControlPortData
'Wait for S3=0, S5=0, S6=1.
Do
DoEvents
    StatusPortData = StatusPortRead(BaseAddress)
Loop Until ((StatusPortData And &H68) = &H40) Or Timedout
'If using Byte mode, disable the data outputs.
If RequestedMode = "ByteMode" Then
    BitSet ControlPortData, 5
    ControlPortWrite BaseAddress, ControlPortData
End If
tmrTimedOut.Enabled = False
End Function
```

Listing 13-2: Program code for the PC in Compatibility, Nibble, and Byte modes, with negotiating. (Sheet 3 of 7)

```
Sub ByteModeTransfer
     BitSet ControlPortData, 0
     BitReset ControlPortData, 1
     ControlPortWrite BaseAddress, ControlPortData
     'When S6=0, read the data port and set control bits.
     Do
          StatusPortData = StatusPortRead(BaseAddress)
          S6 = BitRead(StatusPortData, 6)
          DoEvents
          If Timedout Then Exit Sub
     Loop Until S6 = 0
     DataIn = DataPortRead(BaseAddress)
     BitReset ControlPortData, 0
     BitSet ControlPortData, 1
     ControlPortWrite BaseAddress, ControlPortData
     'Wait for peripheral to respond by setting S6=1.
     Do
          StatusPortData = StatusPortRead(BaseAddress)
          S6 = BitRead(StatusPortData, 6)
          DoEvents
          If Timedout Then Exit Sub
     Loop Until S6 = 1
     BitReset ControlPortData, 1
     ControlPortWrite BaseAddress, ControlPortData
     'If S3 =1, the transmission is complete.
     If (StatusPortData And 8) > 0 Then
          ReadAnother = False
          BitSet ControlPortData, 0
          ControlPortWrite BaseAddress, ControlPortData
     End If
End Sub
```

Listing 13-2: Program code for the PC in Compatibility, Nibble, and Byte modes, with negotiating. (Sheet 4 of 7)

```
Sub NibbleModeTransfer
    'When S6=0, read the status port into LowNibble and set C1=1.
    BitReset ControlPortData, 1
    Do
        LowNibble = StatusPortRead(BaseAddress)
        S6 = BitRead(LowNibble, 6)
        DoEvents
        If Timedout Then Exit Sub
    Loop Until S6 = 0
    BitSet ControlPortData, 1
    ControlPortWrite BaseAddress, ControlPortData
    'When the peripheral responds by setting S6=1, set C1=0.
    Do
        StatusPortData = StatusPortRead(BaseAddress)
        S6 = BitRead(StatusPortData, 6)
        DoEvents
        If Timedout Then Exit Sub
    Loop Until S6 = 1
    BitReset ControlPortData, 1
    ControlPortWrite BaseAddress, ControlPortData
    'When S6=0 again, read the status port into HighNibble
    'and set C1=1.
    Do
        HighNibble = StatusPortRead(BaseAddress)
        S6 = BitRead(HighNibble, 6)
        DoEvents
        If Timedout Then Exit Sub
    Loop Until S6 = 0
    BitSet ControlPortData, 1
    ControlPortWrite BaseAddress, ControlPortData
    'When the peripheral responds by setting S6=1, set C1=0.
    Do
        StatusPortData = StatusPortRead(BaseAddress)
        S6 = BitRead(StatusPortData, 6)
        DoEvents
        If Timedout Then Exit Sub
    Loop Until S6 = 1
    BitReset ControlPortData, 1
    ControlPortWrite BaseAddress, ControlPortData
    MakeByteFromNibbles
    'If any of S3 or S5 =1, the transmission is complete.
    If (StatusPortData And &H8) > 0 Then ReadAnother = False
End Sub
```

Listing 13-2: Program code for the PC in Compatibility, Nibble, and Byte modes, with negotiating. (Sheet 5 of 7)

```
Sub ReadByteFromPort (RequestedMode$)
'Read one character from the parallel port
'Uses nibble or byte mode.
Dim S6%
ControlPortData = ControlPortRead(BaseAddress)
Select Case RequestedMode
    Case "NibbleMode"
        NibbleModeTransfer
    Case "ByteMode"
        ByteModeTransfer
End Select
End Sub
```

```
Sub ReturnToCompatibilityMode ()
Dim S6%
BitSet ControlPortData, 0
BitSet ControlPortData, 1
BitReset ControlPortData, 3
ControlPortWrite BaseAddress, ControlPortData
tmrTimedOut.Enabled = True
'Wait for S3=1, S4=1, S6=0, S7=1.
Do
    DoEvents
    StatusPortData = StatusPortRead(BaseAddress)
    Loop Until ((StatusPortData And &HD8) = &H98) Or Timedout
BitReset ControlPortData, 1
ControlPortWrite BaseAddress, ControlPortData
Do
    DoEvents
    StatusPortData = StatusPortRead(BaseAddress)
    S6 = BitRead(StatusPortData, 6)
Loop Until (S6 = 1) Or Timedout
BitSet ControlPortData, 1
'Re-enable the data outputs
BitReset ControlPortData, 5
ControlPortWrite BaseAddress, ControlPortData
tmrTimedOut.Enabled = False
End Sub
```

Listing 13-2: Program code for the PC in Compatibility, Nibble, and Byte modes, with negotiating. (Sheet 6 of 7)

```
Sub tmrTimedOut_Timer ()
Timedout = True
MsgBox "Peripheral not responding", 0
tmrTimedOut.Enabled = False
ReturnToCompatibilityMode
End Sub
```

```
Sub WriteByteToPort ()
'Write one character to the parallel port
'Uses compatibility mode handshaking.
Dim S7%
'Wait for S7 (Busy) to be low.
Do
    StatusPortData = StatusPortRead(BaseAddress)
    S7 = BitRead(StatusPortData, 7)
    DoEvents
    If Timedout Then Exit Sub
    Loop Until S7 = 0
'Write the character.
If Character = "" Then Character = " "
DataPortWrite BaseAddress, Asc(Character)
'Complete the handshake.
BitReset ControlPortData, 0
ControlPortWrite BaseAddress, ControlPortData
Do
    StatusPortData = StatusPortRead(BaseAddress)
    S7 = BitRead(StatusPortData, 7)
    DoEvents
    If Timedout Then Exit Sub
    Loop Until S7 = 1
BitSet ControlPortData, 0
ControlPortWrite BaseAddress, ControlPortData
End Sub
```

Listing 13-2: Program code for the PC in Compatibility, Nibble, and Byte modes, with negotiating. (Sheet 7 of 7)

14

Enhanced Parallel Port: EPP

An Enhanced Parallel Port (EPP) can transfer data at high speeds in both directions. An EPP can distinguish between two types of information, usually defined as data and addresses. Because it can switch directions quickly, EPP is useful for devices that exchange smaller blocks of data with frequent direction switches, such as external disk drives or network interfaces.

Inside the EPP

An EPP can read or write a byte of data in one ISA-bus cycle, or about 1 microsecond, including handshaking. The data lines are bidirectional, and a single control signal determines the direction of the data port. Two other control signals distinguish between address and data information on the data lines.

Intel's 82360SL I/O Subsystem is an early chip that contained an EPP. The chip includes many peripheral functions besides the parallel port, and was used in many laptop computers that used Intel's 80386SL and 80486SL microprocessors.

EPP transfers differ from Compatibility, Nibble, and Byte transfers in that the port's hardware automatically generates control signals and detects responses from the opposite end. There's no need for software instructions to toggle a strobe output or read a busy input. The hardware handshaking enables an EPP to read or write a byte, with handshaking, in one ISA-bus cycle, instead of the four cycles required in Compatibility or Byte mode.

Two Strobes

The EPP's data and address operations use different control signals to latch the bytes into the receiving device. Address reads and writes use *nAStrobe* ($\overline{C3}$), while data reads and writes use *nDStrobe* ($\overline{C1}$). This provides a simple way for the receiving device to distinguish between two types of information.

For example, the sending device might write an address to the receiving device, then write one or more data bytes. The receiving device could then store the received data in a block of memory beginning at the received address.

The IEEE 1284 standard doesn't document all aspects of the EPP. The standard doesn't mention features that are specific to PCs, such as the signals and timing on the expansion bus and the additional register assignments for the port. Other documents, including the data sheets for the controller chips, describe conventions for these.

The Registers

An EPP uses eight registers, five more than the original parallel port. Table 14-1 shows the registers and their functions.

The first three registers are nearly identical to the Data, Status, and Control registers in an SPP. One difference is that in the Status port, bit 0 usually indicates a timeout on an EPP cycle. Some EPPs also emulate PS/2-type ports, where setting Control bit 5 to 1 disables the data outputs and enables using the data lines for simple input. On other EPPs, the Data lines are output-only (SPP type), except when doing EPP transfers.

For EPP transfers, the port uses additional registers. To write a data byte in EPP mode, you write to the EPP Data register (at *base address + 4*) rather than to the base address. Writing to the EPP data register causes the port to initiate a complete data-write cycle. The port's hardware places the byte to write on *D0–D7*, and the port automatically toggles the handshaking signals and detects the peripheral's responses. In a similar way, reading a byte from the EPP Data register initiates a complete data-read cycle at the port.

Address transfers are much the same, except that you write to or read the EPP Address register (at *base address + 3*), which causes the port to initiate a complete

Table 14-1: The EPP's eight registers and their functions.

Register Name	Offset	Use
SPP/PS2 Data	0	Read or write to data lines, no handshaking
SPP Status	1	Read 5 status lines (S3-S7). In EPP mode, an additional bit (0) indicates timeout
SPP Control	2	Read or write to 4 control lines (C0-C3); also contains configuration bits for interrupt enabling (C4) and byte-mode direction control (C5).
EPP Address	3	Read or write to data lines, with handshaking, address cycle
EPP Data	4	Read or write to data lines, with handshaking, data cycle
(varies)	5	May be used for 16/32-bit data transfers, port configuration, or user-defined
(varies)	6	May be used for 16/32-bit data transfers, port configuration, or user-defined
(varies)	7	May be used for 16/32-bit data transfers, port configuration, or user-defined

address-write or address-read cycle. These are identical to the EPP data cycles except that they use a different control signal to transfer the byte into the receiving device.

The function of the registers at *base address + 5* through *base address + 7* vary. On some ports, you can use 16- or 32-bit read or write operations to access the port, and these registers will hold the additional byte or bytes written or read, with the port transferring each byte in sequence.

The base address of an EPP is normally 378h or 278h, with the port using the address range 378h–37Fh or 278h–27Fh. EPPs normally don't use the base address 3BCh, because the video display may use the bytes following 3BEh.

Handshaking

EPP mode supports four operations: address write, data write, address read, and data read. Each has a different handshake.

Four Types of Transfers

On many ports, before accessing the EPP registers and initiating a transfer, Control port bits $\overline{C0}$, $\overline{C1}$, and $\overline{C3}$ must be high. (Remember that the port hardware inverts these bits, so to bring them high, you write 0 to the corresponding register bits.)

Table 14-2 has the timing limits for the signals in the timing diagrams that follow. These are the steps in the four types of EPP transfers described in IEEE 1284:

Address write (forward transfer)

Figure 14-1 shows the signals for an address-write cycle.

1. The peripheral's data outputs are disabled and *nWait* ($\overline{S7}$) is low. The host brings *nWrite* ($\overline{C0}$) low, writes an address to the EPP Address register, which causes the byte to appear on *D0–D7*, and brings *nAStrobe* ($\overline{C3}$) low.

3. The peripheral brings *nWait* high to signal that it's ready to latch the address.

4. The host brings *nAStrobe* high to cause the peripheral to latch the address.

5. When the peripheral is ready for another byte, it brings *nWait* low.

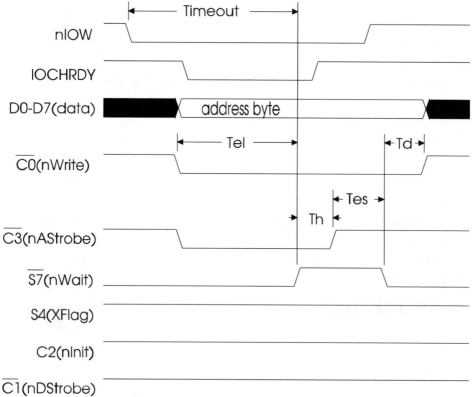

Figure 14-1: An EPP address-write cycle.

Table 14-2: Timing limits for EPP transfers.

Parameter	minimum	maximum
Timeout	0	10 μsec.
Tel	0	10 μsec.
Th	0	1 sec.
Tes	0	125 nanosec.
Td	0	-

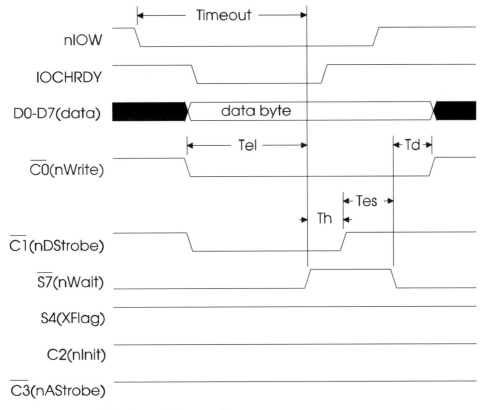

Figure 14-2: An EPP Data Write cycle.

Data write (forward transfer)

Data writes are identical to address writes, except that the host uses *nDStrobe* instead of *nAStrobe*. Figure 14-2 illustrates.

1. The peripheral's data outputs are disabled and *nWait* is low. The host brings *nWrite* low, writes data to the EPP Data register, which causes the byte to appear on *D0–D7,* and brings *nDStrobe* ($\overline{C1}$) low.

3. The peripheral brings *nWait* high to signal that it's ready to latch the data.

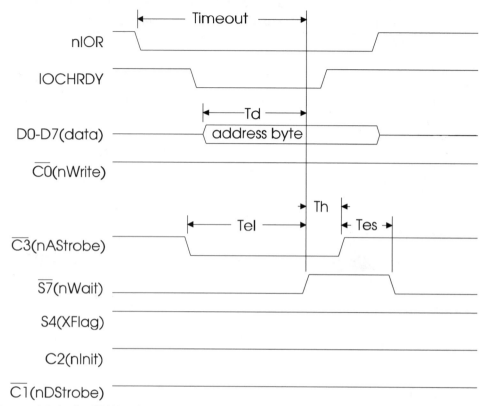

Figure 14-3: An EPP address-read cycle.

4. The host brings *nDStrobe* high to cause the peripheral to latch the data.

5. When the peripheral is ready for another byte, it brings *nWait* low.

Address read (reverse transfer)

For an address-read cycle, the host uses *nAStrobe* as in an address write, but reads the EPP Address register instead of writing to it. Figure 14-3 illustrates.

1. The peripheral's *nWait* is low. The host brings *nWrite* high, disables outputs *D0–D7*, and brings *nAStrobe* low.

3. The peripheral enables its *D0–D7* outputs, writes an address to them, and brings *nWait* high to signal the host that the address is available to be read.

4. The host reads *D0–D7* at the EPP Address register and brings *nAStrobe* high.

5. The peripheral disables outputs *D0–D7* and brings *nWait* low.

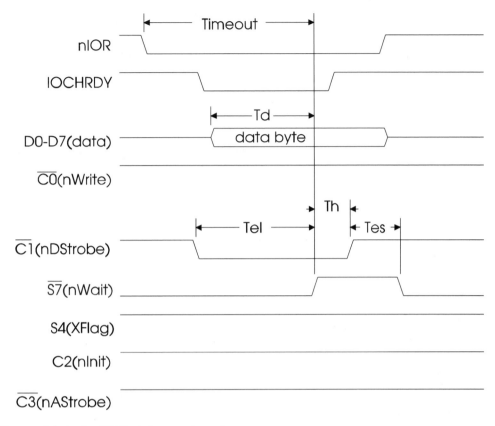

Figure 14-4: An EPP data-read cycle.

Data read (reverse transfer)

Data reads are identical to address reads, except that the host uses *nDStrobe* instead of nAStrobe. Figure 14-4 illustrates.

1. The peripheral's *nWait* must be low. The host brings *nWrite* high, disables outputs *D0–D7,* and brings *nDStrobe* low.

3. The peripheral enables its *D0–D7* outputs, writes data to them, and brings *nWait* high to signal the host that the data is available to be read.

4. The host reads *D0–D7* at the EPP Data register and brings *nDStrobe* high.

5. The peripheral disables outputs *D0–D7* and brings *nWait* low.

Switching Directions

In EPP mode, changing direction doesn't require any special negotiating. You can mix read and write cycles without extra steps to set the direction. When *nWrite* is low, the peripheral must immediately disable its *D0–D7* outputs so the host can write to the peripheral, and the peripheral must respond to the host's strobe by reading *D0–D7*. Whenever *nWrite* is high, the host must immediately disable its data outputs so the peripheral can write to the host, and the peripheral must respond to the strobe signal by writing to *D0–D7*.

If you're designing your own peripheral interface and your hardware doesn't support automatic direction switching, you can use otherwise unused lines or software commands to control the direction. The result won't be a fully standard EPP interface, but you can still use EPP mode for the transfers.

Although IEEE 1284 doesn't specify it as a requirement, the PC's EPP hardware automatically toggles the *nAStrobe* or *nDStrobe* output, enables or disables the data outputs when appropriate, and monitors the *nWait* input to see if the peripheral is ready for a new transfer. There's no need to do any of these in software.

Timing Considerations

The minimum time specifications for EPP transfers are very short, so EPP transfers can be very fast. The only restriction on the width of *nAStrobe* and *nDStrobe* is that they are wide enough that the receiving device can detect them. On a PC, a complete EPP transfer can take place within one I/O cycle on the ISA bus, so port accesses can take place at bus speeds, or around 1 Megahertz on most systems. If necessary, an EPP transfer can take much longer, however. The timing specifications allow the *nDStrobe* and *nAStrobe* pulses to be as long as 1 second.

An important timing limit is that the peripheral must bring *nWait* high within 10 microseconds after *nDstrobe* or *nAStrobe* goes low. If *nWait* doesn't go high within the time allowed, the timeout bit (*S0*, or Status port bit 0) will be set to 1 and the transfer will abort.

The reason for this timing constraint is that, unlike simple port reads and writes, in an EPP transfer, the system bus's I/O read or write cycle won't complete until *nWait* has gone high. The cycle must complete within 15 microseconds to allow memory refresh. Other system resources may be waiting to access the system bus as well.

Simple port reads or writes in SPP or PS/2 mode don't have this constraint. The CPU pulses $\overline{IOR}$ (I/O Read) or $\overline{IOW}$ (I/O Write) low briefly and the operation completes in one bus cycle, without concerning itself with whether or not the transfer with the peripheral completes.

In an EPP read or write, when $\overline{IOR}$ or $\overline{IOW}$ goes low, the EPP's hardware brings the system bus's *IOCHRDY* (I/O Channel Ready) line low. This causes the CPU to hold $\overline{IOR}$ or $\overline{IOW}$ low. The EPP brings *IOCHRDY* high when the EPP's *nWait* input goes high, or if a timeout occurs before *nWait* goes high. Only then does $\overline{IOR}$ or $\overline{IOW}$ return high to complete the cycle, freeing the system bus for use by other components. If Status bit 0 is low when the cycle ends, the transfer was a success.

If you're designing your own peripheral circuits, to prevent timeouts, a falling edge on a strobe input must cause the peripheral to bring *nWait* high within 10 microseconds!

IEEE 1284 says that the peripheral may use its *Intr* (*S6*, or Status bit 6) output to interrupt the host. However, it doesn't specify a protocol for using interrupts, so this is left to the programmer. You could use the interrupt line to signal the PC to read an incoming byte, or write the next byte to the peripheral.

EPP Variations

Among EPPs, there are variations in the timing of data transfers in the PC's I/O cycle, in how to clear the timeout bit, and in the use of the direction bit in the Control register.

Use of *nWait*

One variation in EPPs is the result of a difference between IEEE 1284's EPP protocol and the original EPP as implemented in Intel's 82360SL chip. The original type is sometimes called type *EPP 1.7*, while ports compatible with IEEE-1284's signaling are type *EPP 1.9*. Many newer EPPs can emulate either.

The types differ in their use of *nWait*. An EPP 1.7 host doesn't wait for *nWait* to be low before it brings *nAStrobe* or *nDStrobe* low. If *nWait* is high when the strobe goes low, *IOCHRDY* won't go low and the transfer will complete in one bus cycle, without waiting for the peripheral to bring *nWait* high, and the timeout bit won't be set. Because of this, an EPP 1.7 peripheral should ensure that *nWait* returns low before *nDataStrobe* or *nAddressStrobe* goes low to begin the next transfer, or the peripheral should be able to detect the strobe even if *nWait* is high. Otherwise, the host may think it executed a successful EPP read or write cycle, when in fact the peripheral wasn't ready.

The timing constraint is also slightly tighter for EPP 1.7, with timeouts determined by the width of the $\overline{IOW}$ or $\overline{IOR}$ pulse, rather than by the time between $\overline{IOW}$ or $\overline{IOR}$'s going low and *nWait*'s going high.

If you're having trouble with EPP transfers, and your controller chip supports both EPP types, switching to the other EPP type might help. When there is a choice, type 1.9 is usually the default.

Clearing Timeouts

IEEE 1284 doesn't specify it, but Status bit 0 usually is a timeout bit that indicates a failed EPP transfer. Unfortunately, the method for clearing the timeout bit varies with the controller chip. On SMC's '665 and '666 Super I/O controllers, you clear *S0* by writing 1 to it. Writing 0 to *S0* has no effect. On National Semiconductor's Super I/O, after reading 1 at bit 0, another read of the Status register clears the bit. If an application is going to run on many different systems, or if you're not sure of which method to use, you can do both: write 1 to the timeout bit, then read it again. You might also write 0 to the bit to attempt to clear it, in case any chips use the conventional method of clearing a bit!

Clearing the timeout bit is essential. On SMC's '665 and '666 (and possibly other chips), a set timeout bit will block all reads and writes to the port, in any mode, until the bit is cleared either by software or a system reset.

IEEE 1284 specifies that the peripheral should bring *nWait* low within 125 nanoseconds after *nDStrobe* or *nAStrobe* returns high. If a peripheral may take longer and the host is EPP type 1.7, the host's software should check *nWait* before beginning a read or write cycle.

Direction Control

Some EPPs allow both automatic and software control of Control bit 5. As in PS/2 mode, when Control bit 5 is 0, the Data outputs are enabled, and when it's 1, the Data outputs are tristated and the host can read external signals on the Data lines.

SMC's Super I/O toggles its direction bit (Control port bit 5, *C5*, or PDir) automatically, and *C5* should be *0* before beginning an EPP transfer. During EPP cycles, the chip brings *C5* low whenever *nWrite* is low and the data outputs are enabled.

National's Super I/O supports automatic direction control (the default), and also includes a configuration bit that allows the software to control *C5*. Under software control, the program must bring *C5* low before a write cycle, and high before a read cycle. Using software control, when *C5*=0, you can write to an EPP register and read back what you've written without causing a complete EPP read cycle. When *C5*=1, you can read an EPP register without causing a complete EPP write cycle. This offers a way of testing for the presence of the EPP registers without

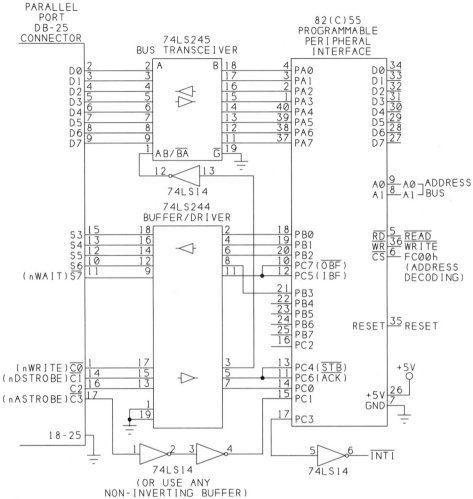

Figure 14-5: Circuit for performing EPP transfers.

having anything connected to the port. But because other port controllers don't include this ability, it's of limited general use.

An EPP Application

Figure 14-5 shows a circuit that can use EPP mode to exchange data with a micro-controller. As in the previous examples, an 82C55 interfaces the microcontroller to the parallel port. Listing 14-1 is excerpts from program code that transfers blocks of 16 bytes using EPP data writes and reads.

```
Dim StatusPortData%
Dim ControlPortData%
Dim TimedOut%
Dim DirectionSet%
Dim DataIn%
Dim LowNibble%
Dim HighNibble%
Dim ReadAnother%
Dim Character$
```

```
Sub cmdReadDataFromPort_Click ()
'Read characters from the parallel port.
'Display the received characters on the form.
Dim CharNumber%
CharNumber = 0
TimedOut = False
lblDataInDisplay.Caption = ""
DirectionSet = DirectionRequest("PeripheralToPc")
tmrTimedOut.Enabled = True

'Read bytes at the port.
'After each byte, read the status port.
'Stop reading if S3 =1 (indicates end of transmission)
ReadAnother = True
Do Until ReadAnother = False Or TimedOut = True
    DoEvents
    ReadByteFromPort
    lblDataInDisplay.Caption = _
     lblDataInDisplay.Caption + Chr$(DataIn)
    CharNumber = CharNumber + 1
Loop
    If Not (TimedOut) Then
     MsgBox "Successful transfer", 0, "Result"
    End If
CharNumber = 0
tmrTimedOut.Enabled = False
'Re-enable the data outputs.
DirectionSet = DirectionRequest("PcToPeripheral")
End Sub
```

Listing 14-1: Transferring blocks of 16 bytes using EPP data reads and writes.
(Sheet 1 of 5)

```
Sub cmdWriteDataToPort_Click ()
Dim CharNumber%
TimedOut = False
tmrTimedOut.Enabled = True
ControlPortData = ControlPortRead(BaseAddress)
BitSet ControlPortData, 1
ControlPortWrite ControlPortData, BaseAddress
'Write the characters in the text box to the parallel port.
For CharNumber = 1 To 16
    If Not (TimedOut) Then
     'Write each character in sequence
     Character = Mid$(txtDataOut.Text, CharNumber, 1)
     If Character = "" Then Character = " "
     WriteByteToPort
    End If
Next CharNumber
If Not (TimedOut) Then
    MsgBox "Successful transfer", 0, "Result"
End If
tmrTimedOut.Enabled = False
End Sub
```

Listing 14-1: Transferring blocks of 16 bytes using EPP data reads and writes.
(Sheet 2 of 5)

```
Function DirectionRequest% (Direction$)
Dim S3%
Dim C3%
Direction = LCase$(Direction)
ControlPortData = ControlPortRead(BaseAddress)
BitSet ControlPortData, 1
'Set Control port bits to match the selected direction.
'For control bit 5,
'0 enables the data outputs, 1 tristates the outputs.
Select Case Direction
    Case "pctoperipheral"
     BitSet ControlPortData, 3
     BitReset ControlPortData, 5
     C3 = 1
    Case "peripheraltopc"
     BitReset ControlPortData, 3
     BitSet ControlPortData, 5
     C3 = 0
    Case Else
    End Select
ControlPortWrite BaseAddress, ControlPortData
tmrTimedOut.Enabled = True
Do
    'Wait for the peripheral to acknowledge the
    'direction change.
    StatusPortData = StatusPortRead(BaseAddress)
    S3 = BitRead(StatusPortData, 3)
    DoEvents
    If TimedOut Then Exit Function
Loop Until C3 = S3
If C3 = S3 Then tmrTimedOut.Enabled = False
End Function
```

```
Sub Form_Load ()
Startup
DirectionSet = DirectionRequest("PcToPeripheral")
'Timeout limit for peripheral.
tmrTimedOut.Interval = 5000
tmrTimedOut.Enabled = False
EPPDataPort0Address = BaseAddress + 4
'Initial test data
txtDataOut.Text = "0123456789ABCDEF"
End Sub
```

Listing 14-1: Transferring blocks of 16 bytes using EPP data reads and writes.
(Sheet 3 of 5)

```
Sub ReadByteFromPort ()
'Read one character from the parallel port.
'Uses EPP mode.
Dim S7%
Dim S3%
Dim DataPortData%
'Wait for S7=0.
Do
    StatusPortData = StatusPortRead(BaseAddress)
    S7 = BitRead(StatusPortData, 7)
    If ReadEppTimeoutBit(BaseAddress) = 1 Then
     tmrTimedOut_Timer
    End If
    DoEvents
    If TimedOut Then Exit Sub
Loop Until S7 = 0
'Read the byte
DataIn = DataPortRead(EPPDataPort0Address)

'Check the timeout bit.
'If it's set, clear it and display the timeout message.
Dim ByteTimeout%
ByteTimeout = ReadEppTimeoutBit(BaseAddress)
If ByteTimeout = 1 Then
    tmrTimedOut_Timer
End If

'If S3 =1, the transmission is complete.
StatusPortData = StatusPortRead(BaseAddress)
If (StatusPortData And 8) > 0 Then
    ReadAnother = False
End If
End Sub
```

```
Sub tmrTimedOut_Timer ()
'On timeout, display a message and switch
'direction to PC-to-peripheral.
TimedOut = True
MsgBox "Peripheral not responding", 0, "Warning"
DirectionSet = DirectionRequest("PcToPeripheral")
tmrTimedOut.Enabled = False
End Sub
```

Listing 14-1: Transferring blocks of 16 bytes using EPP data reads and writes.
(Sheet 4 of 5)

```
Sub WriteByteToPort ()
'Write one character to the parallel port.
'Uses EPP mode.
Dim S7%
Dim ByteTimeout%
'Wait for Busy (S7)=0, then write a byte to the data port.
Do
    StatusPortData = StatusPortRead(BaseAddress)
    S7 = BitRead(StatusPortData, 7)
    DoEvents
    If TimedOut Then Exit Sub
Loop Until S7 = 0
If Character = "" Then Character = " "
DataPortWrite EPPDataPort0Address, Asc(Character)

'Check the timeout bit.
'If it's set, clear it and display the timeout message.
ByteTimeout = ReadEppTimeoutBit(BaseAddress)
If ByteTimeout = 1 Then
    tmrTimedOut_Timer
End If
End Sub
```

Listing 14-1: Transferring blocks of 16 bytes using EPP data reads and writes.
(Sheet 5 of 5)

The Circuit

The circuit is similar to Chapter 13's Compatibility-and-Byte-mode circuit. The 82C55's Port A provides the Data lines, Port B provides four of the Status outputs, and Port C provides the Control inputs and the other Status output. A 74LS245 transceiver interfaces Port A to the PC's Data port. A 74LS244 buffer/driver interfaces the 5 Status lines and 3 of the Control lines to Ports B and C. The fourth Control line uses another buffer.

The EPP uses just one pair of handshaking signals for both read and write operations. For data transfers, *nDStrobe* ($\overline{C1}$) is the host's, or PC's, strobe output and *nWait* ($\overline{S7}$) is its busy input. In contrast, the 82C55's strobed I/O modes use separate handshaking signals for each direction.

In Figure 14-5, the 82C55's outputs $\overline{OBF}$ and *IBF* connect together and through a buffer to *nWait*, and inputs $\overline{STB}$ and $\overline{ACK}$ connect together and through a buffer to *nDStrobe*. Connecting the $\overline{STB}$ and $\overline{ACK}$ inputs has no ill effects, but connecting two outputs ($\overline{OBF}$ and *IBF*) normally isn't a good idea. However, a solution is to use the 82C55's Mode 1, configure the 82C55 so that unused bits on Port C are inputs, and switch Port A from input to output as needed. When Port A is configured as input, $\overline{OBF}$ becomes an unused input, and when Port A is configured as output, IBF becomes an unused input. With this arrangement, the PC must request a direction switch from the peripheral, and can't switch direction without warning.

The nWrite ($\overline{C0}$) signal is the direction control for the '245. The host's EPP automatically brings nWrite low when it requests to read a byte, and high after the byte is read. A 74HC14 inverts nWrite so it has the correct polarity for controlling the transceiver's direction. The 82C55 doesn't use this bit at all. (You can eliminate the inverter by wiring the '245 so that its A pins connect to the 82C55 and the B pins connect to the cable to the PC.)

Programming

The example program does data transfers only, using nDStrobe ($\overline{C1}$). Bits $\overline{C3}$ and S3 are direction-control bits. as in the earlier Compatibility/Byte mode example. $\overline{C3}$ and S3 are normally high.

Bit S3 is unassigned in the EPP, so it's available for other uses. If you want to use $\overline{C3}$ as an address strobe, you could use C2, which is unused in the EPP, as the direction control. The 82C55 has no built-in way to detect the difference between the two strobe signals, however, so there is no simple way to do both types of transfers and distinguish between them.

When the PC performs an EPP write, the 82C55 detects nDstrobe's going low and brings nWait high. The 82C55's Mode 1 brings its IBF output high within 150 nanoseconds after its $\overline{Stb}$ input goes low. Even after adding delays due to the transceiver and cable, the response easily meets the EPP's 10-microsecond requirement.

In response to nWait's going high, nDStrobe returns high. This causes the 82C55 to interrupt the 8052, which then reads the byte from the 82C55's Port A input buffer. The read operation brings nWait low again. Because the 8052 can be slow to read the byte, the host's program reads nWait and waits for it to go low before starting a new transfer.

When the host wants to read a byte, it brings $\overline{C3}$ low. The 82C55 responds by switching Port A to Mode 1, output, bringing S3 low to acknowledge the switch, and writing the first byte to the 82C55's Port A.

As with an EPP write, the 82C55 detects nDstrobe's going low and brings nWait high. This time, however, nWait is controlled by the 82C55's $\overline{OBF}$ output, rather than IBF. Again, the 82C55 responds within 150 nanoseconds.

In response to *nWait*'s going high, *nDStrobe* returns high. This causes the 82C55 to interrupt the 8052, which then writes another byte to 82C55's Port A. The write operation brings *nWait* low again.

15

Extended Capabilities Port: ECP

The Extended Capabilities Port, or ECP, offers another fast way to transfer data at the parallel port. Like an EPP, an ECP transfer can take place in one ISA-bus cycle, or about 1 microsecond. An ECP conventionally has a 16-byte buffer to hold data to be sent and data received. For the fastest transfers, an ECP may use data compression to pack information into fewer bytes. Direct memory access allows the CPU to do other things while the data is being transferred between the buffer and memory.

Besides being fast, ECP transfers are flexible. Unlike EPPs, the ECP's hardware handshaking has no automatic timeout, and transfers can slow to accommodate slower peripherals. Like EPPs, ECPs can also emulate SPPs and PS/2-type ports. ECPs also include a Fast Centronics mode for improved communications with SPP peripherals. Many ECPs can do EPP transfers as well.

This chapter describes the ECP and its abilities, and includes an example application for exchanging data with a microcontroller, using ECP transfers.

ECP Basics

As with the EPP, many of the ECP's conventions aren't documented in the IEEE-1284 standard. There's no mention of the ECP registers or FIFO use in the PC. Much of the additional information is contained in document from Microsoft titled *The IEEE 1284 Extended Capabilities Port Protocol and ISA Interface Standard*. (See Appendix A.) The data sheets for the controller chips include much of this information as well.

Some of the features of the ECP, including DMA support and the ability to cause hardware interrupts under new conditions, were first introduced in IBM's PS/2 port.

The FIFO

In the host, the ECP typically has a 16-byte FIFO, a first-in, first-out, byte-wide buffer that stores data to be sent or data received. The CPU can write a series of bytes to the buffer, and the port circuits take care of the details of writing them in sequence to port's Data outputs. First-in, first-out means that the FIFO sends the bytes in the same order it receives them. In the opposite direction, the buffer stores a series of received bytes, and the CPU doesn't have to worry about reading each byte before the next one arrives. When the software reads the bytes from the FIFO, they are in the same order that the FIFO received them.

If the PC is sending data to a slow peripheral, the PC can write as many as 16 bytes to the FIFO and then go on to other things. The ECP will transfer the bytes automatically, as the peripheral is ready for them. In a similar way, if a fast peripheral wants to send data to a PC, the PC's FIFO will store up to 16 received bytes, which the PC can read at its leisure.

Depending on the speed of the peripheral, the speed of port-to-port transfers may be even faster than one byte per ISA-bus cycle. For example, if the peripheral isn't ready to receive data, the PC's FIFO may store 16 bytes to be written. When the peripheral is ready, the PC's port will transfer the data to the peripheral at whatever speed both ports can handle.

The peripheral has its own FIFO, which works in much the same way. The FIFO doesn't have to be 16 bytes; some peripheral controllers have 64-byte FIFOs.

Data and Commands

An ECP uses control signals to distinguish between two types of read and write cycles: data and commands. For forward (host-to-peripheral) transfers, the control signal is $\overline{C1}$ (*HostAck*). For reverse (peripheral-to-host) transfers, it's $\overline{S7}$ (*Periph-*

Ack). In both cases, the signal is high when the device is sending data, and low when sending a command.

In command bytes, when bit *D7* is 1, bits 0-6 are a channel address, and when *D7* is 0, bits 0-6 are a run-length count used in data compression.

Data Compression

ECPs include hardware support for a simple method of data compression, *run-length encoding*, which can reduce the number of bytes needed to transfer a block of data. The method is most effective when the data contains many identical bytes in sequence, as do many graphics files.

Instead of transferring the identical bytes individually, the sending device first writes a command byte that tells the receiving device how many times to repeat the byte that follows, then writes the data byte. For example, instead of sending the byte *F0h* five times, the sending device first writes *5* to the ECP Address FIFO (at offset 0). This tells the receiving device to store five copies of the next data byte. The sending device then writes *F0h* to the data FIFO (at offset 400h). The receiving device sees five bytes of F0h, as if there had been five identical read cycles.

Many ECP chips (like SMC's Super I/O) have built-in support only for decompressing the data on the receiving end. Software is responsible for compressing the data before transmitting.

DMA Use

IBM's Type 3 PS/2 port was an early port that supported direct memory access (DMA), and ECPs can use DMA as well.

DMA is a way of reading and writing blocks of data independently from the CPU. All PCs have a DMA controller that can transfer blocks of data between memory and ports. To perform a DMA write operation, the software writes the starting address of the source and the number of bytes to write to the DMA controller. The DMA controller asks for control of the system bus by bringing the CPU's *Hold* input high. When the CPU responds by bringing its *HldA* output high, the DMA controller writes each byte in sequence to the port.

A DMA read operation is similar, with the controller storing the starting address of the destination and the number of bytes to read.

During the DMA transfer, the CPU can perform internal operations, but it can't access the system bus until the DMA transfer completes and the DMA controller brings *Hold* low again, giving control back to the CPU. Because the CPU must refresh the system RAM every 15 microseconds, DMA transfers must take no longer than this before giving control of the bus back to the CPU. For this reason, the data sheet for SMC's Super I/O warns that the port should do no more than 32 DMA cycles in a row.

Registers

An ECP requires six registers in the PC. Table 15-1 shows the registers and their functions. Besides the SPP's three registers, the added ECP registers are at *base address + 400h, base address + 401h,* and *base address + 402h.*

The functions of some of the registers vary depending on which of the ECP's internal modes is selected. For example, in mode 011 (ECP), a write to the base address will cause the port to attempt an ECP address-read cycle. For simple port writes to the base address, the ECP should be in mode 000 or 001 (SPP or PS/2).

In order to access the added ECP registers, the port circuits have to decode at least eleven port address lines. The parallel ports on early PCs decoded only 10 lines (*A0-A9*). This allowed up to 1024 (400h) byte-wide ports. On these early PCs, if you access a port with a higher address, the hardware ignores all address bits above *A9*. The result is redundant addressing—you can access a port at 378h by writing to any of a number of addresses, including 378h, 778h, B78h, or 378h plus any multiple of 400h.

ECPs must decode an eleventh address line, *A10,* so that (using the example address) a port at 778h is distinct from one at 378h.

A port that supports both ECP and EPP will use 11 registers in all: the three SPP registers, plus the five EPP registers at the *base address + 3* through *base address + 7,* and the three ECP registers beginning at *base address + 400h.*

Extended Control Register (ECR)

The Extended Control Register (ECR) holds configuration information for the ECP, including the currently selected mode. Table 15-2 shows the functions for each of the bits in the register.

Internal Modes

ECP-capable ports support SPP and PS/2 transfers as well as ECP transfers. In addition, ECPs support a Fast Centronics mode for improved forward transfers with SPPs. Many ECPs can also do EPP transfers. Table 15-3 shows the modes.

You select a mode by writing a value to bits 7, 6, and 5 of the ECR, at *base address + 402h.* In mode 000, the ECP behaves like an SPP. In mode 001, it

Table 15-1: ECP registers.

Register Name	Offset	ECP mode(s)	Description
Data	000	000, 001	SPP/PS2 Data
EcpAFIFO		011	ECP Address FIFO
DSR	001	all	SPP Status
DCR	002	all	SPP Control
CFIFO	400	010	Parallel Port Data FIFO (Fast Centronics)
EcpDFIFO		011	ECP Data FIFO
TFIFO		110	ECP Test FIFO
CnfgA		111	Configuration A
CnfgB	401	111	Configuration B
ECR	402	all	Extended Control Register

behaves like a PS/2-type port, with a bidirectional data port. Many ECPs support mode 100, which causes the port to emulate an EPP.

The following sections discuss the remaining modes: ECP, Fast Centronics, Test, and Configuration.

ECP Transfers

An ECP can do both forward (host-to-peripheral) and reverse (peripheral-to-host) transfers. In either direction, the byte transferred may be data or a command.

Table 15-4 lists the timing limits for the ECP transfers in the timing diagrams that follow.

Forward transfers

Figure 15-1 shows the signals for an ECP forward transfer. The transfer works like this:

1. At the peripheral, *nAckReverse* (*S5*) high. *PeriphAck* ($\overline{S7}$) is low when the peripheral is not busy.

2. At the host, *HostClk* ($\overline{C0}$) is high. Control bit 5 should be 0, to enable the data outputs.

3. The host writes a byte to the ECP Data FIFO or ECP Address FIFO. If there are no other bytes ahead of it in the FIFO, the byte is placed on *D0–D7*. The host brings *HostAck* ($\overline{C1}$) high for data and low for an address/command, and brings *HostClk* low.

4. The peripheral brings *PeriphAck* high.

5. The host brings *HostClk* high.

6. The peripheral reads *D0–D7* into its FIFO and brings *PeriphAck* low to complete the transfer.

Reverse Transfers

Figure 15-2 shows the signals for a reverse transfer. The transfer works like this:

1. At the peripheral, *nAckReverse* (*S5*) is high, and *PeriphAck* ($\overline{S7}$) is low when the peripheral is not busy.

2. At the host, *HostClk* ($\overline{C0}$) is high and *HostAck* ($\overline{C1}$) is high.

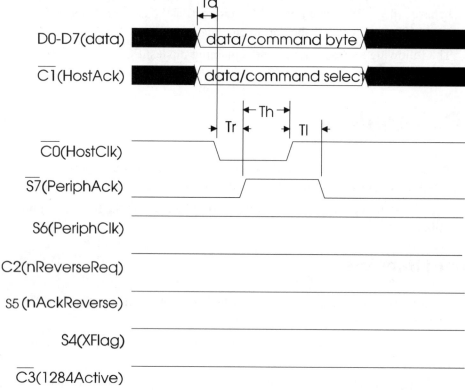

Figure 15-1: ECP forward transfer.

3. The host brings Control bit 5 high, to disable the data outputs. The host brings *HostAck* low.

4. After a delay of at least 0.5 microseconds, the host brings *nReverseReq* ($\overline{C2}$) low.

5. The peripheral brings *nAckReverse* low.

6. The peripheral enables its Data outputs and writes a byte to the ECP Data FIFO or ECP Address FIFO. If there are no other bytes ahead of it in the FIFO, the byte is placed on *D0–D7*. The peripheral brings *PeriphAck* high for data and low for an address/command, and brings *PeriphClk* low.

7. The host brings *HostAck* high.

9. The peripheral brings *PeriphClk* high.

10. The host reads *D0–D7* into its FIFO and brings *HostAck* low to complete the transfer.

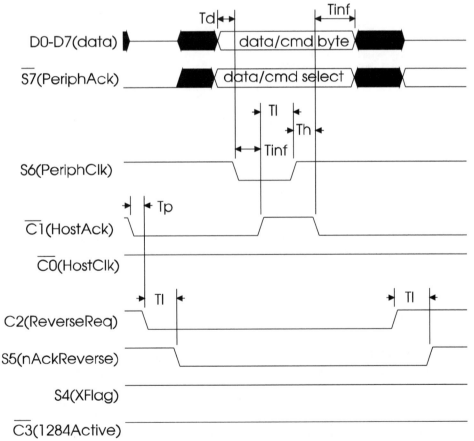

Figure 15-2: An ECP switch to reverse (peripheral to PC) direction, reverse transfer, and switch back to forward direction..

Table 15-2: The ECR (extended control register) configures the ECP.

Bit	Name	Read/ Write	Description
0	FIFOEmpty	Read only	1=empty. 0=at least 1 byte of data present.
1	FIFOFull	Read only	1= full. 0=at least 1 free byte remains.
2	ServiceIntr	R/W	1=Disables DMA and service interrupts. 0=Enables service interrupt. Set to 1: If dmaEn=1, during DMA transfers. If dmaEn=0 and direction=0, when the number of free bytes in the FIFO is equal to or greater than the FIFO's threshold. If dmaEn=0 and direction=1, when the number of bytes in the FIFO is equal to or greater than the FIFO's threhold. After the bit has been set to 1, it must be cleared to 0 to re-enable interrupts.
3	dmaEn	R/W	1=DMA enabled. 0=DMA disabled.
4	nErrIntrEn	R/W	1= No interrupts at nError (S3). 0= Falling edge of nError generates interrupt.
5,6,7	ECP mode select	R/W	See Table 15-3

Switching Directions: Host-to-peripheral

To switch back to the host-to-peripheral direction:

1. The host brings *nReverseReq* high.

2. The peripheral disables outputs *D0–D7*, brings *PeriphClk* high (if not high already), and sets *PeriphAck* high if the peripheral is busy, low if not busy.

3. The peripheral brings *nAckReverse* high.

Timing Considerations

As in EPP mode, the port hardware automatically takes care of the handshaking at the host, so you can read or write a byte in one I/O cycle on the PC.

The timing requirements for the peripheral are quite loose. In a forward transfer, there is no specified limit on how long the peripheral may take to bring *PeriphAck* high in response to *HostClk*'s going low, and when *HostClk* returns high, the peripheral may take as long as 35 milliseconds to bring *PeriphAck* low again. In a reverse transfer, after the peripheral brings *PeriphClk* low to send a byte and the

Table 15-3: ECP internal modes.

Mode (bits 7,6,5 of ECR)	Description
000	SPP (original)
001	PS/2 (Byte, Bidirectional)
010	Fast Centronics
011	ECP
100	EPP
101	Reserved
110	Test
111	Configuration

host brings *HostAck* high in response, the peripheral may take as long as 35 milliseconds to bring *PeriphClk* high again. In reality, the host's port hardware doesn't monitor the timings, so the software can allow the peripheral as long as it wants to respond to the host.

If the peripheral doesn't complete a transfer within a defined amount of time, the host should abort the transfer and return the interface to the state it was in before the transfer. The host can find out whether or not a transfer has completed by reading the number of bytes in the FIFO. Checking for a timeout ensures that the host's port doesn't stall as it waits for the peripheral to respond. The timeout period can be any amount, however.

Interrupt Use

In ECP mode, several events can cause a hardware interrupt at the parallel port. In order to use the interrupt, the selected IRQ level must be enabled at the host's interrupt controller, and the interrupt must be enabled at the parallel port, as described in Chapter 10.

These are the events that can trigger an interrupt:

1. DMA transfers. When *serviceIntr*=0, *dmaEn*=1, and the DMA terminal count (*TC*) is asserted in a DMA cycle.

2. ECP output. When the ECR's *serviceIntr*=0, *dmaEn*=0, *C5*(Control Port bit 5)=0, and the number of free bytes in the FIFO is equal to or greater than the FIFO's threshold.

3. ECP input. When *serviceIntr*=0, *dmaEn*=0, *C5*=1, and the number of bytes in the FIFO is equal to or greater than the FIFO's threshold.

4. On Error. When *nErrIntrEn*=0 and *nError* goes low, or if *nError* is low when *nErrIntrEn* is set low.

Table 15-4: Timing limits for ECP transfers.

Parameter	minimum	maximum
Td	0	-
Th	0	1 sec.
Tl	0	35 msec.
Tp	0.5μsec.	-
Tr	0	-
Tinf	0	infinite

5. Ack. When *C4* (Control port bit 4) =1 and *nAck* goes high. This is the conventional parallel-port interrupt.

Using the FIFO

ECP transfers require a way to monitor the state of the FIFO. For forward transfers, the host needs to know whether or not there is room in the FIFO for another byte, and for reverse transfers, the host needs to know when there are bytes waiting to be read.

There are three ways to determine the FIFO's state. In the first, which I'll call Polled I/O, the host periodically reads the FIFO's state from the ECR. In the second way, Programmed I/O, when the FIFO reaches its threshold, the ECP generates an interrupt that causes the host to read or write to the FIFO. An in the third way, DMA, the host's DMA controller is programmed to transfer data to or from the FIFO. The settings of *dmaEn* (bit 3) and *serviceIntr* (bit 2) in the ECR determine which method is enabled.

Polled I/O

In polled I/O, before doing a forward transfer, the host reads Bit 1 of the ECR. If it reads 1, the FIFO has at least one free byte, and the CPU can write to the port. If it reads 0, the FIFO is full and the CPU should wait. For reverse transfers, the host's CPU polls Bit 0 of the ECR. If it reads 0, there is at least one byte of data in the FIFO to be read. If it reads 1, the FIFO is empty and there is nothing to read.

This is the simplest mode to program, because it doesn't require interrupts or accessing the DMA controller. However, it's not the most efficient.

To use Polled I/O, set *dmaEn*=0 and *serviceIntr*=1.

Interrupt-driven Programmed I/O

In interrupt-driven programmed I/O, the port generates an interrupt when the FIFO has a predetermined number of bytes. For port reads, the interrupt occurs when the FIFO has at least *16 - threshold* bytes. The host's interrupt-service routine then reads the bytes from the FIFO. For port writes, the interrupt occurs when the FIFO has *threshold* or fewer bytes, and the host's interrupt-service routine writes more bytes to the FIFO.

The port's controller chip may allow setting of the FIFO threshold from 1 to 16 bytes. On SMC's Super I/O, you set the threshold by writing *threshold - 1* to bits 0-3 of the chip's *CRA* (Configuration Register A). (This is the controller chip's Configuration Register A, which requires the special access code described in Chapter 11, not the read-only Configuration Register A accessed in the ECP's Configuration mode.)

For reverse transfers, the host must read the FIFO often enough to prevent it from overflowing with incoming data. A large threshold is safest, because it causes the host to read the FIFO when it has fewer bytes in it, so there's less chance that the FIFO will overflow while waiting for the host to read it. If the FIFO fills slowly, the threshold can be smaller, with the advantage that the host will need to read the FIFO less often.

For forward transfers, the threshold size is less critical. A large value will help ensure that the FIFO always has data to send, and blocks of data will transfer more quickly, but the host will be interrupted more often to write to the FIFO. With a small value, the host will have fewer interrupts, with the risk that the FIFO may be empty at times, with nothing to send.

The threshold value doesn't affect the writing of the bytes in the FIFO to the port pins. As soon as the FIFO receives bytes from the host, the port's hardware begins writing them in sequence to the port pins; the port doesn't wait for the FIFO to fill before transferring bytes to the connector.

Visual Basic doesn't include the ability to write interrupt-service routines, so if you want to use interrupts, you'll need to program in C or another language that enables you to do so, or use a DLL or Ocx with this ability.

To use Programmed I/O, set *dmaEn*=0 and *serviceIntr*=0.

DMA

In a DMA transfer, the host sets the direction and programs the system's DMA controller with a count and memory address to read or write. The host then sets *dmaEn*=1 and *serviceIntr*=0, and the DMA controller transfers data to or from the ECP's FIFO. When the DMA controller reaches its terminal count, it causes an interrupt and sets *serviceIntr*=1, which disables DMA.

To use DMA transfers, the ECP must have an assigned DMA channel and IRQ level. Again, Visual Basic alone doesn't allow programming of interrupt-service routines, though a Visual Basic program can communicate with a Vxd or DLL that services hardware interrupts. Appendix A lists sources for more information on programming DMA transfers in a PC.

Other ECP Modes

Three additional ECP modes are Fast Centronics, Test FIFO, and Configuration.

Fast Centronics

Fast Centronics, also called *Fast* mode or *Parallel Port FIFO* mode (010), allows quicker data transfers when communicating with SPP peripherals. In this mode, the host writes data to the FIFO and the hardware performs the SPP handshake, writing a byte and pulsing *nStrobe* when *Busy* is low. Figure 15-3 shows the signalling for this mode.

In Fast Centronics mode, there's no need to do the handshaking in software, and the use of the FIFO makes it easy for the host to write a series of bytes to the port without having to wait for the peripheral to respond. The peripheral doesn't know or care whether the host's handshaking is generated by hardware or software, so in most cases, it behaves as usual. Fast Centronics is too fast for some peripherals, however, and these require SPP mode.

This mode does forward transfers (PC-to-peripheral) only. The IEEE 1284 standard doesn't mention Fast Centronics mode, but Microsoft's ECP document describes it, and ECP controller chips include it.

Test Mode

Test mode allows reading and writing to the FIFO without generating handshaking signals or writing to the port pins. This mode is intended for testing port speed, or throughput, and determining at what rate the host should read and write to the FIFO to prevent its overflowing.

Configuration Mode

ECP mode includes two configuration registers that hold information about the chip's support of data compression, use of interrupts and DMA, and the thresholds and current state of the FIFO. Some of the register functions vary depending on the chip, while others should be the same on all ECP-capable ports.

Configuration Register A (cnfgA):

Read-only. Returns 10h, which indicates that the port is an 8-bit (byte) implementation.

Configuration Register B (cnfgB):

Bit 7. Compress. Read-only. 0 = doesn't support hardware RLE compression. (The chip may support hardware RLE decompression, however.)

Bit 6. intrValue. Read-only. State of the port's IRQ line on the ISA bus.

Bits 5,4,3. On some chips, selects an IRQ level.

Bits 2,1,0. On some chips, selects a DMA channel.

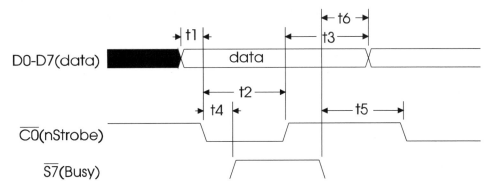

Parameter	Description	min (nsec.)	max (nsec.)
t1	Data valid to *nStrobe* active	600	
t2	*nStrobe* pulse width	600	
t3	Data hold from *nStrobe* active	450[1]	
t4	*nStrobe* active to *Busy* active		500
t5	*Busy* inactive to *nStrobe* active	680	
t6	*Busy* inactive to Data invalid	80[1]	

[1]If another data transfer is pending, Data is held until *Busy* goes inactive or time t3, whichever is longer. If no transfer is pending, Data is held indefinitely.

(Timings are from SMC's FDC37C665/6 Super I/O data sheet.)

Figure 15-3: Timing diagram for Fast Centronics transfers.

An ECP Application

An ECP application can use a circuit identical to the Compatibility, Nibble, and Byte-mode circuit of Chapter 13. As usual, an 82C55 is the interface between a microcontroller and a PC's parallel port, and the example application reads and writes blocks of bytes. The only difference is that the Status and Control signals have different names to reflect their new functions in the ECP interface.

All of the 82C55's ports are configured in Mode 0 (simple I/O), with no automatic handshaking. The 8052's control program toggles and reads the handshaking signals when appropriate.

Listing 15-1 is excerpts from a program that does ECP transfers with this circuit. The program uses polled, programmed I/O, checking FIFO full or FIFO empty before each transfer. This isn't the fastest, most efficient use of an ECP, but it does illustrate what the software needs to do to perform simple ECP transfers. As in previous examples, the program transfers blocks of 32 bytes.

```
Function CheckFIFOEmpty% ()
'Bit 0 of the Ecr indicates FIFO empty.
'1=empty; 0=not empty
Dim FIFOFull%
EcrData = VbInp(EcrAddress)
If BitRead(EcrData, 0) = 1 Then
    CheckFIFOEmpty = True
Else CheckFIFOEmpty = False
End If
FIFOFull = BitRead(EcrData, 1)
End Function
```

```
Function CheckFIFOFull ()
'Bit 1 of the Ecr indicates FIFO full.
'1=full; 0=not full
Dim FIFOFull%
EcrData = VbInp(EcrAddress)
If BitRead(EcrData, 1) = 1 Then
    CheckFIFOFull = True
Else
    CheckFIFOFull = False
End If
End Function
```

Listing 15-1: Code to perform ECP forward and reverse transfers. (Sheet 1 of 5)

```
Sub cmdReadDataFromPort_Click ()
'Read characters from the parallel port.
'Display the received characters on the form.
Dim CharNumber%
CharNumber = 0
TimedOut = False
lblDataInDisplay.Caption = ""
DirectionSet = DirectionRequest("PeripheralToPc")
tmrTimedOut.Enabled = True
'Read bytes at the port.
'After each byte, read the status port.
ReadAnother = True
'Empty the FIFO
Do
    FIFOEmpty = CheckFIFOEmpty()
Loop Until FIFOEmpty = True
Do Until CharNumber = 32 Or TimedOut = True
    DoEvents
    FIFOEmpty = CheckFIFOEmpty()
    If FIFOEmpty = False Then
     DoEvents
     DataIn = DataPortRead(ECPDataPortAddress)
     lblDataInDisplay.Caption = lblDataInDisplay.Caption _
      + Chr$(DataIn)
     CharNumber = CharNumber + 1
    End If
Loop
    If Not (TimedOut) Then
     MsgBox "Successful transfer", 0
    End If
lblDataInDisplay.Caption = ""
'Set C2 to tell peripheral to stop sending
BitSet ControlPortData, 2
ControlPortWrite BaseAddress, ControlPortData
CharNumber = 0
tmrTimedOut.Enabled = False
'Re-enable the data outputs.
DirectionSet = DirectionRequest("PcToPeripheral")
End Sub
```

Listing 15-1: Code to perform ECP forward and reverse transfers. (Sheet 2 of 5)

```
Sub cmdWriteDataToPort_Click ()
Dim CharNumber%
Dim FIFOFull%
TimedOut = False
tmrTimedOut.Enabled = True
DirectionSet = DirectionRequest("PcToPeripheral")
tmrTimedOut.Enabled = True
'Write the characters in the text box to the parallel port.
For CharNumber = 1 To 32
    Do
     DoEvents
     FIFOFull = CheckFIFOFull()
    Loop Until (Not (FIFOFull)) Or (TimedOut = True)
    'Write each character in sequence
    Character = Mid$(txtDataOut.Text, CharNumber, 1)
    If Character = "" Then Character = " "
    DataPortWrite ECPDataPortAddress, Asc(Character)
Next CharNumber
Do
    DoEvents
    FIFOEmpty = CheckFIFOEmpty()
Loop Until FIFOEmpty Or TimedOut
If Not (TimedOut) Then
    MsgBox "Successful transfer", 0
End If
tmrTimedOut.Enabled = False
End Sub
```

Listing 15-1: Code to perform ECP forward and reverse transfers. (Sheet 3 of 5)

```
Function DirectionRequest% (Direction$)
Dim S3%
Dim PeripheralResponse
'Use the ECP's PS2 mode to switch directions.
SetEcpMode (PS2)
Direction = LCase$(Direction)
ControlPortData = ControlPortRead(BaseAddress)
BitSet ControlPortData, 0
BitSet ControlPortData, 3
'Set Control port bits to match the selected direction.
'For control bit 5,
'0 enables the data outputs, 1 tristates the outputs.
Select Case Direction
    Case "pctoperipheral"
     BitReset ControlPortData, 1
     BitSet ControlPortData, 2
     PeripheralResponse = 1
    Case "peripheraltopc"
     BitSet ControlPortData, 1
     BitSet ControlPortData, 5
     ControlPortWrite BaseAddress, ControlPortData
     BitReset ControlPortData, 2
     PeripheralResponse = 0
    Case Else
    End Select
ControlPortWrite BaseAddress, ControlPortData
tmrTimedOut.Enabled = True
Do
    'Wait for the peripheral to acknowledge the
    'direction change.
    StatusPortData = StatusPortRead(BaseAddress)
    S3 = BitRead(StatusPortData, 3)
    DoEvents
    If TimedOut Then Exit Function
Loop Until S3 = PeripheralResponse
If S3 = 1 Then
    tmrTimedOut.Enabled = False
    'Enable the data outputs only after the peripheral
    'has acknowledged the direction change to
    'PC-to-peripheral.
    BitReset ControlPortData, 5
    ControlPortWrite BaseAddress, ControlPortData
End If
SetEcpMode (ECP)
End Function
```

Listing 15-1: Code to perform ECP forward and reverse transfers. (Sheet 4 of 5)

```
Sub Form_Load ()
ECPDataPortAddress = BaseAddress + &H400
EcrAddress = BaseAddress + &H402
'Timeout limit for peripheral.
tmrTimedOut.Interval = 5000
tmrTimedOut.Enabled = False
'Initial Ecr setting (PS2 mode, no DMA or interrupts)
VbOut EcrAddress, &H30
DirectionSet = DirectionRequest("PcToPeripheral")
Do
    DoEvents
    FIFOEmpty = CheckFIFOEmpty()
    DataIn = DataPortRead(ECPDataPortAddress)
Loop Until FIFOEmpty
End Sub
```

```
Sub tmrTimedOut_Timer ()
'On timeout, display a message and switch
'direction to PC-to-peripheral.
TimedOut = True
MsgBox "Peripheral not responding", 0
DirectionSet = DirectionRequest("PcToPeripheral")
tmrTimedOut.Enabled = False
End Sub
```

Listing 15-1: Code to perform ECP forward and reverse transfers. (Sheet 5 of 5)

16

PC-to-PC Communications

The original purpose of the parallel port was to enable communications between a PC and a peripheral. Another use that has become very popular is transferring information between PCs. You can use a PC-to-PC link to transfer files without having to use floppy disks. You can even set up a 2-computer network where one computer can access the files and even run programs that reside on the other computer.

MS-DOS and Windows 95 have PC-to-PC communications abilities built-in. Traveling Software's LapLink is an example of commercial software that adds parallel- and serial-port communications abilities to a pair of computers.

A PC-to-PC Cable

Connecting two PCs' parallel ports requires a special cable. In most cases, the cable will have a 25-pin male D-sub connector on each end. An ordinary male-to-male D-sub cable won't do, though, because the wires on a PC-to-PC parallel cable don't connect straight-across, pin-for-pin.

In a PC-to-peripheral link, the host's Control outputs connect to inputs on the peripheral, and the host's Status inputs connect to outputs on the peripheral. On powerup, the Data lines are outputs on the host and inputs on the peripheral. If you connect the parallel ports to two PCs straight together, you end up with inputs connected to inputs, and outputs connected to outputs.

The solution is to use a special bidirectional parallel cable, often sold as LapLink or Bidirectional parallel cables. Because they transfer data a nibble at a time, I'll call this type of cable a Nibble-mode bidirectional parallel cable. Table 16-1 shows the wiring for the cable. On each PC, five Data outputs ($D0–D4$) connect to the five Status inputs ($S3–\overline{S7}$) on the other computer. The cable should include all eight ground wires. You can use the information in the table to make your own bidirectional cable or adapter.

The four Control lines ($\overline{C0}–\overline{C3}$) are normally unused. If you're connecting to SPPs whose Control bits have open-collector outputs, you could wire the Control bits straight-through and gain four more bidirectional lines that you can use in programs you write. This is an unconventional use of the bits, however, and it won't work on all ports.

Dos and Windows Tools

Operating-system tools for parallel-port transfers include DOS's Interlnk and Windows 95's Direct Cable Connection.

MS-DOS's InterInk

MS-DOS version 6 added the ability to redirect disk and parallel-port operations from one computer (called the *client*) to another (called the *server*), using a simple parallel or serial connection between the computers. The client can read and write to disks and LPT devices on the server.

DOS provides two programs for this purpose: *Interlnk.exe* and *Intersvr.exe*. You also need either a bidirectional Nibble-mode cable connected to a parallel port on each computer, or a null-modem serial cable connected to a serial port on each computer. The parallel link is faster, but you can use the serial link if you don't have parallel ports to spare, if the computers are too far apart for a parallel link, or if you don't have the required parallel cable handy. Also, if only one of the computers has the *Interlnk* and *Intersvr* files, you can use *Interlnk* to copy files over a serial link (but not a parallel link).

Table 16-1: Wiring for nibble-mode PC-to-PC parallel-port cable.

Computer A		Direction	Computer B	
Pin	Register Bit		Register Bit	Pin
2	D0	→	S3	15
3	D1	→	S4	13
4	D2	→	S5	12
5	D3	→	S6	10
6	D4	→	S7	11
10	S6	←	D3	5
11	S7	←	D4	6
12	S5	←	D2	4
13	S4	←	D1	3
15	S3	←	D0	2
18-25	-	GND	-	18-25
1	C0	no connection	C0	1
14	C1	no connection	C1	14
16	C2	no connection	C2	16
17	C3	no connection	C3	17

Using *Interlnk*, the client can read, write to, copy, move, and delete files on the server. The client can send files to a printer connected to the server and access other LPT devices that are controlled with MS-DOS functions. (See Chapter 2 for more on MS-DOS's LPT functions.)

To use *Interlnk*, you connect a cable, then install the device driver on the client. To install *Interlnk* on Lpt1, you add this statement to the config.sys file and reboot:

```
device=c:\dos\interlnk.exe /lpt1
```

The `/lpt1` switch tells the driver where the cable is connected.

To block remote access to the parallel ports, add `/noprinter` to the end of the command above:

```
device=c:\dos\interlnk.exe /lpt1 /noprinter
```

By default, *Interlnk* redirects three drives on the server. To change this number, add a `/drives:n` switch to the end of the command:

```
device=c:\dos\interlnk.exe /lpt1 /drives:2
```

At the server, start the server program by typing:

```
intersvr
```

The server computer requires no changes to its *config.sys* file.

The client can then access disks and parallel ports on the server.

The client assigns its own letters to the server's drives, beginning with the letter after the client's final drive. For example, if the client uses drives A through E, drive *A* on the server becomes drive *F* on the client; drive *B* on the server becomes drive *G* on the client, and so on up. At the client, saving a file to drive F will cause the file to be saved to the server's drive A.

The *Interlnk* connection will be active automatically if the client reboots while the server is running, or if the client makes one of the server's redirected drives the active drive (by typing *drive letter:* at the command prompt). You can also activate the connection by typing *interlnk* at the client's command prompt.

If only one computer has the *Interlnk* files, you can use *intersvr*'s `rcopy` command to copy files from one computer to another. At the computer with Interlnk, type:

```
intersvr /rcopy
```

and follow the on-screen instructions. However, this command only works on serial links.

Direct Cable Connection

Windows 95 has much greater built-in PC-to-PC communications abilities with its *Direct Cable Connection* (DCC). DCC creates a simple network between two computers. Both computers must be running Windows 95.

With DCC, one computer is the *host*, and the other is the *guest*. The guest has access to the resources of the host, similar to the Interlnk's client and server, but with greater abilities. The guest can access files, drives (including CD-ROM drives, which aren't supported with Interlnk), and printers on the host. In addition, with DCC, the guest can run applications on the host, though performance will be limited by the speed of the link. If the host is connected to a network, the guest can access the network, and the host can access shared resources on the guest.

As with Interlnk, to use DCC, you need either a free parallel port on each computer or a free serial port on each computer, plus an appropriate cable. For parallel connections, DCC can use the Nibble-mode bidirectional cable described above. It can also use a special Direct Parallel Universal Cable from Parallel Technologies. This smart cable is useful if the ports on both computers are capable of bidirectional, EPP, or ECP data transfers. The Universal cable automatically detects the port types at each end and configures itself for the fastest data transfers possible. If ECP mode is available on both ports, DCC will use it.

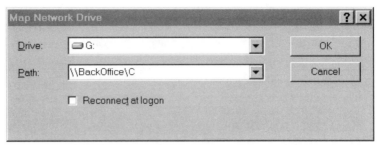

Figure 16-2: The *Map Network Drive* icon in *My Computer* enables you to designate a letter to refer to a drive on the remote system.

DCC will use hardware interrupts if the ports have them available; otherwise, it will operate without interrupts.

As with Interlnk, a serial DCC link uses a null-modem cable.

Both computers must have Dial-up Networking and Direct Cable Connect installed. To find out if these are installed, go to *Control Panel, Add/Remove Programs, Windows Setup, Communications, Details.* To add an item, click the appropriate check box, then *OK*, and follow the instructions.

To establish a Direct Cable Connection, click on the *Start* menu, *Programs, Accessories, Direct Cable Connection.* At each computer, on-screen prompts guide you through selecting a port and selecting host or guest. If the connection fails, Windows Help includes a *DCC Troubleshooter* that helps resolve many common problems.

The host must specify which resources it wants to share, and what type of sharing to enable. You can choose to share individual files, folders, or drives. The shared access can be read-only or full (read/write). To enable sharing, in *My Computer,* right-click the file or drive to share and select *Properties, Sharing* (Figure 16-1). Click on *Shared As* and enter a name, which can be the same as the drive or file name, and select an *Access Type.* When a resource is shared, its icon includes an outstretched hand, so the shared resources are easy to identify in a list.

When the DCC is established, the *View Host* button on the DCC window enables you to view and access the shared resources on the host. To select a folder, click on it as usual.

Another way to view and access the host is to map a drive to an unused drive letter on the guest. The host must have a name, which you specify in its Control Panel under *Network, Identification, Computer Name.* In *My Computer,* click the *Map Network Drive* icon. Select an unused drive letter, and type the path of the drive you want to access, as Figure 16-2 shows. The double backslash (\\) tells the system that the path is on the remote system. In the illustration, *BackOffice* is the

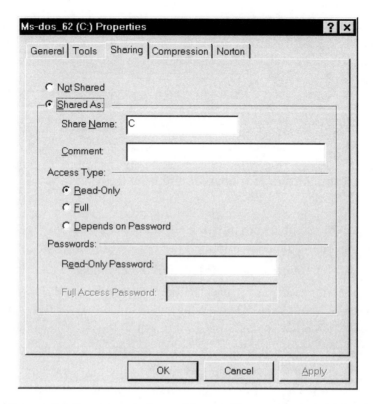

Figure 16-1: In the properties screen for a drive or file, you can enable sharing with a Direct Cable Connection.

name of the host. Don't add a colon (:) after the drive letter. The drive then appears along with other system drives in My Computer.

Briefcase

If you use more than one computer to work on a set of files, Windows 95's Briefcase helps you maintain a single, up-to-date version of each file. If Briefcase isn't installed, you can add it in the *Control Panel, Add/Remove Programs*.

A common use for the Briefcase is when you use a portable computer and a desktop computer to work on the same files. You can use Briefcase to synchronize, or maintain up-to-date copies, of files that reside on both computers. To use the Briefcase, establish a Direct Cable Connection with the portable computer as guest and the desktop computer as host. At the guest, use *View Host* to see the shared resources. Copy the files you'll want to synchronize to the guest's Briefcase. The Briefcase uses the syntax *\\hostname\path\filename* for the host's files. Now you can disconnect the DCC link and work with the files on the guest computer.

When you want to synchronize the files, re-establish the DCC link. In the guest's Briefcase, under the Briefcase menu item, select *Update All* or *Update Selection.* If the two versions of a file differ, Briefcase will display the filename and date and time information and ask if you want to update the older file. If you answer yes, both computers will have identical, up-to-date versions of the file. If both versions have changed, Briefcase allows you to select which version to use, or skip the update entirely. If you no longer want to update a file, select *Split From Original*, and the Briefcase will no longer attempt to synchronize it.

(You can also use the Briefcase without DCC, to synchronize files on a hard disk and a floppy that you use with another computer.)

A PC-to-PC Application

Any two PCs with parallel ports can use Nibble mode to exchange data. Listing 16-1 shows the code for a program that enables two PCs to transfer files. Although you can use Interlnk or Direct Cable Connect for this purpose, you might want to include file transfers as part of another application, and this example shows a way to do it. It uses Visual Basic's Common Dialog control to display and select files to send and to select filenames for received files.

Both PCs run identical programs. Each PC initializes to an idle condition. To send a file, the user clicks a *Send File* command button, which brings up a Common Dialog box that enables the user to select a file to send. When the file is selected, the program writes the filename, the file length, and then the file itself to the selected parallel port.

At the receiving end, a Timer subroutine reads the status port periodically. When Status port bit 6 = 0, it means that the opposite end is sending a file. The receiving PC reads the filename and brings up a Common Dialog box with the transmitted filename as the default. Figure 16-3 illustrates. The user can then save the file under this name or another name, and select a directory. The program then reads the file length and stores the bytes in the requested file.

When the transfer is complete, both PCs return to the idle state, monitoring Status bit 6 for an incoming file.

A couple of factors limit the speed of the file transfers. To ensure that the program doesn't hang if the opposite end stops responding, the program includes many timeout checks and a DoEvents in each loop that waits for a response. Also, the transmitting end has to divide each byte into nibbles, and the receiving end has to recombine them. See Chapter 3 for tips for speeding up Visual-Basic programs.

Chapter 16

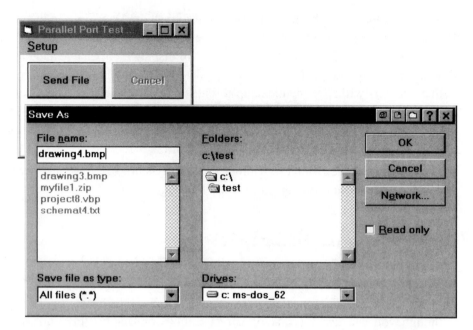

Figure 16-3: Visual Basic's Common DIalog control makes it easy to select files to transmit and filenames for received files.

You can use the same data-transfer technique to exchange blocks of data, as in earlier examples, rather than files. And of course, you can use the file-transfer technique in this example with PC-to-peripheral transfers.

```
Dim StatusPortData%
Dim TimedOut%
Dim LowNibble%
Dim HighNibble%
Dim FileLengthByte%(0 To 3)
Dim S6%
Dim TimedOutInterval&
Dim TransferCancelled%
```

```
Sub cmdCancelTransfer_Click ()
'Simulate a timeout to cause the transfer to end.
TransferCancelled = True
tmrTimedOut.Interval = 1
InitializeToIdleCondition
End Sub
```

Listing 16-1: Two PCs can use nibble mode to transfer files. (Sheet 1 of 10)

```
Sub cmdWriteFileToPort_Click ()
'Allow the user to select a file from a common-dialog box.
'Then write the filename, file length, and the file itself to
'the parallel port.
Const OFN_FILEMUSTEXIST = &H1000&
Dim ByteNumber&
Dim ByteToWrite%
Dim SelectedFile$
Dim CharacterRead$
Dim FileLength&
Dim FileNameToSend$
tmrWatchForIncomingFile.Enabled = False
tmrTimedOut.Interval = 0
TimedOut = False
On Error GoTo ErrorHandlerWr
cdlFileToSend.Filter = "All files (*.*)|*.*"
cdlFileToSend.Filename = ""
cdlFileToSend.Flags = OFN_FILEMUSTEXIST

'Get the selected file from the common dialog box.
cdlFileToSend.Action = 1
cmdWriteFileToPort.Enabled = False
'Write the filename and length to the port.
SelectedFile = cdlFileToSend.Filename
FileLength = FileLen(SelectedFile)
DivideFileLengthInto4Bytes (FileLength)
cmdCancelTransfer.Enabled = True
lblProgress.Caption = "Waiting for response..."
'Extract the filename from SelectedFile, which includes a path.
FileNameToSend = GetFilenameToSend(SelectedFile)
'Write the filename to the port.
For ByteNumber = 1 To 12
    WriteByteToPort Asc(Mid$(FileNameToSend, ByteNumber, 1))
Next ByteNumber
'Write the file length to the port.
For ByteNumber = 0 To 3
    WriteByteToPort FileLengthByte(ByteNumber)
Next ByteNumber
```

Listing 16-1: Two PCs can use nibble mode to transfer files. (Sheet 2 of 10)

```
'Enable the timeout timer.
tmrTimedOut.Interval = TimedOutInterval
lblProgress.Caption = "Transferring file..."
Open SelectedFile For Input As #1
For ByteNumber = 1 To FileLength
    'Read 1 character from the file; send its ASCII code
    WriteByteToPort Asc(Input$(1, #1))
Next ByteNumber
If Not (TimedOut) Then
    lblProgress.Caption = "Successful transfer"
End If
GoTo EndTransferWr

ErrorHandlerWr:
TransferCancelled = True
Resume EndTransferWr

EndTransferWr:
Close #1
If TransferCancelled = True Then
    DisplayCancelMessage
End If
InitializeToIdleCondition
End Sub
```

```
Sub DisplayCancelMessage ()
lblProgress.Caption = "Transfer cancelled."
TransferCancelled = False
End Sub
```

Listing 16-1: Two PCs can use nibble mode to transfer files. (Sheet 3 of 10)

```
Sub DivideByteIntoNibbles (ByteToDivide%)
'Divide a byte into low and high nibbles.
'Each nibble is stored in a byte.
'Bit 3 is the strobe.
'Bits 5-7 are unused.
'Original bit 0 = Low Nibble bit 0
'Original bit 1 = Low Nibble bit 1
'Original bit 2 = Low Nibble bit 2
'Original bit 3 = Low Nibble bit 4
'Original bit 4 = High Nibble bit 0
'Original bit 5 = High Nibble bit 1
'Original bit 6 = High Nibble bit 2
'Original bit 7 = High Nibble bit 4
Dim Bit0%
Dim Bit1%
Dim Bit2%
Dim Bit4%
Bit0 = ByteToDivide And 1
Bit1 = ByteToDivide And 2
Bit2 = ByteToDivide And 4
Bit4 = (ByteToDivide And 8) * 2
LowNibble = Bit0 + Bit1 + Bit2 + Bit4
Bit0 = (ByteToDivide And &H10) \ &H10
Bit1 = (ByteToDivide And &H20) \ &H10
Bit2 = (ByteToDivide And &H40) \ &H10
Bit4 = (ByteToDivide And &H80) \ 8
HighNibble = Bit0 + Bit1 + Bit2 + Bit4
End Sub
```

```
Sub DivideFileLengthInto4Bytes (FileLength&)
FileLengthByte(0) = FileLength And &HFF
FileLengthByte(1) = ((FileLength \ &H100) And &HFF)
FileLengthByte(2) = ((FileLength \ &H10000) And &HFF)
FileLengthByte(3) = ((FileLength \ &H1000000) And &HFF)
End Sub
```

```
Sub Form_Load ()
StartUp
InitializeToIdleCondition
End Sub
```

Listing 16-1: Two PCs can use nibble mode to transfer files. (Sheet 4 of 10)

```
Function GetFileLength& ()
GetFileLength = FileLengthByte(0) + FileLengthByte(1) * &H100 _
  + FileLengthByte(2) * &H10000 + FileLengthByte(3) * &H1000000
End Function
```

```
Function GetFilenameToSend$ (SelectedFile$)
'SelectedFile contains the filename and path.
'Extract the file name only into FileNameToSend.
'FilenameToSend is 12 characters. Extra characters are spaces.
Dim Character$
Dim CharacterNumber%
Dim ByteNumber%
Dim FileNameToSend$

FileNameToSend = ""
ByteNumber = Len(SelectedFile)
'Starting from the right, find the filename in the string.
Do
    Character = Mid$(SelectedFile, ByteNumber, 1)
    FileNameToSend = Character & FileNameToSend
    ByteNumber = ByteNumber - 1
Loop Until ByteNumber = _
  Len(SelectedFile) - 13 Or ByteNumber = 0 Or Character = "\"
If Character = "\" Then
    FileNameToSend = _
     Right$(FileNameToSend, Len(FileNameToSend) - 1)
End If
'Pad the filename with spaces until it has 12 characters.
For CharacterNumber = Len(FileNameToSend) + 1 To 12
    FileNameToSend = FileNameToSend & " "
Next CharacterNumber
GetFilenameToSend = FileNameToSend
End Function
```

Listing 16-1: Two PCs can use nibble mode to transfer files. (Sheet 5 of 10)

```
Sub InitializeToIdleCondition ()
TimedOutInterval = 5000
tmrTimedOut.Interval = TimedOutInterval
tmrTimedOut.Enabled = False
tmrWatchForIncomingFile.Interval = 1000
'Initialize D3 (strobe) to 1.
DataPortWrite BaseAddress, 8
'Wait for the opposite end to set D3=1 (not busy).
Do
    StatusPortData = StatusPortRead(BaseAddress)
    S6 = BitRead(StatusPortData, 6)
    DoEvents
Loop Until S6 = 1
tmrWatchForIncomingFile.Enabled = True
cmdWriteFileToPort.Enabled = True
cmdCancelTransfer.Enabled = False
End Sub
```

```
Function MakeByteFromNibbles% (LowNibble%, HighNibble%)
'Get the 8 bits from LowNibble and HighNibble
'and arrange them into a byte.
Dim Bit0%
Dim Bit1%
Dim Bit2%
Dim Bit3%
Dim Bit4%
Dim Bit5%
Dim Bit6%
Dim Bit7%

Bit0 = BitRead(LowNibble, 3)
Bit1 = BitRead(LowNibble, 4) * 2
Bit2 = BitRead(LowNibble, 5) * 4
Bit3 = BitRead(LowNibble, 7) * 8
Bit4 = BitRead(HighNibble, 3) * &H10
Bit5 = BitRead(HighNibble, 4) * &H20
Bit6 = BitRead(HighNibble, 5) * &H40
Bit7 = BitRead(HighNibble, 7) * &H80
MakeByteFromNibbles = _
   Bit0 + Bit1 + Bit2 + Bit3 + Bit4 + Bit5 + Bit6 + Bit7
End Function
```

Listing 16-1: Two PCs can use nibble mode to transfer files. (Sheet 6 of 10)

Parallel Port Complete

```
Function ReadByteFromPort% ()
'Read a byte of data at the status port, in 2 nibbles.
tmrTimedOut.Enabled = True
'When S6=0, set D3=0.
Do
    LowNibble = StatusPortRead(BaseAddress)
    S6 = BitRead(LowNibble, 6)
    DoEvents
    Loop Until (S6 = 0) Or TimedOut
DataPortWrite BaseAddress, 0
'When the peripheral responds by setting S6=1, set D3=1.
'LowNibble holds 4 bits of data.
Do
    LowNibble = StatusPortRead(BaseAddress)
    S6 = BitRead(LowNibble, 6)
    DoEvents
Loop Until (S6 = 1) Or TimedOut
DataPortWrite BaseAddress, 8
'When S6=0 again, set D3=0.
Do
    HighNibble = StatusPortRead(BaseAddress)
    S6 = BitRead(HighNibble, 6)
    DoEvents
Loop Until (S6 = 0) Or TimedOut
DataPortWrite BaseAddress, 0
'When the peripheral responds by setting S6=1, set D3=1.
'HighNibble holds 4 bits of data.
Do
    HighNibble = StatusPortRead(BaseAddress)
    S6 = BitRead(HighNibble, 6)
    DoEvents
Loop Until (S6 = 1) Or TimedOut
DataPortWrite BaseAddress, 8
ReadByteFromPort = MakeByteFromNibbles(LowNibble, HighNibble)
tmrTimedOut.Enabled = False
End Function
```

Listing 16-1: Two PCs can use nibble mode to transfer files. (Sheet 7 of 10)

```
Sub ReadFileFromPort ()
'This subroutine runs when tmrWatchForIncomingFile detects
'an incoming file.
'Read the filename and display it in a Common Dialog box.
'When the user has selected a filename and path, read
'the file length and store the file in the selected filename.
Dim FileLength&
Dim ByteRead%
Dim ByteNumber&
Const OFN_OVERWRITEPROMPT = &H2&
Dim FileReceived$
Dim CharacterToWrite$
tmrWatchForIncomingFile.Enabled = False
tmrTimedOut.Interval = TimedOutInterval
cdlFileReceived.Filter = "All files (*.*)|*.*"
cdlFileReceived.Filename = ""
cdlFileReceived.Flags = OFN_OVERWRITEPROMPT
On Error GoTo ErrorHandlerRd
FileReceived = ""

'Read the filename and display the common-dialog box.
For ByteNumber = 1 To 12
    FileReceived = FileReceived & Chr$(ReadByteFromPort())
Next ByteNumber
cdlFileReceived.Filename = FileReceived
cdlFileReceived.Action = 2
lblProgress.Caption = "Receiving file..."
cmdCancelTransfer.Enabled = True
Open cdlFileReceived.Filename For Output As #1

'Read the file length.
For ByteNumber = 0 To 3
    FileLengthByte(ByteNumber) = ReadByteFromPort()
Next ByteNumber

'Read and store the file.
If Not (TimedOut) Then
    FileLength = GetFileLength()
    For ByteNumber = 1 To FileLength
     CharacterToWrite = Chr$(ReadByteFromPort())
     Print #1, CharacterToWrite;
    Next ByteNumber
    lblProgress.Caption = "Successful transfer"
End If
```

Listing 16-1: Two PCs can use nibble mode to transfer files. (Sheet 8 of 10)

```
GoTo EndTransferRd

ErrorHandlerRd:
TransferCancelled = True
Resume EndTransferRd

EndTransferRd:
Close #1
If TransferCancelled = True Then
    DisplayCancelMessage
End If
InitializeToIdleCondition
End Sub
```

```
Sub tmrTimedOut_Timer ()
TimedOut = True
lblProgress.Caption = "Remote system not responding"
tmrTimedOut.Enabled = False
End Sub
```

```
Sub tmrWatchForIncomingFile_Timer ()
'When not sending a file, poll Status bit 6.
'If S6=0, the opposite end is sending a file.
StatusPortData = StatusPortRead(BaseAddress)
S6 = BitRead(StatusPortData, 6)
If S6 = 0 Then ReadFileFromPort
End Sub
```

Listing 16-1: Two PCs can use nibble mode to transfer files. (Sheet 9 of 10)

```
Sub WriteByteToPort (ByteToWrite%)
'Write a byte to the data port, in 2 nibbles.
'The remote system reads the data at its status port.
'The data bits are D0, D1, D2, and D4.
'D3 is the strobe.
DivideByteIntoNibbles (ByteToWrite)
tmrTimedOut.Enabled = True
'When S6=1 (not busy), write the low nibble and set D3=0.
Do
    StatusPortData = StatusPortRead(BaseAddress)
    S6 = BitRead(StatusPortData, 6)
    DoEvents
Loop Until (S6 = 1) Or TimedOut
DataPortWrite BaseAddress, LowNibble
'When the peripheral responds by setting S6=0, set D3=1.
Do
    StatusPortData = StatusPortRead(BaseAddress)
    S6 = BitRead(StatusPortData, 6)
    DoEvents
Loop Until (S6 = 0) Or TimedOut
DataPortWrite BaseAddress, LowNibble + 8
'When S6=1, write the high nibble and set D3=0.
Do
    StatusPortData = StatusPortRead(BaseAddress)
    S6 = BitRead(StatusPortData, 6)
    DoEvents
Loop Until (S6 = 1) Or TimedOut
DataPortWrite BaseAddress, HighNibble
'When the peripheral responds by setting S6=0, set D3=1.
Do
    StatusPortData = StatusPortRead(BaseAddress)
    S6 = BitRead(StatusPortData, 6)
    DoEvents
Loop Until (S6 = 0) Or TimedOut
DataPortWrite BaseAddress, HighNibble + 8
tmrTimedOut.Enabled = False
End Sub
```

Listing 16-1: Two PCs can use nibble mode to transfer files. (Sheet 10 of 10)

Appendix A

Resources

This section lists a variety of resources that you may find useful in your parallel-port explorations. Many of the items are ones I used in my research for this book. For additions and updates to this list, visit Lakeview Research on the World Wide Web at *http://www.lvr.com*, where I host a page devoted to the latest parallel-port information and products.

Parallel-port Documents

IEEE Std 1284-1994. *IEEE Standard Signaling Method for a Bidirectional Parallel Peripheral Interface for Personal Computers.* 1994. Sponsored by the Microprocessor and Microcomputer Standards Committee of the IEEE Computer Society. The official document describing the parallel port's five modes of communication and negotiation protocol. IEEE Standards:

Phone: 800-678-4333, 908-981-0060
Fax: 908-981-9667
WWW: http://stdsbbs.ieee.org/

"*Extended Capabilities Port Protocol and ISA Interface Standard*" A document from Microsoft Corporation Windows Developer Relations that describes the parallel port's ECP mode, including register use in the PC. This document has been included on the Archive disk of the *Microsoft Developer Network Developer's Library CD-ROM* (under *Specifications*).

Manufacturer's data sheets for parallel-port controller chips contain a wealth of information about the parallel port and its use. They're often available for viewing or downloading from the manufacturer's Web site.

Hardware-related Resources

These include sources for parallel-port-related products and resources for learning about the PC's hardware and electronics in general.

Hardware Products

Universal cable, for fast PC-to-PC transfers using parallel ports, from Parallel Technologies:
Phone: 800-789-4784 206-869-1136
WWW: http://www.lpt.com/lpt/

There are many sources for electronic components and parallel-port cards, switches, extenders, and similar devices. The following vendors have good selections of these:

Digi-Key. Chips and other electronic components.
Phone:
Fax:
WWW: http://www.digikey.com/

Jameco. Chips, components, and parallel-port cards, switch boxes, and extenders.
Phone:
Fax:
WWW: http://www.jameco.com/

JDR. Chips, components, and parallel-port cards, switch boxes, and extenders.
Phone:
Fax:
WWW: http://www.jdr.com/

Warp Nine Engineering (formerly FarPoint), source for parallel-port expansion cards that support EPP and ECP modes, cables.

http://www.fapo.com/

Books about Electronics

The Personal Computer from the Inside Out, Third Edition by Murray Sargent III and Richard L Shoemaker. 1995, Addison-Wesley, 800 pages. A classic, detailed reference to the PC's hardware. Also includes a primer on assembly language, an introduction to digital logic, a chapter on computer control and monitoring, and even project construction tips.

The Art of Electronics, Second Edition, by Paul Horowitz and Winfield Hill. 1989, Cambridge University Press, 1125 pages. An essential, complete introduction to electronic circuits of all types.

High-Speed Digital Design: A Handbook of Black Magic, by Howard W. Johnson and Martin Graham. 1993, Prentice Hall, 447 pages. A technical but very readable guide to a difficult topic. Covers cable and interface design.

Software-related Resources

These include resources to help in writing Windows and other programs, plus programming languages and other software products.

Windows Programming

Visual Basic Programmer's Guide to the Win32 API, by Daniel Appleman. 1996, Ziff-Davis Press, 1518 pages. The definitive reference for using the Windows API in 32-bit Visual-Basic programs. Contain many insights and tips beyond simply documenting the API.

Visual Basic Programmer's Guide to the Windows API, by Daniel Appleman. 1993, Ziff-Davis Press, 1020 pages. Same as the previous listing, but for Windows 3.1 programming.

These three books show what's involved in writing VxDs and other Windows device drivers:

Systems Programming for Windows 95: C/C++ programmer's guide to VxDs, I/O devices, and operating system extensions by Walter Oney. 1996, Microsoft Press, 715 pages.

Writing Windows VxDs and Device Drivers by Karen Hazzah. 1995, R & D Publications, 352 pages.

Writing Windows Device Drivers by Daniel A. Norton. 1992, Addison-Wesley, 434 pages.

The Windows Interface Guidelines for Software Design. 1995, Microsoft Press, 556 pages. How to design programs with user-friendly, consistent interfaces that conform to the Windows guidelines.

Microsoft's Developer's Network. A wealth of information and programming tools from Microsoft, on CD-ROM. Available in several levels. All but the lowest level includes the Device Developer's Kit, which is essential if you want to create VxDs.

WWW: http://www.microsoft.com

General Programming

Code Complete by Steve McConnell. 1993, Microsoft Press, 857 pages. A tutorial on how to write functional, maintainable programs.

Programming Languages

Visual Basic. The language of choice for Basic programming under Windows.
WWW: http://www.microsoft.com

Power Basic DLL compiler. Create compiled DLLs in Basic.
PowerBasic, Inc.
Phone: 800-780-7707, 408-659-8000
Fax: 408-659-8008
WWW: http://www.powerbasic.com

Delphi. An object Pascal compiler. The language is not too different from Basic, but Delphi is a compiled, not interpreted, language and includes an in-line assembler and other features not found in Visual Basic. You can use Delphi for an entire project, or use it to create compiled DLLs for use with Visual-Basic programs.

WWW: http://www.borland.com

Other Software Products

These vendors offer Ocx's for Port I/O and detecting hardware interrupts:

BlueWater Systems
Phone: 800-962-2114, 206-771-3610
Fax: 206-771-2742
WWW: http://www.bluewatersystems.com/

TetraDyne Software
Phone: 408- 377-6367
Fax: 408-377-6258
WWW: http://www.wintech.com

Appendix B

Microcontroller Circuit

Several of the examples in this book use an 82C55 programmable peripheral interface chip as an interface between a PC's parallel port and a microcontroller. Figure B-1 shows a microcontroller circuit that can interface to an 82C55.

The microcontroller is an 80(C)52-Basic, with a Basic-52 interpreter in ROM. The design is similar to that used in many microcontroller applications. The circuit includes the microcontroller chip, address decoding into eight 8K blocks, RAM for temporary storage of data and Basic programs, and a serial interface for connecting to a PC. To these components you can add EPROM or other nonvolatile memory for program storage and I/O circuits similar to the examples in this book.

The companion disk for this book includes Basic-52 program code for the example circuits that use an 82C55, along with a microcontroller circuit similar to this one. The circuit is reprinted from my *Microcontroller Idea Book*, which has more details about the circuit and how to use it.

Other 8051-family microcontrollers can use similar circuits, and the 82C55 can interface in a similar way to other microcontrollers.

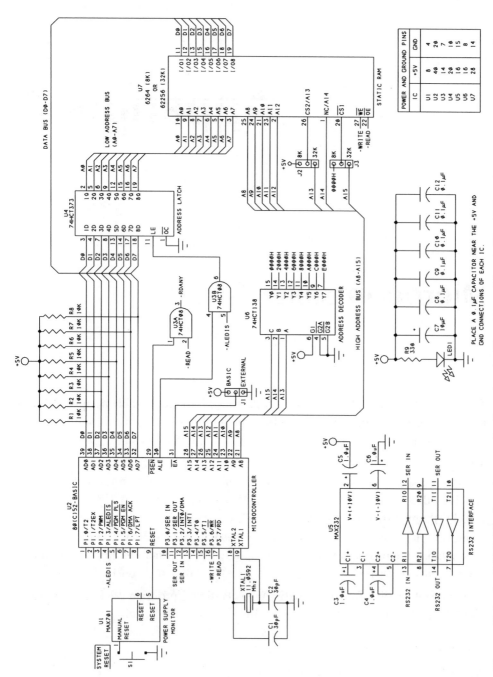

Figure B-1: An 8052-Basic microcontroller circuit. (Reprinted from *The Microcontroller Idea Book* by Jan Axelson.)

Appendix C

Number Systems

Programming of parallel-port applications often involves using number systems other than the familiar decimal system. Hexadecimal and binary numbers are useful because they offer an easy-to-read way of expressing the bit- and byte-oriented values that parallel-port applications often use. For those who are new to number systems, or rusty on them, this appendix offers an introduction or review.

About Number Systems

A number system is a way to express quantitative information. Each of the number systems described below has a different base: 10, 2, or 16. Among other things, the base determines how many characters are needed to express a given quantity.

Decimal Numbers

The decimal number system used in everyday (non-computer) life has ten digits (0-9). Each digit in a number represents a value raised to a power of 10.

This table shows the value of each digit in the decimal number 632:

Decimal digit	6	3	2
Digit multiplier	10^2	10^1	10^0
Digit value	600	30	2

Binary Numbers

In the binary number system, each digit represents a value raised to a power of 2. The numbers use only two of the ten decimal digits, 0 and 1.

Binary representations are useful when you need to see the value of each bit in a byte. For example, you might want to set, clear, toggle, or read a bit in one of the parallel port's registers. Visual Basic's logical operators offer a way to control and display individual bit values.

This table shows the value of each digit in 10 0111 1000, which is the binary representation of the decimal number 632:

Binary bit	1	0	0	1	1	1	1	0	0	0
Bit multiplier	2^9	2^8	2^7	2^6	2^5	2^4	2^3	2^2	2^1	2^0
Bit value (decimal)	512	0	0	64	32	16	8	0	0	0

Hexadecimal Numbers

In the hexadecimal, or hex, number system, each character represents a value raised to a power of 16. There are 16 characters, with the letters A through F representing the decimal values 10 through 15.

Each character in a hex number represents 4 bits. This makes hex numbers a convenient, compact way to express 8- or 16-bit numbers. In Visual Basic, a leading &h indicates a hex value:

```
&h278
```

Other common ways of indicating hex values are with a trailing h:

```
278h
```

with a leading 0x:

```
0x278
```

or with a leading $:

```
$278
```

Visual Basic's Hex$ operator displays a value in hexadecimal:

```
debug.print Hex$(632)
278
```

This table shows the value of each character in 278h, which is the hexadecimal representation of the decimal number 632:

Hex character	2	7	8
Character multiplier (decimal)	16^2	16^1	16^0
Character value (decimal)	512	112	8

ASCII Hex format

Some devices expect to receive information as ASCII codes, with each code representing a text character. If you try to send numeric data as bytes from 0 to 255 to a device like this, the device will interpret each byte as its ASCII code, and this can cause unwanted effects. For example, the value *0Ah* may cause the device to do a line feed, or a *7* may sound a bell. A solution is to use ASCII hex format, which uses a pair of ASCII characters to represent each byte of information. The only characters used are 0–9 and A–F. For example:

Value to write (1Fh):	1	F
Character's ASCII code	31h	46h
Byte to send (binary)	00110001	01000110

Instead of sending one byte to represent a value from 0 to 255, the sending device sends two, one for each character in the hex number that represents the byte. In the example above, the value to transmit is 1Fh, but the sending device sends two bytes: 31h, the ASCII code for 1, and 46h, the ASCII code for F. The receiving device treats the values like ordinary text. After the values have been received, the receiving device can process or use the data any way it wants, including translating it back to binary data.

One common use for ASCII hex files is to send binary codes for programming EPROMs or loading programs into RAM for testing on microcontroller systems. Intel Hex and Motorola S-record formats both store data in ASCII hex format, along with error-checking and other information.

Kilobytes and Megabytes

Two popular and sometimes confusing terms for dealing with quantities in the computer world are kilobyte (K) and Megabyte (M).

In the metric system of measurement, kilo means 1000, but in the computer world, it commonly refers to 1024, which is 2^{10}, or 400h. An 8K RAM chip actually stores 8192 bytes, not 8000.

In a similar way, in the metric system, Mega means a million, but in the computer world, it commonly refers to 1,048,576 (2^{20}, or 1000h). One Megabyte equals 1024 kilobytes.

Multipliers

And finally, here's a review of the prefixes often used to express component values and other quantities in electronics:

Prefix	Description	Multiplier
M	Mega-	1,000,000
K	kilo-	1,000
m	milli-	1/1000
μ	micro-	1/1,000,000
p	pico-	$1/10^{-12}$

Index

H

handshake
    reason for **223**
    See also specific modes
hardware interrupt **194–199**
hardware, port **11**
Harris Semiconductor **144**
HCMOS
    drivers **107**
    logic **93**
    power supply **124**
    See also logic families
Hewlett Packard GPIB **14**
hexadecimal numbers **330**
high-side switch **139**
Hold, CPU **287**
host
    defined **205**
    Direct Cable Connection **308**
HostAck **286, 290**
HostBusy
    in Byte mode **250**
    in negotiating **212**
    in Nibble mode **228**
HostClk
    in Byte mode **250**
    in ECP mode **289, 292**
HostLogicHigh **115**
hysteresis **108**

I

I/O cycle **45**
IBM PC **2**
    8255 in **233**
IEEE **203**
    ISA-bus standard **46**
IEEE 1284 **203–207**
    compliant cable **115**
    connector **10, 112**
    negotiating **210–212**
    supplement **221**
    supplement to **218**
    transceiver chip **109**

IEEE 1394 **14**
IEEE 488, compared to parallel port **14**
impedance
    characteristic **121**
    output **107, 108**
inductive coupling **118**
infrared interface **14**
ini file **61**
Init. See nInit
initialization data **61**
inp function **26**
inpout DLL **27**
input
    applications **149–163**
    bits **17–24**
    detecting external **189–199**
    expanding **152**
    latch **150**
    See also Byte mode, Nibble mode, ECP,
        EPP
INT 17h **34**
INT 21h **35**
Intel
    80386SL/486SL **267**
    82360SL I/O Subsystem **267**
interfacing **105–124**
interference, cable **118**
Interlnk **306–308**
interlocked handshake **205**
interpreter **48**
interrupt
    and VxDs **44**
    enable bit **22, 57**
    hardware **194–199**
    in ECP mode **293, 295–296**
    in EPP mode **275**
    use of **5**
    variation in use **226**
interrupt service routine. See ISR
inverted signals **20**
inverting bit
    in hardware **98**
    in software **56**
IOCHRDY, in EPP mode **274**
IOR and IOW **45, 274**

Index

IrDA **14**
IRQ **5–6**
    See also interrupt
ISA bus **2**
    IEEE standard for **46**
    speed **45**
ISA-compatible port **3**
ISR **194–199**

K

kilobyte **331**

L

language, programming
    port I/O in **26–31**
    speed **47–50**
Laplink cable **306**
latch, input **150**
LED
    for viewing bits **86**
    interface **86, 135**
Level 1 & 2 devices **106–110**
level detecting **155**
LF347 quad op amp **162**
line printer driver **32**
Linear Technology **139**
Linefeed, auto **22**
LM339 quad comparator **155**
logic families **93, 98**
    and transmission-line effects **120**
    output characteristics **107**
    speed **111**
logic output
    as switch **134**
loop, as timer **186**
LP324 op amp **124**
LPT
    defined **5**
    ports, accessing **31–37**
LPT4 **25**
lptprogs.ini **61**
LSTTL **93**
    drivers **106**

    See also logic families **105**
LTC1156 quad MOSFET driver **139**

M

magnetic coupling **118**
mapping **309**
mask byte **57**
matrix, switch **144**
Max186 ADC **181**
Max456 crosspoint switch **148**
Max756 step-up converter **127**
Maxim Semiconductor. See individual chips
    (Max-)
Megabyte **331**
memory, under Windows **41**
Microchip PIC **232**
microcontroller
    8052-Basic **236–237**
    circuit **327**
    in peripherals **232**
microprocessor. See CPU
Microsoft
    Diagnostic **6**
    ECP document **286**
    Plug and Play **6**
    See also individual products
Microwire **166**
mode
    Byte **249–258**
    Compatibility **223–228**
    disabling **209**
    ECP **285–298**
    EPP **267–284**
    Fast Centronics **296**
    IEEE 1284 **204–210**
    negotiating **210–212**
    Nibble **228–231**
modification, bidirectional **100–103**
MOSFET **138–141**
motherboard port **11**
msd.exe **6**
MS-DOS
    and PCs **2**
    device drivers **40–42**